THE NEW POLITICS OF
ONLINE FEMINISM

The New Politics of Online Feminism

AKANE KANAI

DUKE UNIVERSITY PRESS
Durham and London
2 0 2 6

Project Editor: Livia Tenzer
Designed by A. Mattson Gallagher
Typeset in Arno Pro, Comma Base, and Goldich
by Copperline Book Services

Library of Congress Cataloging-in-Publication Data
Names: Kanai, Akane, author.
Title: The new politics of online feminism / Akane Kanai.
Description: Durham : Duke University Press, 2026. | Includes
bibliographical references and index.
Identifiers: LCCN 2025022046 (print)
LCCN 2025022047 (ebook)
ISBN 9781478033219 (paperback)
ISBN 9781478029755 (hardcover)
ISBN 9781478061977 (ebook)
Subjects: LCSH: Feminists—Australia. | Young women—
Australia. | Online social networks. | Intersectionality
(Sociology) | Feminism—Australia.
Classification: LCC HQ1221 .K36 2026 (print) |
LCC HQ1221 (ebook)
LC record available at https://lccn.loc.gov/2025022046
LC ebook record available at https://lccn.loc.gov/2025022047

CONTENTS

ACKNOWLEDGMENTS

This book was written while I was on a research fellowship funded by the Australian Research Council, at Monash University in Australia, on Kulin Nations country. This fellowship, over four years, allowed me the time to do the research and thinking required to write. It began during lockdown in the middle of the COVID-19 pandemic, was put on hiatus when I went on parental leave, and was then completed in the midst of an overseas move uprooting my partner, toddler, and dog from one hemisphere to the other. And so this book has seen times of smooth and bumpy travel, of acceleration, stasis, and slow motion.

This book is about cultures of knowledge, while also aiming to produce knowledge. You need time and space to write. But the sustained *social* dimension of knowledge production in the attention so generously given to my ideas has also been a condition of possibility for this book. The intellectual support from friends and thoughtful strangers, ranging from informal chats over coffee and wine to the input of anonymous peer reviewers and deep questions from conference audiences, has been instrumental to feeling that what I am saying is a *legitimate perspective* and can be shared. This kind of legitimation, I think, is quite rare and precious, particularly in considering the quandaries my participants faced in establishing their own "epistemic status," as Maria do Mar Pereira would say. So, my first thank-you goes to my participants for bringing their generosity and good faith to this project. I share their quandaries and fears of exposure, of overstepping, of failing to do feminism right; indeed, the ambitious title of this book ("The *New* Politics") feels somewhat too big for my small academic niche. But this book is not about *new* as in a neat break with the past; it is more about defining a shift in feminist relationalities that might be particular but I don't think is random or arbitrary.

Thank you to Christina Scharff and Maria do Mar Pereira for their ongoing engagement, and deep reading of my work over some years. I also want to acknowledge Jonathan Dean for supporting my work and introducing it to Maria, allowing us to begin our intellectual collaboration. Thank you to Ros Gill, Esther Tordjmann, Zala Volcic, Maura Edmond, and Brett Hutchins, who all read chapters of this book at varying stages of its life cycle, and to Julia Coffey, with whom I worked on a small project on online feminism and conflictual feelings that helped to give birth to this book.

Natasha Zeng, one of my first PhD students, was my project research assistant. Her care, insight, and sheer trustworthiness contributed immensely to this research. I want to also highlight the generative conversations with my other PhD students during the fellowship: Niamh White, Jae Roh, Natasha Dimitrovska, Shirley Chen, Berwyn Kwek, and Zoe Condliffe. And to Heather Tyas, Sophia Brill, Jodie Wood, and Terri Matthias at the School of Media, Film and Journalism at Monash University, who helped me with all the day-to-day of research administration—I couldn't have completed this project without you!

Before having my baby, I don't think I had ever fully understood in an embodied sense how autonomy is relational: you cannot write, finish your train of thought, or even finish your meal until someone else is looking after your small child. My thanks to my partner Ben and our bigger biological and nonbiological family who have been with us to witness and share in the profound changes that Noa has brought to our lives. And thank you to Noa, for helping me to think differently.

INTRODUCTION

Knowing Right from Wrong

I know I'm not a bad feminist for moving in [with my boy-
friend], but ... how do I be a feminist and be in a heterosexual relationship and, and live with him and try not to repeat
patriarchal ideas in my relationship and like, in my life?

Alice, age 26

I met Alice a year before she moved in with her boyfriend. Earnest, bright,
and articulate, she was a graduate student researching sustainability in the
creative industries, in Perth, a sunny metropolitan center on the west coast
of Australia. She was passionate about her burgeoning research and was
pondering the possibility of further study, or working for a nonprofit with
similar goals. But her larger personal project was feminism: a feminism
that was a whole worldview, expanding into understanding race, climate
change, popular culture, presidential scandals and the rise of the far right in
the United States, and massacres in Israel-Palestine, Lebanon, and Ukraine.
More than a simple career trajectory, the obligation to practice feminism
in the best way possible informed her personal lifestyle, choices, and am-
bitions. It led to a proliferation of questions that continually tested her in
binary terms of authenticity and hypocrisy, success and failure, goodness
and its opposite. Was it feminist to desire travel and overseas adventure,

given the very real climate crisis? Was it feminist to work in a sector that was so intertwined with capitalism, even if you had good intentions? How could you be feminist and be in a monogamous, long-term heterosexual relationship? Fed by a social media environment in which examples of feminist women "getting it wrong" were all too common, Alice agonized over how she could practice a feminism responsive to all the crises she strove to acknowledge. She often felt "overwhelmed by her womanhood," as she shared in the group workshop where I first met her.

Like other relatively resources-rich young women in my project, white middle-class Alice was seeking a way to buoy her identity to a position resisting the status quo. As sociologists such as Zygmunt Bauman have argued, living in the "liquid modernity" (2000) of Western economies means people like Alice are increasingly less embedded in social structures, and therefore are left on their own in designing their biographies. Certainly, while social structures have far from disappeared, the young feminists I spoke to grew up with cultural messaging foregrounding the abundance of life choices, at the same time that they were urged to see themselves as the future voices of social change. Growing up with social media and feeling the duty to "use her voice," Alice, similarly, felt passionately about the misogyny, racism, and denial of climate crisis that continued to frame high-profile culture wars across the Anglo-American news cycle. Social media, for her and others, was a central means of witnessing and engaging with the wrongs of the world. Structural issues ranging from police brutality to the underpayment of women in fast fashion felt extremely personal and were accessed from their phones on and off throughout the day, while commuting, at work, on the sofa, and in bed when they woke up. Such mediated connection, while seemingly voluntary, was also an obligation: How could you be feminist and care about such big-picture issues and then turn away from them, as fatiguing and distressing as it was to always be connected to social media? And how could you be feminist if you didn't know what was happening, when it was so important and seemingly so simple to educate yourself on matters of importance?

To be feminist in an age of social media, for many of my participants, was to feel pressured, pushed and pulled in many directions. As online culture changes the scale and contexts of communication, media studies scholars have highlighted the logics of "connective action" (Bennett and Segerberg 2012), and the guiding possibilities for "fighting back" through the structures of social media platforms: hashtags, organized counterpublics, and platforms for reporting harassment and assault (Jackson et al.

2020; Mendes et al. 2019). Yet, in the murkier temporalities and spaces of everyday life, the young feminists I spoke to struggled to orient and ground themselves. They lived not just with "discomfort," as the now popular social justice credo goes, but in a constant state of unease and emotional contradiction. Alice felt guilty about her social media detoxes, when she would consciously periodically delete apps such as Instagram and TikTok from her phone. She loved fashion but tried to never buy new clothes, knowing about the exploitation of women garment workers. She scrutinized her devotion to paid work, seeing it as a capitulation to the capitalist wheel. When I spoke to her, I wasn't sure that she did indeed know that she was not a bad feminist for moving into her boyfriend's flat.

Alice was not unique. My young feminist participants didn't simply feel unmoored; they felt increasingly under the microscope. To identify as feminist was not necessarily to feel liberated from constraints. Rather, it often meant you felt responsible for your own shackles and those of others. And in accepting this responsibility, it often meant feeling more, not less, bound to restrictive measures and practices of gender, incessantly circling around the questions *Am I a good person? Did I do bad? Could I be better?* in the broader project of producing a feminist self that somehow registered and embodied the right reaction to the diverse harms witnessed through one's screen. In this loop, an outward gaze absorbed a general outline of violence and backlash taking place across different contexts; it then turned inward with an intense, exacting energy. One's everyday practices and selfhood became the locus of responsibility, blame, and change; there were no excuses, given what was happening in the world. Against the everyday spectacle of extremism and violence, the only option was to know, and do better.

In Anglo-American media culture, as Sarah Banet-Weiser (2018) has written, feminism has more recently achieved a certain point of "popularity" in comparison with its more ambivalent representations of the early twenty-first century. From the 1990s to the early 2000s, scholars noted the tendency for feminism to be represented in highly individualized ways, if at all, and often in direct repudiation of the collective gains of the 1970s and 1980s, in what Rosalind Gill (2007) analyzed as a "postfeminist" sensibility. Representations of "top girls" proliferated in commercial media, highlighting personal ambition and achievement under capitalism (McRobbie 2009). Such representations often directly disavowed what was characterized as a dowdy, overprotective feminism of the Western second wave. Empowered women didn't need feminism; they could solve their own problems to overcome sexism through ingenuity and sheer will-power ("manifesting their desires," to borrow the motivation-speak that came slightly later).

This postfeminist status quo, however, has seen a shift in recent years. Feminism is now marketable across feminized domains of consumer culture, from luxury brands to fast-moving consumer goods. In the late 2010s, Dior began producing T-shirts using direct slogans from second wave feminist activism; *Vogue* has continued in this vein in highlighting women as agents of change. The words *feminism* and *feminist* are commonsense identifiers in popular reality TV franchises such as *The Real Housewives*; and feminism and women's self-flourishing are no longer seen as at odds. Operating in an "economy of visibility," according to Banet-Weiser (2018), feminism and women's aspiration, confidence, and competence are increasingly conflated across brand culture and lifestyle media. As feminism has become increasingly au fait in media culture, it can now seem naïve or even ill-informed, for women at least, to reject it in a blanket fashion.

In this book, I chart some connections in these individualized dynamics for young feminists who have grown up with social media, and for whom social media was a central, everyday means of connecting with feminism and feminist ideas. Yet I also outline transformations in the understood significance of feminism. For my participants, feminism often did not give a confidence boost; rather, it was associated with a continual punitive scrutiny, of the self, but also of others, and an ongoing imperative to be in the right when you were always at risk of getting it wrong. Far from popular mediated representations of a happy feminist simplicity, equating feminist confidence and positivity with self-worth (Orgad and Gill 2021), social media feminist cultures propagated ongoing mechanisms for self-measurement and continual self-modification, in tandem with an individualized ideal of goodness. In the invocations of "good" and "bad" feminism that frequently haunted my participants' observations, what struck me was how these categories often neatly mapped onto a historical "bedrock" (Hall 1988, 141) of representations of good and bad women. Good feminists, named as intersectional feminists, negated themselves, were grateful for their privilege, included others, and were "nice." While one aspired to be good, to take everybody into account, one was always only one thoughtless misstep away from being bad, being selfish, not knowing one's place, taking up too much space. And not knowing one's place, or one's lane, based on one's identity traits was a cardinal sin in the identity politics of social media.

Drawing on ethnographic work with fifty young feminists based in Australia who shared their social media use with me over three points in time over 2021–22, I want to highlight how social media heightened the personal stakes of feminism. Social media feminist culture required all feminists to stay connected, keep up to date on relevant trends and events, and continually work on improving their feminist selves. In the insistence on a singular right but many wrongs, on the imperative to have the complete picture and never leave anything out, and to consistently present the same polished face to the world, these knowledge cultures set ever-higher but ever-narrower personal standards of what being feminist meant. The result was that, for many of my participants, feminism became a set of rules, and relatedly, an ongoing means of regulating conduct. To be feminist in what I term these "online knowledge cultures" was to continually demonstrate awareness of the ever-shifting parameters around appropriate identity practices, curating one's media consumption to align with a "perfect" intersectional politics, and avoiding those singled out as "problematic." It was to be able to describe your gendered needs and vulnerabilities with the right language but continually defer them to show you were appropriately aware of your privilege and did not take up too much space or attention. Indeed, there was a sense that claiming the identity of feminist meant you were always already empowered. My participants, who were predominantly women and gender-diverse people, showed how participation in feminist social media cultures recast them as responsible guardians of feminism rather than its legitimate beneficiaries.

In everyday life, then, feminism on social media was not only about participating in activism, petitions, or awareness-raising, accessing feminist news and debates, or even encountering concepts such as *toxicity* and *patriarchy* and adjectives such as *problematic* and *complicit*. Under the guise of achieving a better, more "intersectional" feminism, social media recast feminism as a universalizing knowledge project, centered on refashioning the feminist knower themselves. And in the age of answers notionally being one Google search away, and given the saturation of feminist discourses throughout institutional and everyday media culture, being a feminist knower and being devoted to ongoing learning became a default position for normativity and belonging. Further, I want to highlight how the call of this social media feminism was intensively gendered in its address. It required "good girls." By this, I mean not that it was relevant only to girls, or that it was explicitly styled for women only, but that it emerged with acute salience for my participants in the aftermath of ideals of "empowered girls"

(Dobson and Harris 2015) and inclusive leadership in the institutionalized youth cultures in which they were often embedded. It revived historically embedded expectations of women's primary responsibility for care and social reproduction, now presented in a refreshed form as contemporary responsibilities of inclusion. This goodness also drew on cultural fantasies of Western middle-class femininity (Daniels 2021; Moreton-Robinson 2006; Sullivan 2014) in underscoring claims to moral authority. Producing binaries of whiteness and color as ahistorical, transnational phenomena, my young Australian participants were invited to conflate their experiences with those of their usually North American counterparts, adopting a bird's-eye view of scandals, tragedies, and other phenomena that rapidly rolled through their social media feeds.

Identities thus took on certain rigidities. But the notion of goodness was mobile, able to incorporate ever-shifting, higher standards of intersectionality, while maintaining the risk of moral opprobrium, and indeed, misogyny, if you slipped up and were bad. I thus foreground goodness rather than perfection in my analysis here, in order to give a sense of classed and racialized salience of this gendered ideal, as well as the heightened stakes of failure in the binary landscape of social media. To be imperfect on social media meant you could be therapeutically framed as trying to be better. But if you weren't good, as demonstrated by the ritual social media fury catalyzed by the mistakes of famous women, you could be violently put in your place.

FROM EMPOWERMENT TO INCLUSION

I should now better situate the cultural context from which I speak and how this inflects the question of diversity within feminism that is central to the arguments of this book. As Ien Ang (2003) neatly puts it, Australia's "main social institutions and basic cultural orientations are identifiably Western, and as a nation it is categorized in the international order as a part of 'the West'" (201). Yet its position as a settler colonial nation located south of the Asian continent has always complicated the felt security of this whiteness, placing Australia "on the periphery of the Euro-American core," and producing a sense of "non-metropolitan, post-colonial whiteness" (201). Whiteness has often been described as "fragile" in terms of its reactivity in being challenged (Daniels 2016), but in the context of this book, I am noting in particular how this uncertainty renders antipodean whiteness highly dependent on transnational Anglo-American sources of media. In a "double reflection" (Gülçiçek 2024) imagining Australia as an extension but not epicenter of the West, a crucial place is given to American popular culture, debates, and concepts in local progressive political identities seeking to define themselves against parochial examples of whiteness as sources of cultural "cringe" (Phillips 2006). This can render Australian feminisms more amenable to postnational notions of multicultural feminist community in which differences between the United States and the United Kingdom, Canada, and Australia are minimized but registered sequentially as more "forward-thinking" or "backward" on a line of progress.

Australia's settler colonial foundations also produce a political imaginary centering an Anglo-Celtic majority as natural and authoritative mediators of diversity within its borders (Hage 2000). Simultaneously paying penance for the "original sin" of colonization (Ang 2003, 202; see also Ahmed 2004b), and welcoming contemporary diversity, such an imaginary separates the "bad" past and "good" present, obfuscating how the histories of both colonized Indigenous peoples and racialized settlers were intertwined in programs of genocide, land appropriation, indentured labor, regulation of sexuality, and Eurocentric border control (Curthoys and Mitchell 2020; Lo and Kanamori 2013; Stephenson 2007). Against this backdrop, the centrality of white women as "mediators" of Australian feminism has sharpened the sense of feminism as inclusive mission, such that Indigenous feminists such as Aileen Moreton-Robinson have forcefully articulated that they do not want to be "included" in white feminism (2000a; 2000b, 174), and certainly not a version of feminism in which the experience of racialized people in the United States is seen as more foundationally instructive than the history of racial oppression in Australia (2000b, 2006). As I discuss further in chapters 1 and 2, this can also render local, everyday practices of whiteness more invisible even as or, particularly when race is explicitly discussed, when it becomes something to be identified textually, in media elsewhere.

There is a rich breadth of scholarly work that examines how feminist digital activism responds to the challenges of misogyny arising through differing geopolitical and national histories, using online groups, hashtags, and platform affordances (Beta 2022; Dimitrovska 2024; Errázuriz 2021; Jeong and Lee 2018; Mendes et al. 2019; Pain 2021; Yin and Sun 2021). The Hollywood-led online activism around #MeToo in 2017 that fueled significant transnational conversation and feminist activity online and offline shows that ideas that travel are not simply spread but recreated and made to matter through the politics of emplaced, lived histories and contexts. This book aims to contribute to understandings of the contextual transformation of what feminism is, and does, by analyzing social media feminism as a set of knowledge cultures (Cetina 2007) informing everyday life. In a moment when feminist television, film, art, and online content have proliferated, to identify as "feminist" in the West is increasingly to adopt a knowing position through practices of appraisal, evaluation, position, and distinction. In the Australian national context, such knowledge cultures are driven by Anglo-American mediated events and analysis, and, more broadly, by the cultural shift in the West whereby feminism's significance is not primarily defined by discrete forms of activism but as a style or genre (Cattien 2019) of cultural production, consumption, and identification. Through this lens, I examine how social media feminism as an everyday knowledge culture has its own contextual rules and logics, and provides frameworks through which to understand personal experience, setting personal expectations and political priorities. I am influenced by a wealth of scholarship that has shown how feminism, in Western social contexts, is often highly mediated, and how such mediation, often through commercial and privatized channels, has ambivalent effects.

In contrast to its varied histories, mobilizations, disputes, and contestations, scholars have observed how commercial Anglo-American media culture from the late twentieth century onward has tended to privilege a simplified, individualized account of feminism. Addressed most directly to women as its subjects, feminism has been articulated as a personalized but malleable set of aspirations and practices, spanning a focus on hard work and achievement under capitalism (McRobbie 2020), "confidence" (Orgad and Gill 2021), and consumption and visibility (Savolainen et al. 2022), all of which coalesce in an increasing lack of distinction between "influencing" and "activism" online (Scharff 2023a). Thus, as popular culture has incorporated, repudiated, and reformed feminism according to accounts of postfeminism (Gill 2007), popular feminism (Banet-Weiser 2018), and fourth wave feminism (Rivers 2017), the co-constitution of neoliberalism and feminism has led to the intensification of practices of self-governing addressed to women: self-monitoring, benchmarking, self-branding, and working on making one's feelings fit the relentless positivity of empowered femininity.

Recently, Angela McRobbie (2015) has also argued that there has been a turn to "perfection" and "resilience" (2020) in the endless competition with oneself required in the new sexual contract. Women must benchmark themselves and achieve against continually raised measures of improvement. Rosalind Gill (2023) observes the sharpening of expectations of feminine perfection as social media both normalizes and heightens the stakes of visibility. These demands of perfection speak to an internalized continual self-surveillance as social surveillance becomes part of the fabric of a media culture structured by the expansion of norms of celebrity. Thus the impetus to perfect how one practices identity has only intensified with the increased personalization of media in the growth of social media and convergent culture. Those traditionally addressed as media consumers are recast as active participants and cocreators of a media environment promoting "permanent visibility" (Bartky 1997, quoting Foucault), involving the scrutiny and surveillance not just of those nominally famous but, potentially, of everyone.

From studies of digital culture focusing on antiracism, I also continue critical engagement with how the Internet draws on and reforms structures of racialization. Safiya Noble and Brendesha M. Tynes (2016) make a call for intersectional critical race technology studies, given the pregiven whiteness and maleness of the Western Internet. It is important to understand how intersectionality operates in practice, rather than "in theory" (Noble and Tynes 2016; Bailey and Trudy 2018; Steele 2021; Steele et al. 2023). While feminist spaces might seem prima facie to offer spaces of counterculture to this dominant culture, as Jessie Daniels (2016, 2021) has noted for some time, such whiteness also continues to shape feminist spaces as an unspoken norm. This book shows how this continues notwithstanding and even precisely due to the fact that certain popular discourses of "popular intersectionality" (Schindel 2024) have now saturated broader culture. Such movements dovetail with the rise of "wokeness" as a marker of identity (Sobande et al. 2022), increasingly producing a (white) subject who is always visibly ready to acknowledge their privilege and "clear the floor" for others. While derided by an increasingly vocal right-wing constituency, both the pressures and the trending nature of the display of a progressive, inclusive "woke" identity signal the amenability of intersectional ideas, in the current moment, to commercial culture (Kanai and Gill 2020). For this reason, it is not enough to insist that feminism can be "corrected" by intersectionality in this conjuncture (Nash 2019; see also Dean 2023); it is crucial to understand how the intersectionality of popular culture, social media culture, and institutional culture produces its own common sense that carries far more weight in everyday practice than scholarly debates over its definitional accuracy (Cho et al. 2013).

The dynamics of the popularization of intersectionality and the continuation of whiteness and neoliberalism as normal, have, of course, been identified by scholars such as Sara Ahmed (2004a, 2004b, 2012), Patricia Hill Collins (2015), Gail Lewis (2013), Chandra Talpade Mohanty (2003, 2013), and Jennifer C. Nash (2019) in relation to how intersectionality has traveled in the transnational, neoliberal academy, not to mention Kimberlé Crenshaw, in conjunction with other critical race scholars appraising the field (Cho et al. 2013; Andrews et al. 2023). My work is indebted to the intellectual labor of these scholars. What I aim to further highlight in my focus on the experience of online knowledge cultures, and in aiming to apply an intersectional analysis to the empirical transformations of intersectionality as a concept, are the multifaceted consequences of its travels. Therefore, I identify not only how claims to good, inclusive white authority may be strengthened through the invocation of intersectionality but also how social media knowledge cultures produce intersectionality as a personal benchmark, a form of self-governance that may be used to throw individual legitimacy into question, either through self-scrutiny or by an unknown critical audience poised to call out failings. How intersectional can you make your everyday actions? How intersectional *can you be*?

Indeed, where the implicit driving message of past decades of popular feminist media culture has been "how to be an empowered woman," the question of how to uplift more marginalized others has now become ascendant as this empowerment has now seemingly been achieved. This turn to intersectionality arises in this gendered context of regulation, and is shaped by the inclusive-expansive logics of social media. For my participants, this required that they be always already aware of the local and global, and be able to react in an informed fashion to the miscellaneous and the catastrophic. In short, as social media brought the world into my participants' feeds, the world was brought into the ambit of their personal feminism. Participants lived with an ambient, repetitive sense of potential deficit, with the injunction to react and act in the right way in connection with the flow of events. In seeking to be a good intersectional citizen, you could always learn more; you could always be left behind. In the rhythms of social media culture, where it has become all-important to be fully informed, even as the impossibility of being fully informed also presents itself (Andrejevic 2013), this produced existential conundrums. It provided a measure of goodness and badness that was felt intensely by most (though not all) white participants in my study, while my participants of color were more likely to feel such anxieties projected onto them.

Take Alice. She had been using social media since she was in high school, mainly Instagram and Tumblr; she now, like many others, had a love-hate relationship with social media, regularly deleting apps from her phone, only to reinstall them sometime later. Margot, another young white woman in my study, similarly spoke of the "toxicity" of TikTok in presuming the worst of every social citizen; she referred to a time when she was "offline" with relief. And yet you could not indefinitely remain offline, if you wished to remain part of feminism's march toward progress. These pressures were acknowledged by everyone in my study, regardless of gender identity. But because of the implicit centrality of women to feminism, and the singular emphasis on inclusion as good feminist practice, these pressures operated more intensively for women participants whose racial and class identities were deemed privileged. For these participants, the question of how to comfortably inhabit the subjectivity of being a feminist woman seemed to pose more distressing questions than it solved.

Thus, the version of intersectional feminism that circulated as best practice, in highlighting white women as the most privileged beneficiaries of feminism, and inclusion as the endpoint of such intersectionality, thus paradoxically centered young white women just as they were told to disavow their identities. They were to speak out against injustice whenever witnessed, involving a self-conscious appointment of authority and willingness to enforce the feminist "law." But they were also to include, consider all others before the self, and practice a self-conscious negation ("You're not supposed to center yourself, that's a big no-no," as Bella, one of my participants, put it). These practices also relied on a quantitative, classificatory imagination of identity, ranking legitimacy as a multiplication of vectors of oppression.

This "popular intersectionality" (Schindel 2024) led to much skepticism from my participants of color as to what "intersectionality even meant anymore." Such an intersectional framework required white women to act as feminism's guardians, holding the power to include, and to call out. For some of my white participants, this indeed seemed to buttress messages that they heard since childhood that they were born to be leaders. Middle-class, self-identified extravert Gabi, for example, seemed to feel confident in adopting the role of good intersectional leader, making sure that "everyone had a seat at the table"; this version of intersectionality reinforced her rightful place in being a spokesperson; she saw no contradiction in being a white woman leader who "amplified" others' voices. For others, like soft-spoken Alice, it created continual existential anxieties—of trying but failing, of never living up to her best intentions.

For this reason, it should not have surprised me when Alice revealed the personal reassurance provided by Abbie Chatfield, an Australian femi-

I.1 Abbie Chatfield, "Do I Want It or Is It Capitalism?" Instagram post, September 15, 2021. Screenshot by author.

nist influencer and former *Bachelor* contestant (see figure I.1). Blonde, attractive Chatfield was a clear stalwart of commercial media, mixing her own podcast and social media presence with hosting and judging on reality TV, and brand ambassadorships. She had always proudly positioned herself against the derisions of high-culture commentators. Most importantly, Chatfield gave emotional and personal *license*. She was a personality who refused shame, and spoke with a sense of legitimacy and curiosity without purporting to be an authority. She embraced "low" culture in continued work on reality TV, and following horrifying social media bullying after her appearance on *The Bachelor*, she had emerged triumphant as a media personality in her own right. Although Chatfield was starkly different in her career trajectory, personality, and feminist practice, Alice said, "I think she's really amazing. And I think she is a big reason why I've been able to broaden my understanding of feminism and . . . what it, what it means to be a woman."

What speaking to Alice, Jessica, and others illustrated to me was the centrality of social media, both as a source of continual information through which one was meant to stay "on the pulse" of feminism, and in its direct governing of the emotional life of young feminists and young women, in particular. Feminism was not experienced as something separate from the pressures of body image, academic achievement, workplace success, and so on; rather, in its mediated structuring of everyday life and as an overarching benchmark against which to measure one's practices, feminist social media culture was something from which my young participants often, guiltily, needed to detox.

THEORIZING EVERYDAY FEMINIST KNOWLEDGE CULTURES

Before going on to outline the arguments of this book in more detail, I clarify two premises on which they are based. First, the significance of a personal feminist identity for young feminists was shaped by the centrality of online culture in their everyday experience. The continual dipping in and out, the lingering feelings and changes in position after passing time in these social media, and the ongoing urge to stay connected mean that social media occupied a continual thread in the experience of the everyday. Second, through being led by what my participants defined as their "feminist social media feed," this book focuses on dispersed online feminist cultures involving the circulation of resources, culture, and artifacts that seek primarily to inform and provide perspectives, and were defined as feminist from the viewpoints of my participants themselves. Most often, this involved showing me social media content on their phones. This book features the content my participants shared, but it has mostly been rescreenshot by me for the purposes of consistent image quality and anonymization. Participants shared brief snapshots into what they had noticed in the last week, or carefully saved or favorited assemblages of posts they had thought were noteworthy, such as the Instagram grid in figure I.2.

At other times, my participants would talk about scandals and social media flare-ups that had too many posts to actually document but left a deeply felt imprint. Stepping sideways from the focus of much scholarship on self-identifying activists and discrete feminist campaigns and platforms, this view highlights how digital culture is in fact implicated in the everydayness of feminism, a feminism that sometimes involves only a "minimal agency" (Lugones 2003). Indeed, as social media hummed in the background of the everyday for my participants, I contend that more broadly,

Good stuff
12 saved posts

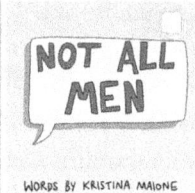

1.2 "Good stuff" Instagram collection, February 20, 2025. Screenshot by author.

online feminist culture is experienced not primarily as activism but as a sensibility directed toward the constant reception of "updates," corresponding to the requirements of digital citizenship in the Information Age. Having an ambient, 360-degree awareness of what is happening becomes an important baseline of belonging in contemporary feminism, despite the fact that such awareness is also premised, among other things, on exclusions of class (Scharff 2023b) and significant labor (Gleeson 2016; Mendes 2022).

Consequently, one of this book's central contentions is that knowledge and being in the know become indelible parts of contemporary feminist culture when social media is a routine element of everyday experience. Given the glut of information online—or "infoglut," as Mark Andrejevic (2013) has put it—together with the identity focus of neoliberal cultures more broadly, the ability to identify, classify, and position becomes more important than a deep expertise in any corpus of knowledge itself. In short, knowing what is happening, and the right position to take on it, become dominant heuristics and ways of managing how to belong in feminist cultures connected with social media.

This book, then, does not necessarily position these online feminist knowledge cultures as a circuit of marginal, or subaltern, knowledges, although they sometimes are. Seeing such knowledge cultures as entangled with the messiness of everyday life, existing forms of inequality and privilege as distributed through my participants' experiences, and the consumer capitalist rhythms of social media, online everyday feminism is positioned as a space of power relations with its own processes of domination and peripheralization. As scholars ranging from Charlotte Brunsdon (2005) to Srila Roy (2015, 2022) have argued, feminism, perhaps, has always been entangled with the governing of identity, both of self and of others. Contemporary feminisms in diverse locations are shaped by governing forces like situated neoliberalisms, while also carrying their own histories that shape how feminist subjects make intelligible and normalize certain "standards" of empowerment. Such insights underline the importance of understanding how feminism is always already entangled with power relations, especially when the everyday, as a site of media saturation, is increasingly colonized by capitalist practices of surveillance and value extraction. Thus, everyday feminist spaces are not simply subsumed by power, but neither are they purely spaces of resistance, as Margaret Davies (2008) neatly surmises.

Continuing a long feminist preoccupation with the everyday and with the mundane, in connection with insights into how seemingly private sites are causally connected to public forms of power (Enloe 2011), this book mobilizes this lens to understand the situation of young people in which distinctions between online and offline and producers and consumers of ideas and images become more tenuous. Maria Lugones's view of agency lends itself to thinking through the politics of the minute negotiations of the everyday, as the digital, in the locations that my participants inhabit, becomes an unremarkable and taken-for-granted element of daily routine and sociality. It is useful because it corresponds to the conditions of my participants' lives, but it also powerfully attests to the complexity of the ways in which identity is subject to power:

a variegated,
dominated,
in resistance to a variety of intermeshed and interlocking
    oppressions,
aggregate that
pulls in different ways,
sometimes in unison,
but more often in many directions (19)

This kind of agency is located within simultaneous spatialities and temporalities of resistance and oppression that encounter, overlay, and crisscross each other, meaning that "a person may be both oppressed and resistant *and act in accordance with both logics*" (25; my italics). In Lugones's view, the necessary simultaneity of the logics of domination and resistance means that it is futile to conceptualize or desire a pure agency "against" domination, in contradistinction to the ressentiment articulated in common liberal articulations of resistance. Like Ahmed's (2006) queer phenomenology, central to the analysis of political orientation and possibilities of movement in this book, this perspective is relational, multidirectional, and refuses a bird's-eye view in understanding the possible movements and negotiations from an embodied and located position.

This diffuse approach thus eschews neat distinctions between space and actor, agent and object, that can implicitly inform accounts of online identity politics and activism. That is to say, although I refer to Instagram and TikTok, Facebook and Twitter (now X), I do not necessarily understand them as pregiven, discrete spaces into which my participants enter and exit. Space, as political geographers note, is fundamentally a question of relationality and temporality, rather than physical or virtual coordinates (Goonewardena et al. 2008). Further, the naturalization of certain spaces as "empty" or as "occupied" is often a political endeavor (Veracini 2011) that shapes who may play "host," who is a "guest," or who is displaced. As Lugones (2003) writes, there is no position on the map that is not criss-crossed by power, as "your spot lies at the intersection of all the spatial venues where you may, must, or cannot live or move. Those intersections also spatialize your relations and your condition with respect to the asymmetries of power that constitute those relations" (21).

The position that you occupy, in short, is shaped by the complex power relations that follow you and unfold wherever you go. Such a view, focusing on the politics of spatiality invited through social media, not just "in" it, permits the identification of new kinds of feminist relationality and selves that are imagined and practiced day to day. These include, as I discuss in this book, the imagined belonging in a vaguely transnational, multicultural feminist "community" in which there are certain rules and expectations for membership; new identity practices as a feminist involving continued learning, ongoing measurement, aspiration, and self-motivation; and relational practices with acquaintances, strangers, and loved ones. Such relationality is not bounded by the borders of each so-called platform (a label, which as Rianka Singh and Sarah Sharma (2019) note, can obfuscate more than it clarifies in its claim to neutral, flat space).

My use of the framework of everyday knowledge cultures is to describe and take seriously my participants' practices of knowledge seeking and accumulation. I also situate this drive to know within the classed social allocation and withholding of "epistemic status" (Pereira 2017), just as online culture conflates knowledge with access to information. In this vein, this book attends to how knowledge is enacted through its multifaceted mobilization—to gain access to resources, to make oneself intelligible, to handle the everyday. The everyday world, according to Philomena Essed (1991) in her germinal book on everyday racism, "is a world in which one must learn to maneuver and a world that one must learn to handle. . . . This at least includes knowledge of language, norms, customs and rules, and knowledge to use the means and resources that make living possible (or successful) in a given environment" (48).

Essed highlights the role of knowledge, both explicit and implicit—and its connection to means and resources—in navigating and orienting the self. In this book, then, I attend to explicit knowledge articulated and translated in the citation of concepts—*intersectionality*, *patriarchy*, and *privilege* as terms that circulate and are given by participants—as well as the tacit, implicit, and embodied knowledges that underpin knowledge practices.

METHODOLOGICAL AND PERSONAL FOUNDATIONS

Attending to the highly contextual, active, and everyday negotiation of feminist knowledge requires grappling with messiness, circling back, and revision. This book has notably been a challenge to write. I met with my participants three times over the space of two years, once in a group setting and twice in follow-up interviews, to give participants the possibility to revise and revisit their narratives—something that I had noticed was not easy on social media—and in order to track shifts over time. These interviews were designed as semistructured but in practice were led by what my participants sought to point out as meaningful in their feeds, and in their lives. Given the status of feminism as a set of beliefs without a clear canon (McRobbie 2009), I was thus oriented by what my participants defined as what "feminist social media" was for them. My participants engaged with a diverse range of social media—almost all with Instagram, and many with TikTok. YouTube was used by some who were devoted to watching long, thoughtful treatises on popular culture, and Facebook feminist groups were used by those who hadn't yet quit but otherwise had mostly abandoned Facebook. Many had loved but ceased to use Tumblr. Participants used social media to keep abreast of updates from news media, NGOs, and community organizations. In this instance, social media was more of a channel to relay happenings from elsewhere. But social media was also engaged with as a world of its own, with its own culture, reference points, debates, and movements, as with the content produced by the queer, feminist, and antiracist influencers participants followed. And sometimes an offline event would catalyze and then become dominated by its discursive life on social media—such as with the Met Gala faux pas of supermodel Cara Delevingne and politician Alexandria Ocasio-Cortez, or the Hollywood litigation launched by Johnny Depp against Amber Heard in 2022.

The challenge of this book has also stemmed from trying to understand and contextualize, as best I could, the diverse life experiences of my participants themselves. These feminist young people had a variety of histories, backgrounds, and predilections. They were at different stages of their experience of youth, aged nineteen to twenty-eight in the first year of this project, often meaning different experiences of employment, educational institutions, and, simply, life stages. They were students, writers, retail and hospitality workers, administrative and corporate professionals, and advocates at NGOs. While much research in youth studies with a social justice bent presumes the researcher has significantly more cultural and economic capital than participants (see also Stiegler 2024), this was not always the case for some of my participants who had impressive CVs and stellar career trajectories. Many had histories—as well as fresh experiences—of family, partner, and stranger violence. Some, despite setbacks, had clearly been high achievers throughout their lives and smoothly proceeded from school to university to full employment; others had had life events interrupt their educational and employment journeys; for others, class, disability, chronic illness, and neurodivergence had always narrowed what was practically possible. Most were Australian-born, but some were migrants working or who had worked toward permanent residency and citizenship. Ethnicities included Anglo-Celtic, Uruguayan, Bosnian, Venezuelan, Indian, Filipina, Indonesian, Timorese, French, German, Singaporean, Chinese, Nigerian, Taiwanese, Lebanese, Indigenous/Torres Strait Islander, Persian, Malay, Mauritian, Italian, and Greek, and, I note, these cultural designations did not always neatly map onto racial self-identifications of "person of color" (POC), "Black/Blak," or white. Though identities did not necessarily remain stable through the timeline of the project, approximately half identified as queer, and the vast majority were cisgender women, an identity I share. Those who had moved across gendered lines described themselves as trans women, trans masc, nonbinary, or questioning. All, however, had been personally addressed by mediated discourses of femininity for a substantial time in their lives, even if they did not currently identify as women or as femmes. In this book's emphasis on knowledge cultures, I signal racial or ethnic identity consistently when I quote my participants, and note class in relation to knowledge practices and position taking. I have adopted this admittedly imperfect practice to harness the insights of Lorraine Code (2006) and Maivân Clech Lâm (1994) in relation to how whiteness is central in the authorization of knowledge; and I draw on the work of Beverley Skeggs (2004), who explains how class is enacted through perspectives and practices that are then communicated as legitimate *knowledge*.

The broader challenges of this book, I must note, are also to do with grappling with my own perspective and the responsibilities of being a feminist scholar. Much of the time I felt straightforward empathy for and with my participants (if such straightforwardness is possible, given the problematic history of empathy, as Carolyn Pedwell [2014] has written). Meeting with them several times, I recognized but was materially distanced from the pain, the struggles, the anxieties, and the joys they shared with me, insulated by my position as a researcher enjoying full-time employment who did not need social media in the same way as my young participants for my social life and connections with the world. But both as a privileged researcher and as a daughter of Japanese migrants in Australia, a settler colonial state in which fears of "the yellow peril" have been formative in national culture, I sometimes felt unease in the face of accounts of expertise and authority, practices that reinforced whiteness even and particularly as participants took care to acknowledge their white privilege and how they "couldn't know" the experience of a person of color. Sometimes I wished I could simply inhabit the position of just supporting what my participants said. I wondered if it was mean-spirited to question the intersectional intentions of some. I wanted (and want) to be a good feminist researcher—a "nice lady"—and take their words at face value. But my very desire for simpler feelings, and a simpler orientation to feminist work, reminded me of the complicated nature of power and identities. It also reminded me of how I was connected to my participants' own fears of anticipating conflict and punishment, their struggles to articulate their own perspectives in the mediated regulation of diversity.

In our differing positions, I am immensely grateful for the consistent, ongoing generosity and openness of my participants. This book would literally be nothing without them. For this reason, I think it most important, rather than dwelling on my own agonizations, to say something about the shared struggles of negotiating contemporary feminism in an age of seeming information abundance and ever-present scrutiny. For these young people, what emerged was a clear sense of the challenges of finding a sustainable but not sterile political orientation. For young people who are addressed as feminism's subjects of the future, being a contemporary feminist is often experienced as a continual series of individual "shoulds" and "oughts" in line with the "always on" rhythms of social media. The urgency of these challenges is also unevenly gendered; as Rosalind Gill and Christina Scharff (2011) have argued, women are often positioned as neoliberalism's ideal, flexible, self-improving subjects. This book shows how the pressures of mediated feminism operate differently according to the contextual complexity of one's own inhabiting of intersections. But there were clear patterns. The discourse of individual feminist responsibility, while not explicitly *naming* women as an audience, clearly addressed my women participants on a personal, felt level. The intensity of this responsibility was also shot through by what one of my nonbinary participants termed an "uptick in misogyny" in a mediated world where criticism and abuse travels quickly, without context, without warning. As feminism becomes a set of expectations of cleaning up the world, it also becomes burdened with misogynistic expectations that devalue the work of care, and that view women as sites of intervention and blame, to be stripped of their privilege when progress isn't quick enough or falls short.

THE ORGANIZATION OF THIS BOOK

By now, I hope it is clear that the "new" politics described in this book are situated very much in existing social and cultural stratifications and histories. But as I describe in the first two chapters in part I of this book, these politics also derive from a preoccupation with the constantly new and a desire to stay on top of continual updates and hot-button topics. Part I outlines the cultural and conceptual norms of online feminist knowledge cultures, beginning by situating the deeply felt, embodied expectations of being a good feminist knower. In chapter 1, "Everyday Reactivism, or, Never Look Away," I track the moral imperative for online feminists to rapidly and correctly react to whatever they are presented with. This required my young participants to be "always ready": ready to use what resources were on offer; to always already know about the issues that they were accessing through their social media feeds; and to immediately take a visible stance to show where they stood. In short, they were required to show the right feelings, positions, and hot takes in relation to a range of issues; such feelings were connected to the display of knowledge. Young people felt intense pressures not only to check all boxes but to do so continuously, rapidly, in response to the flows and rhythms of online culture. Such orientations required significant and constant emotional energy connected to the demands of always already knowing and furnished a standard of being algorithmically tuned into the pain of the world. Removing oneself from this interpellating stream of content, while pragmatically necessary at times, was seen as deviating from a rule. As one white participant guiltily put it when discussing her deliberate withdrawal from online culture at times: "I realize that I have the privilege to disconnect from issues." This vigilant orientation also led to the felt need to have a stance on particular issues.

For my younger participants in particular, the felt imperative to take a stand was draining—as well as anxiety provoking, given the constantly looming threat of punitive reactions ranging from shunning to abuse. With the exception of those working in collectives or for professional social justice organizations, the continuous stretching across numerous issues and the potential fallout meant that most participants did not regularly post or talk publicly on social media. The god's-eye view of the world accessed through digital culture opened up a flow of often US-centered content that one "had to know" but that did not necessarily open pathways for local action. "Social justice burnout," as evinced a number of my participants, "is real"; and digital culture, while offering rich experiences to learn from—serving as a personal "woke manual," as one participant put it—also opened the door to continual demands beyond the pressures and stresses from study, work, and other areas of participants' lives.

In chapter 2, "In Your Lane and Knowing Your Place," I outline how feminist social media culture lays a common ground for participation, requiring that you know where you belong in the landscape of identity oppression. This common ground was often defined, simply, as "intersectionality," and set the contemporary boundaries, relationalities, and inhabitable positions of feminist culture for my participants. It was the most cited concept by my cohort overall; it indexed inclusive feminist futures moving beyond an exclusionary past. In a sense, it was both a map—and a compass. It told you where you were but also directed you where to look. But its uses often diverged from its critical origins, as Sumi Cho, Kimberlé Crenshaw, and Leslie McCall (2013) have noted, paradoxically, in its rapid and frequent circulation, and in the desire for a better, up-to-date feminism, becoming a static concept limiting room to move and maneuver.

Broadly, intersectionality, as it circulated in social media culture, explained belonging and exclusion to my participants, directing them to particular concerns, and making certain deficits visible. But the application of intersectionality operated differently because of the unequal terrain that my participants negotiated. My white participants were invested in showing intersectionality as a framework "close to hand" (Ahmed 2019); they evinced an earnestness to display a full embrace of the concept that translated into following people of color online and buying their art and writing (see also Edmond 2022). For my white middle-class feminists, intersectional feminism was an idealized feminism, something that served or "platformed" others, putting them on the map, echoing the "deference politics" critiqued by Olúfẹ́mi O. Táíwò (2022). But because of intersectionality's practical translation as infinite inclusion and acknowledgment of injury, this openness had to be defined and tabulated in order to be manageable, particularly when participants were frequently overwhelmed by the continuous online flow of claims of need, harm, and oppression to which they were exposed. This in turn was shaped by what Paul Gilroy called the turn to "generic racial identity," in which a "fantasy version of African-American culture" is exported via global consumer culture, turning the historical differences of the world into a single, Western-oriented currency capturing "privilege" versus "disadvantage" (Gilroy and Yancy 2015).

Online, this meant that the application of an intersectional framework involved the counting of multiple oppressions as though they were fungible units, seen in participants' fears of claiming and overclaiming oppressions and attention in the online economy. The obverse of this was that "privileged" categories such as whiteness moved to the background, with other "disadvantaged" intersections being brought forward, shielding whiteness from visibility. More broadly, then, intersectionality was not simply a framework to be mobilized in connection with participants' encounters with injustice. Rather, it was a synecdoche for how feminists positioned themselves in an imagined relationality with other feminists, constructing relations of who always already belonged in feminism and who needed to be welcomed into belonging.

Part II of the book explores in more detail the patterns of personal negotiation of these recognized frameworks and rules. Chapter 3, "Leadership Journeys and Intersectional Resources," explains how the understanding of a journey of self-empowerment and inclusive leadership was ingrained as a means of navigating the feminist intersectional grid; but the material resources and conditions to do so sustainably were often not to hand. In much feminist media studies literature, scholars have identified the push for empowerment and "girlpower" as one of the central and dominant translations of feminism in the public sphere (Banet-Weiser 2018; Dobson and Harris 2015; Edell et al. 2018), and this was reinforced by feminist social media culture carrying high expectations of individual agency and its instrumentalization through the visible use of voice online. Leadership was something that my participants discussed across differing class backgrounds and ethnicities, as injunctions to "be the change" were indeed pervasive in the cultural and institutional environments that shaped my young participants' lives.

Leadership thus provided a lens through which participants understood the direction of their lives. It required them to be individual role models, and set an ascending line they were meant to climb. It also brought significant pressures and an associated vocabulary of continual growth and self-improvement through which to describe their experience. As Shani Orgad and Rosalind Gill (2021) have argued, the language of confidence has become omnipresent in feminized media culture. Of course, this vocabulary and relationality did sometimes seem to fit the trajectory of some of my participants. But sometimes the disjuncture between this narration of ongoing empowerment and its palpable lack of self-confidence was striking to me, as I discussed with one white working-class participant in particular. The sheer accessibility of the language of individual leadership and self-empowerment often obscured the real material, classed, and gendered challenges that my feminists were negotiating.

This leadership claim was also underlined by the language of inclusion, bringing people to the table, inevitably centering a speaker who was "better off" than the named subject of inclusion. Privileged feminists thus were directed to negate or background their own experiences, and enthusiastically embrace inclusion as the pillar on which their authority rested. Their included counterparts notably showed a much more ambivalent orientation in connection with intersectional leadership. As Mariana Ortega (2006) describes in the "great wanting" for white feminists for intersectionality, intensified by the accessibility and "always on" nature of social media culture, disadvantaged identities and experiences could be converted into resources for others' intersectional journeys of leadership and discovery. These journeys could mean the experience of extension for some, and the experience of fixing, objectification, and classification for others. But the young feminists who were also more "privileged" on paper—that is, white, middle-class, ambitious, and talented—showed how they also were used up and burned out in their efforts to actually embody feminist leadership in fighting the everydayness of harassment and abuse of power in their organizations. They, too, were frozen in place in other ways. For many, in the inward-looking gaze of the intersectional grid, men, with the exception of obvious, high-profile abusers, were largely exempt from everyday scrutiny; these young women thus were understood as the most privileged feminist identities in this grid, creating ongoing anxieties in the compulsion to account for themselves.

Chapter 4 is simply named "Don't Be That Girl." It describes how my young feminists' identities were centrally regulated by this injunction, which circulated repetitively, implicitly, and explicitly through pop culture news cycles in their social media feeds. In feminist social media cultures that simultaneously promoted the twin imperatives to be visible and to scrutinize, to be publicly visible meant you were always possibly about to be taught a lesson about right and wrong. And yet, while it was underlined that right and wrong were clear, inhabitable positions, the line between getting it right (being authentic and correct) and getting it wrong (being "fake" or "performative") was often slippery in practice. This was because the position of feminist guardian meant you had to remain constantly vigilant and ready to react; it promoted a lens of readiness to critique, or to ostracize, on the basis of a heuristic of red flags. Certain identities were more likely to trigger these flags, on the basis of one's being presumed to be more open or more closed, more privileged or more disadvantaged. The more visible, and thus, presumably privileged, a woman was in popular culture, the more likely she would, at some point, attract such critique. An ever-moving social media feast of famous women who were denounced as problematic, or simply fake, showed how identities were turned into texts to be analyzed, magnifying women's absences and missteps, often under the guise that they needed to be taught an intersectional lesson. To elude this disciplining was a feat: in the words of one of my participants on a feminist public figure she followed on Instagram, "She literally hasn't fucked up once and that I cannot believe."

The gendered nature of these everyday practices of critique, ostracization, and denunciation illustrated the paradox my participants found themselves in. To be feminist was to adopt ever-higher standards of what could be expected of individual women, as certain types of feminism were conflated with certain types of women that were constantly put under the microscope and found wanting. This had a direct impact not only on my participants who were women but also on the spheres of possible action for my participants of other genders who did not possess socially recognized masculine entitlements to space. Combined with unsustainable demands of being in the know and the anxieties of continual public comparison and anticipated callouts, this produced an untenable position for many. "Girlboss" feminism was unanimously rejected, but often most vehemently by young women who indeed sought to be leaders. White middle-class participants, in particular, adopted a sophisticated, mobile lexicon of disavowal. In the constant dance of association/disassociation in these connective cultures of judgment, to protect your own position as a good feminist, you could not align yourself or show an affinity with a woman or feminist in the public eye without carefully demonstrating your knowledge of their potential problematic elements and associations. As Ahmed (2012) notes in relation to the unhappy performativity of declarations, a description of a problem can be protective; you might insulate yourself against critique.

The final part of this book makes the argument for slowing down and lowering the stakes of everyday feminism, and resetting the terms of the relationship among structure, the individual, and the everyday. Too often, the most accessible imaginaries of feminist collectivity for my participants were in fact hierarchical, competitive, and demanding: an aggregate of individual actions rather than a complex tapestry of interdependence. They lived in a mediated world where they were continually confronted with the increasingly mainstream circulation of extreme and blatant cis- and transmisogyny. They were always on. My participants found it difficult to rest. They had punishing expectations of their own individual political efficacy, in a world where paying attention to one's own needs was a gratification to be always deferred. In chapter 5, "Quiet Publics and Lowercase Feminism," I suggest that feminisms in the local, repetitive domains of the everyday should be oriented toward mutual sustenance. This requires a more modest view, alive to the possibilities of felt connections or "little bridges." These included spaces that were not formally activist or feminist but instead offered low-stakes, welcoming social spaces, such as trans-inclusive sporting groups and university social clubs. In the space and time to listen, podcasts became quiet publics of low-risk feminist sociality. They provided a temporality and spatiality of connection for embodied actors whose dialogue could not simply be reduced to an informational text, scrolled past in a matter of seconds. In the plurality of voices they often showcased, they also provided positions that could be tried out, thought through, and compared with one's own personal experience. Importantly, apart from the podcast as a medium, these spaces could not necessarily be replicated en masse, but the practices that created such spatiotemporalities *could* be adopted in the everyday. Their delimited duration and place-based nature was part of the important work of grounding, bridging, and allowing spaces of co-presence and co-dwelling.

My participants were pushed to always move on: from one news event, scandal, or problematic situation to another; from occupying the position of being a beneficiary of feminism to being an agentic guardian of it. In chapter 6, "Registering Experience: Moving Between, but Not Moving On," I suggest that in everyday contexts, what most benefited my feminist participants was a sense of being brought back to earth, without being cut down from a lofty height, a grounding that enabled them to practice not a purportedly intersectional bird's-eye view but a continual transversal gaze from self to other (Yuval-Davis 2023). I show how this movement allowed for a sense of being held, and for comparison, reflection, and the space to learn from nonidentical experiences. This was particularly powerful for participants with disabilities, chronic illnesses, and reproductive and sexual health issues, and for those who wondered why their intimate relationships always made them feel less than worthy. A feminist framework helped them to sense that a lack of credibility and legitimacy was *not their fault*. While hardly a silver bullet, it helped them to not give up, to continue the search for adaptive measures, the right diagnosis, more respect. As such, the most potent aspects of online feminist knowledge cultures did not necessarily lie in the big concepts of "patriarchy," "intersectionality," "neoliberalism," and so on. In the everyday, what enlivened my young feminists was a general, nonspecific affective shift in feeling what was unfair and what ought to be the norm. Feminism was also most sustaining as a sense of permission and mutual attention. What was most rewarding in university classrooms, in vernacular niches of online discussion, and even in the group workshops of my project was the acknowledgment and legitimacy of partial knowing and attending to personal experience. Specific experience-focused, anonymous spaces of online discussion also validated attending to the minutiae of everyday experience, theorizing from the bottom up, as opposed to applying a category across the board. Such affective orientations did not have the same appearance of an aggregate of thousands of "likes" or comments but allowed my feminist participants a temporality and spatiality that permitted them to pause, catch their breath, and go on.

This final observation signals that we cannot give up on the possibilities of mediated or online feminism, but we do need to better understand the material everyday conditions in which young people are situated, to more rigorously conceptualize what is possible and sustainable in the rhythms and spatialities of the everyday. In particular, everyday feelings are crucial to understanding the politics of commonsense knowledges, their effects, and how they interweave the personal, the social, and the structural. We cannot reduce knowledge, mediated online or otherwise, to a "tool" or "resource," or to abstract ideas that can be picked up or discarded, and divorced from the self. Feminist knowledge engenders certain orientations, and while feminist theorizing of the world can help to explain dating mishaps, relationship breakdowns, violence, being overlooked at work, or emotional exhaustion, it is not something that can neatly be left behind. Despite the clear demands that my participants faced in their "always on" worlds, the fact that they elected to share their time with me, a stranger, at multiple points over several years, I think signifies an investment in feminism that cannot simply be erased or worn away.

In concluding, I make the call that in an increasingly mediatized world, we need more everyday poetry, not more information. By poetry, I refer to Louise Rosenblatt's notion of reading as poetic transaction, requiring spaces of imagining, lingering, and dwelling that counter the objectification of knowledge, identity, and experience into calculable units and linear relationalities. The mandates of transparency, authenticity, and visibility in social media culture translated ideas into binary terms and imbued them with a moralizing force: *passive* or *active*; *feminist* or *patriarchal*; *feminist* or *complicit*; *good* or *bad*. Most disturbingly, the subjectivity of feminist "knower" positioned my young feminists as always already knowing and inoculated against harm, and thus put them to work in highly individualized ways. They were pushed to adopt the language of leadership and inclusion in hollow terms that did not necessarily serve themselves or others; they were encouraged and authorized to turn on women as failing to embody the ever-moving, ever-higher standards of "good" feminism to which they subjected themselves; and they were, paradoxically, prohibited from taking up space on the basis of the gendered politics of their own experience. What they needed were spaces of sociality that helped them to endure without defensiveness, the time to listen and be listened to, and the validation that they, too, were living with and affected by the violence of this current moment.

PART I

Responsible and Responsive

1

EVERYDAY REACTIVISM, OR, NEVER LOOK AWAY

In 2021, I began the first workshops and interviews of my project against the backdrop of the COVID-19 pandemic. Unlike in parts of Europe and North America, where rules on physical circulation had largely relaxed, strict lockdowns were still ongoing in Sydney and Melbourne, Australia's two largest cities, together holding half of the national population. These lockdowns lasted several months, although, when instituted, they were intended to be of indeterminate duration, depending on the containment of the virus. In Queensland, a historically politically conservative state, the rise of COVID-19 cases in the single digits could result in snap lockdowns. Although citizens knew there was a relation between the movement of numbers and such dramatic measures, the exact formula was unknown. Therefore, to be connected to the reporting across social media on a daily basis was to be up to date but also to immerse the self in uncertainty. Movements of citizens beyond their own neighborhoods were regulated and surveilled; illicit movement across interstate borders was penalized and decried in the same fashion as "nonstandard" migration into the country. It was the norm to wait, to watch, to despair as mounting numbers of COVID-19 cases lengthened the lockdowns until an unknown time in the future.

This spatial freezing and control meant that all my initial workshops and interviews were undertaken on Zoom. In this time of uncertainty and shared vulnerability, it felt particularly intimate to be hearing the accounts of strangers, as fear of contagion and physical distancing eliminated possibilities of serendipitous encounters. Such intimacy was enhanced by these online meetings mainly taking place in my young feminists' bedrooms. Particularly if my participants lived with housemates, or at home with their parents, the bedroom afforded relative privacy and comfort. On camera, I would see them propped up in bed with pillows cushioning their back, at a desk in the corner of their room, or sometimes even on the floor. I myself operated out of the study at home, as my newly adopted dog continually burst in and out, closed doors being anathema to her.

This was perhaps an exceptional time of crisis. But in reflecting on my participants' accounts, I want to highlight how crisis constituted a constant in the everyday lived experience of online feminism. Online feminist knowledge cultures, characterized by a rapid flow of constantly new updates surfacing through personal devices, particularly phones, connected my participants to a beating digital heart of feminist consciousness, a quickening, sometimes panicky pulse that made "outside" structural events and wrongs part of one's personal domain of responsibility. But social media was not simply something that participants used to access the world. It was a medium through which the world accessed them. Even when they had carefully set up "bubbles" of select interests and hobbies through their social media accounts, any sense of cocooned boundedness was shot through by continual calls to attention through social media news cycles, and the moral obligation, as a feminist, to always be aware and well positioned in relation to such content.

This chapter explores the twinned injunctions of online feminism: to never look away from the pain in one's online feed; and to react swiftly and authentically to that content, ranging from global crises to the sundry sexist mishap at home. While in some ways, misogynist extremism had never been more visible online, this did not create extra space for politically sincere everyday politics; on the contrary, it created higher stakes and tighter obligations to have the right reaction. The impulse to participate in changing your profile to a black square in solidarity with #BlackLivesMatter might be decried as fake and performative the next day. This continual individual, everyday activism—or "reactivism," as I put it—required my feminists to be always ready: to be vigilant in relation to possible wrongs such as racism, transphobia, and general microaggressions, and to remain alert and aware of particular events, whether in (some) international locations or geographically close to home. It also meant many were constantly managing feelings of guilt, and dreading the possibility of failure or humiliation.

THE OUTSIDE COMING IN

In the emergence of Web 2.0 in the mid-2000s, the social possibilities afforded by youth-based platforms were theorized as akin to young people's bedrooms. In this necessarily culturally specific analysis, private bedrooms were spaces of leisure, exploration, and creativity where the young Internet user had relative freedom, space to invite friends and hang out. Metaphors of domesticity suggesting the bedroom's coziness and intimacy position the young Internet user as "host," in control of space and its rhythms. Paul Hodkinson and Sian Lincoln's (2008) influential exploration of LiveJournal in the emergence of social media portrays "[the] bedroom as a safe place to escape, to spend time alone, to 'chill out,' relax, daydream" (31), exemplified through participant remarks such as "Sometimes I go up [to my bedroom] because I can't be bothered, just to get away, I just get into bed and start thinking" (31).

I begin with this understanding simply to register how significantly the spatiotemporality inhabited by my young participants has shifted. While concerns about the "outside" coming "in" to personal space have existed since the private telephone (Marvin 1990) and the home television (Morse 1998), this early exploration of Web 2.0 media speaks to an era yet uncharacterized by widespread smartphone usage providing ubiquitous and continual access to a social media feed. It hearkens to a radically different embodiment and spatiotemporality. In the world in which my participants lived now, the distinction between outside and inside was highly permeable, as news, strangers, friends, parents were potentially always present, nudging them on a personal device that was always in their hand, in their pocket, or under their pillow.

But beyond the everyday norms of media usage meaning that the outside was always to hand, there were also powerful norms of good feminism that intensified a sense of obligation to always be available to witness what was going on. To be feminist, and to be online, meant normatively to never look away—to never avoid the encounter with the uncomfortable, the horrifying, the painful in terms of how oppression took place in the world.

This standard of conduct emerged in my workshops obliquely, as participants took care to frame their own practices and negotiations around it as personal choices. Bernie, a poet and nonbinary participant of Malaysian descent, stated that "especially when it comes to people sharing their traumas, I understand that sometimes to learn, you have to put yourself in an uncomfortable position and consume content that doesn't make you feel good, because for me . . . empathy is how I grow, empathy is how I learn." Derogation from this duty was to rely on one's privilege, as Bernie explained, and thus maintain existing social hierarchies: "And if I shield myself from those things, then personally I view that as a privileged decision and one that I wouldn't really label as being an ally, you know?"

To be feminist, particularly an intersectional feminist, then, was to keep one's door open in public online space, to continuously expose oneself to the harms that others suffered. To me, it was unclear what kinds of privilege Bernie felt they were relying on, as a visibly non-white migrant whose gender diversity was only partially legitimated in the queer circles they ran in. But Bernie saw this as an important part of living in the world. I had asked a general question about online well-being and mental health, and Bernie had responded, "I feel like sometimes being down is kind of like an inevitable within the environments that we live in."

They didn't put an expectation on themselves to "feel positive" but acknowledged: "I just allow myself to have my bad days, you know, and to understand that as much as we want to do everything and as much as we want to provide aid and provide education, sometimes your mental health just comes first." Mental health was the main accepted justification for derogating from this obligation to never look away. Rosie, a queer white participant who had also been part of Bernie's workshop, and openly admired their eloquence, confessed to me in a follow-up interview: "Recently just because my mental health hasn't been super fantastic. . . I've sort of made a habit on TikTok because of the algorithm [of] not specifically liking really, really dark stuff. And I know Bernie said, sometimes, that people can't turn off—the people who are actually going through the trauma. But I think I also have to be wary of my mental health when I'm in certain states as well." For Rosie, even while looking away, she felt pulled back by the sense that she was somehow shirking her feminist duties. Margot, an upper-middle-class white participant from Sydney, put this requirement in a different way:

There's also sometimes maybe too much information and it's often a lot to process. I feel like sometimes I have to take a step back, but then

I also kind of beat myself up for taking a step back . . . because I know that in my day-to-day life, I do have the privilege of not having to deal with a lot of the issues that I say are happening online. So it's such a privilege for me to step back and be like, "Oh, this is too much" when people are living that day to day in their everyday life.

To step back from the social media front line—from the distress of the world—was understood as a temporary stopgap measure, a moment of guilty respite. This guilt was tied up with a sense that witnessing on social media was an important form of solidarity, as well as an understanding that privilege was something that you could negate, and that you constantly had to disavow. Participants' online feminist participation thus continually hovered between desires to encounter and witness the world, to break open echo chambers of curated comfort, and the need to shelter from the unpredictable but continual social media nudges that blurred distinctions between outside and inside. "Looking away" on social media was to shirk one's obligation as a feminist to care, to witness, to respond. This meant my participants often inhabited a precarious time and space in which the world had access to them at any moment; there was little to no emotional insulation from the wrongs that streamed through their feeds. Being on the pulse through one's phone was thus a personal feminist vocation that spread across time and space.

This demand to be "chronically online," as one participant put it, was intensified in the social rhythms of standby mobilized during the pandemic. Standby, according to Lisa Baraitser and Laura Salisbury (2021), is a form of social organization that is deployed as a response to crisis. It involves waiting by, waiting on, remaining connected, and being ready to act. As time stretched out in the everyday experience of remaining at home, participants felt taut, stressed, and anxious. While most of my young feminists and I could venture a distance of only three miles from our homes, once per day, social media gave a bird's-eye view of what was happening in the world. It became even more important to be glued to the unfolding of global catastrophe and statistics via social media feeds, and the contrast between the seeming standstill of one's own life and catastrophes elsewhere heightened their significance.

For example, the news of the Taliban retaking Afghanistan in 2021, with consequent changes for women's lives in particular, loomed large in many participants' social media feeds. But it was crushing for participants such as Kristen, a young white participant studying gender and film. She said,

"I do get screen overwhelm. I can't. Like with Afghanistan, for example, I can't engage with content that I see on social media with it." By "engaging" Kristen meant considering, reflecting, and actively discussing it. She hadn't completely avoided the news: she shared an example of a *Guardian* article she had read, when I asked her what she had been accessing on social media. I asked her how she felt about the situation, and she responded, "Hopeless. Pretty dire. Yeah. It made me realize how narrow my perspective is and my experiences. And maybe—reflect on my privilege quite a bit as well."

Kristen keenly felt the narrowness of her studies in film that focused largely on the Anglosphere. However, the enormity of the events, while making her feel guilty, also caused her to guiltily recoil from the current of social media making the political situation visible. For Leila, a young, educated Sydney woman who via her family heritage felt directly affected by situations in the Middle East, it was similarly exhausting but also angering. She discussed her feelings in relation to the owner of an Instagram account named "Burqas and Beer" whose frustrated posts connected with her own feelings of fatigue:

> It is exhausting to be a Middle Eastern woman on Instagram right now, seeing everyone, including non–Middle Easterners, posting about your motherland. And it's kind of also triggering in a way to see that kind of content proliferate so widely across people who may not have really been interested up until this point. . . . So it's like, why have you been silent, for example, on the Afghanistan situation when it's been happening for a lot longer than the last two weeks? So I think that's something that really resonated with me. People are only interested especially in the Middle East when something hot is happening.

In the group workshop about a month before our first one-on-one interview, Leila had voiced her feelings of burnout. She had, she said, been a feminist for ten years. She was now twenty-five, and she was exhausted. Leila explained:

> I think that's a feeling that I've been feeling for quite a while. And in fact, it's kind of almost worse when you are a feminist, because, for example, I am the Middle Eastern correspondent for all my friends and, in particular, my feminist friends, because they are trying to understand and educate themselves about that viewpoint—

She went on:

> [and] what better way than to have a friend that you can kind of *tap into* that kind of content and that kind of information, despite the fact I am no expert and my feelings may not be representative of my complete ethnic group.

The emotional fallout of the highly mediated success of the Taliban permeated Leila's social circles, intensifying desires to know and grasp, to get a handle on, that Leila was ambivalent about fulfilling.

As Leila noted, this recent spectacle was just the tip of the iceberg of a decades-long history in which invasion, violence, and contestation had long been present. But in lockdown, the explosive nature of this mediated event made Afghanistan seem new and spectacular, an object that had to be mastered so that a position had to be taken. Notably the feminist obligation to never look away, importantly, was combined with the obligation to react appropriately. Far from Kabul, and even quite some distance from the national decision-makers who crafted a minimal humanitarian package in response, other participants felt the pressure to show their support and galvanize others into action. Bella, an energetic young woman who ran a feminist group on campus, was well versed in the expectations of re-activism in her social circles. She described the stakes of responding on social media in a timely fashion to events in Afghanistan in terms of being evaluated in relation to your integrity as an activist. She saw the benefits of the "waiting game" in which her activist group was able to see critique of those who most quickly reacted and modify their own collective's public stance, but felt ambivalent as to whether such a measured response was really authentic: "By waiting, we were able to see how other people reacted to other people's posts, which is sometimes interesting, because it's like, are you putting yourself in a better position by waiting? Or are you not posting just for the sake of it? Or, or like, is it more or less authentic, which way you do it? I think that's a, that's a big question when it comes to sharing online."

Responses to this spectacular event were thus plotted and evaluated against axes of authenticity and quality. Did you show you were aware of all the dynamics of the crisis in your response? Was your reaction quick enough to be authentic? In this way, the felt urgency around seemingly singular events heightened both the moral obligation to witness and react and the potential judgment of failing to do so in the right way.

And yet the never-ending emergence of crises, all over the world, often worsened by the pandemic, made it imperative to then keep on moving on. Despite the waves of emotion surrounding images of Taliban fighters brandishing guns in the Afghan national assembly, such feelings were then displaced by the seeming urgency of the subsequent Texas abortion criminalization. As some participants ruefully noted, they had been trying to "hold on" to the urgency of Afghanistan, and particularly in relation to the needs of Afghans who needed to be resettled and the women who feared for their lives. Shona, a white working-class law student from rural Western Australia, spoke about sharing fundraising events for Afghan refugees in Australia. Shona acutely felt how her own sense of space-place had changed, moving to Perth, a medium-sized metropolitan center, where she began her studies. As a rural teenager, she used to "see terrible stuff on Facebook that's happening in other countries. And I remember as a teenager, just scrolling past, like it felt like it was a completely other world. Like it had no impact on me."

Now, Shona's new feminist friendship circles called for a sense of passionate proximity to the problem. The outside could no longer be kept separate from the inside: "Like I could have easily have been born in Afghanistan and that could have been, could be me that is going through those atrocities right now. . . . I told these things like to my girlfriend, like what's happening in Afghanistan, like holy shit. I just feel for the women and the children and [she's] like, 'Oh, you care too much. Like you give too much, you care too much.' It's like, no, what about if this was us?" For this reason, she felt she needed to stick with this particular crisis. But it was like holding on to quicksand. As social media feeds were then flooded with new events and images of protests in Texas about abortion, the conversation had moved on, and she was trying to get "on top of" these new problems. Unlike the passive flow Raymond Williams (1990) famously discussed in relation to the disparate synchronicity of television, this flow felt forceful—it carried you along; it created new time-bound imperatives to know, understand, and react.

GOOD REACTIONS

On a recurring basis, my participants were caught between the pulse of what was happening and the exhaustion of trying to keep up. Keeping up meant being agile; you had to be a master of the quick take, as Leila noted in relation to her friends; it was important to know key facts to avoid or ideally skewer any problematic pitfalls in taking a position. Those that exemplified the capacity to do this, for my participants, were feminist accounts on TikTok in particular that swiftly reacted to problematic takes or people via stitched videos. In this genre of action-reaction, a TikTok creator would begin by featuring the ostensibly problematic opinion or statement, followed by their own take of why this ought to be critiqued. A prominent figure emerging in my participants' 2022 interviews was Drew Afualo, an unapologetic American woman of color in her late twenties with several million followers on TikTok (figure 1.1).

According to Crystal, a white, queer, history student, "She has a huge like platform and on TikTok, she'll stitch videos of mostly—actually all men—saying really suss, problematic things. And then she kind of fights fire with fire almost, and attacks them." In a world where Crystal felt overwhelmed by casual sexism and misogyny to which she couldn't respond, at her workplace, and in her broader social media–connected circles of acquaintances, the courage Afualo showed and the license she took in insulting sexists was admirable: "She is iconic. . . . And I think it's because it's, it's funny, it's a bit shocking to see a woman being like, 'You have a receding hairline, don't come talk, don't be fatphobic.'"

Crystal explained this mode of reactionary content production as key to Afualo's popularity. In some ways, Afualo's fame had grown explicitly from this productive friction with the rhythms of misogyny. While Sarah Banet-Weiser (2018) observed some years ago that popular misogyny is often reactive in relation to a more highly visible, popular feminism, it is feasible that the mainstreaming of online misogyny in recent years has now enabled an online genre of explicitly reactionary social media feminism to emerge. Perhaps for this reason, Crystal noted, showing me a recent Twitter post by Afualo, some had compared her to high-profile men's rights influencer Andrew Tate, though Afualo had explicitly refused to entertain any such similarity with the violent misogynist, an American-British former kickboxer and champion of "men's liberation" who had spent time in prison for kidnapping and enslaving women.

This disavowed connection, however, was often responsible for bringing my participants' initial attention to these misogynists, who otherwise would have circulated on the "other side" of TikTok. Jenny, a white, twenty-one-year-old social worker, observed in relation to the reaction content that Afualo generated in response to the "stitched" misogynist content: "When I see what the videos that Drew—I don't know what they call it where she'll show the clip and then she comes in—I don't know what they call

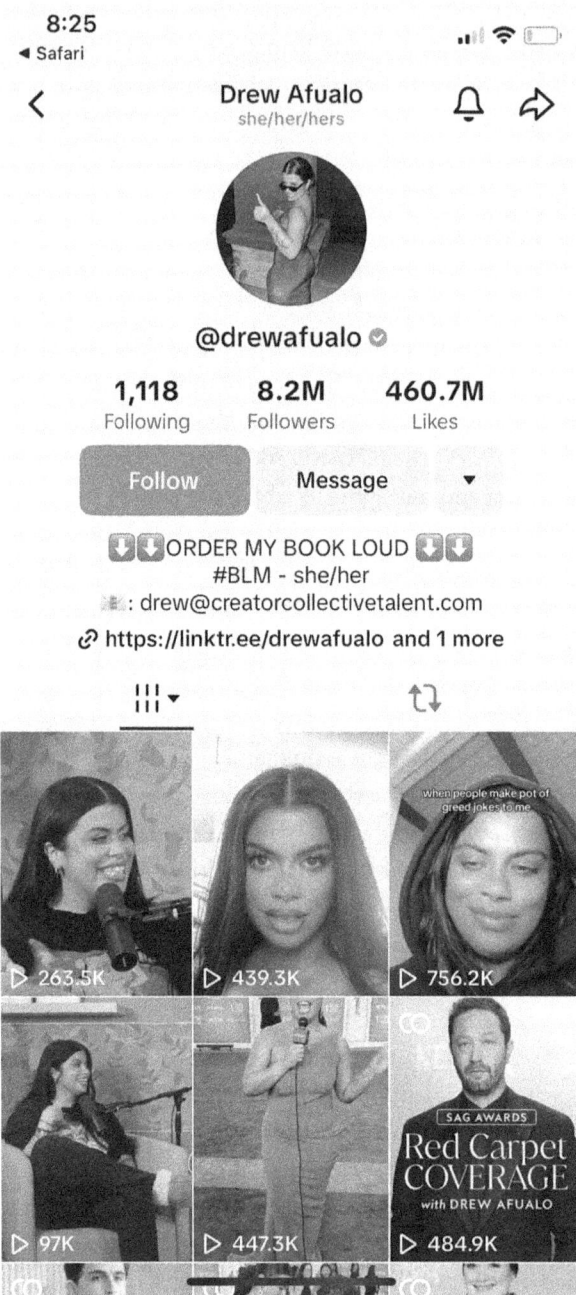

1.1 Drew Afualo's TikTok profile, February 19, 2025. Screenshot by author.

that—I would never have seen those videos before." For others, awareness of Tate similarly came through denunciation by social activist accounts, such as that of Matt Bernstein, a high-profile American queer activist on Instagram. These involved calls for platforms to take responsibility for the megaphone effect afforded to Tate (figure 1.2).

Bernie noted that Tate was very much "in the atmosphere" on progressive TikTok: "Creators have been making videos around him because he's controversial and that's what they do . . . it's in my feed a lot, but people reacting to popular videos, it's definitely a trend. He's definitely a hot-button topic." Progressive creators could thus amplify their own presence by providing speedy, articulate reactions to misogyny and conservatism through which spectators could channel their own sense of frustration and anger. Crystal, the history student and server who had gained much confidence from her undergraduate studies, found herself magnetized to these strong personalities, most often strong women, who consistently "called out" what they saw as wrong and unfair. Abbie Chatfield, a well-known Australian former *Bachelor* contestant and now host of her own podcast, whom I introduced earlier, exemplified this readiness to react and speak out. So did social worker Jenny, who followed her on TikTok: "She's quite outspoken about current things that are happening in the news or in the media at the moment, and looking at them through a gender lens, and sort of analyzing them in that perspective. I like what she stands for. I feel like she's quite genuine."

Bernie appreciated this genre of political analysis on TikTok, and commentators who were able to keep them abreast of new developments and provide smart, ready-formulated takes on them. They shared an example of a TikToker who critiqued the sexist humor of queer rapper Lil Nas X. Bernie thought it was particularly important to be alive to this kind of misogyny, especially as it came from cutting-edge artists who were also positioned as queer ambassadors in popular culture. However, Bernie's watchful orientation also came with a sensitivity to the preoccupations that reaction content could involve. They were concerned about the effects of the proliferation of attention to Tate and similar extremists: "I guess it's a problem that when we see more of this, we normalize it. It's no longer like, 'Holy shit.' I've seen a lot of extremists. I've even noticed within myself that, the first time, I was just so taken aback . . . now I'm resigned. What's it going to be like to have kids that are you know, growing up, listening to this, joking about it. . . . I think it's going to completely desensitize us." Indeed, without a certain desensitization to it, such violence could be hard

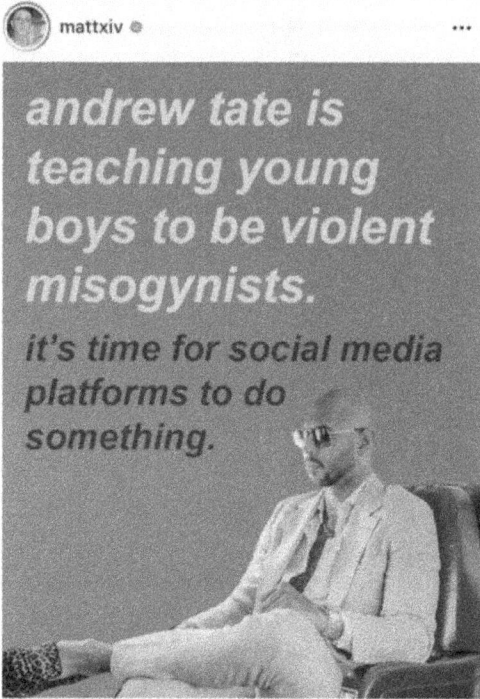

1.2 Instagram post against Andrew Tate, June 20, 2022.
Screenshot by author.

to stomach on an ongoing everyday basis. Some were able to tune out from these shocks to the heart; but for others, the routine social encounters woven into their lives made this impossible. In the everyday, the emergence of different personalities, events, and crises of which one had to be aware came without warning.

This was the case for Marina, who worked as a high school teacher in a Catholic school for boys in the northern suburbs of Melbourne. Of Italian and Greek heritage, and having attended a Catholic school for girls when growing up, she was familiar with the similar social background of boys she taught. But this did not make her job less challenging. Being a teacher multiplied the events, personalities, and general phenomena of which she had to be aware as they bubbled up in chatter between students—namely, in 2022, the popularity of Andrew Tate.

Marina's experience of Tate was more direct than those of the above participants. While still driven by the rhythms of social media, the boundary testing of her students brought Tate's social media circulation into the classroom. Students incorporated Tate into their repertoire of celebrity knowledge and often gleefully name-dropped him in class. She recounted: "Like, you know, if a kid's name is Andrew, they'll call him Andrew Tate, they'll just shout the word Andrew Tate out in class. They will tell me he's a top G, they will ask me, 'What do you think of him?' Like, it, it is getting brought up constantly." Marina felt under siege, with students constantly testing her patience in the name of "humor": "It's one of those things where I've either got kids who find it funny and like to bring him up, they'll set him as their laptop background, they'll try and debate me and sort of say why he's a businessman. . . . [Or] some of them truly listen to this guy and truly they're [like], 'Oh, but no, forget the misogyny stuff.' . . . It's almost like they're in denial or they're almost saying, 'Yeah, but ignore all of that. He's a billionaire.'"

For some of Marina's students, Tate's claims to be a billionaire meant this was worthy of admiration in and of itself. The claim to be self-made meant Tate's "negatives" in terms of histories of violence and assault could be canceled out. When Marina tried to bring these histories to light, she herself was put on the stand for "fake news," for not bringing them credible information: "They're even asking me like, 'Where are you hearing this stuff?'—And I'm like, 'Everywhere.' Like, I don't understand, do I have to come to you with sources? 'Cause look, admittedly I say to my kids when they bring up a stupid claim about something, I'm like, 'Where are you reading this?'" This was itself complicated by the fact that Marina did not wish to spend her spare time trawling videos of Tate's blatant misogyny, and had avoided paying attention to him: "I've just seen a few YouTube clips, I've seen a few things going around on Instagram. It's not like . . . I've never watched a video, I've never watched an interview with him. I don't care to."

This took a toll. In 2021, when I caught up with Marina for her first interview, she had painted a sunny picture of what it was like to put out these fires on a daily basis, in trying to get her high school students to think critically about identity, inequality, and, particularly, gender: "What my mentors have told me in the past is you might not get through to the kid you're talking to, they might be so entrenched in their beliefs. But there'll be three other kids in the room listening.... Sometimes if it's something that's on topic, you can stop the whole class. And then go, actually, guys, let's talk about this again."

But by the time I spoke to Marina again, a year later, in 2022, she admitted that she was at the end of her tether. She could no longer put a positive spin on the exhaustion of being alert to continual minicrises in the classroom and did not have the energy to give to students who often were not coming to her in good faith with questions about the world. This was reflected in her anger when a male colleague approached her to give her a "project" to work on. This project was a boy with ingrained sexist beliefs: "He comes into the staff room and he is like, 'I've got a project' ... and I've gone, 'Oh, *project*. What's that? What do you mean?' And he goes, 'Well I've got a student who's telling me that he doesn't believe, or something along the lines of, he doesn't believe that there's inequality between the genders in Australia.'" The continual grind—and the cycle of patience, endurance, and vigilance in the face of spot fires—caused deep emotional tremors that took the joy out of working: "I just kind of went, it's not a project for me. That's my life. That's not a fun, cool—like, what? ... I was just sort of like, I'm a bit over having to justify my existence and my needs and my gender essentially. I'm a bit over that. That's not fun for me anymore. That's, that's work." Marina was at a dead end. In the face of recurring high-profile controversies around gendered violence, she was now trying to *not* react and to retreat, to save herself.

BAD REACTIONS

It would not be accurate to say that urgency and immediacy always characterized my participants' experiences of connection to the social, particularly during the exemplary experience of waiting during the pandemic. Turning to social media was often commensurate with boredom, as participants sought diversion in a familiar cycle of content. There would be "nothing new" on Instagram, as the algorithm updated to only rarely showing the accounts participants wanted to follow. Boredom and inattention, Jonathan Crary (2001) writes, are the corollary of the sustained attentiveness demanded of citizens in capitalist modernity. That is, bouts of prolonged concentration, together with the openness to diversion, are necessary for capitalism to both harness workers' productivity and colonize their "free time," with online user attention notably being one of the most valuable resources of digital media industries (Jarrett 2015, 2022). This insidiousness was registered by my young participants in their involuntary nature of connection to social media. As Maya explained, you try to avoid it when you're at work, "but then, oh, you scroll down and there's other content, [and] you get distracted."

This "slow" time often felt wasteful and noncathartic; participants would catch themselves magnetized to social media while studying for exams, waiting for the bus, or sitting at their computers at work and then be caught in an aimless cloud of scrolling. Scrolling as an activity required low-level attention; it could be set aside, although you would inevitably return to it; its magnetism would operate as a background hum. But things would sometimes explode and the pace would quicken beyond participants' control. Participants, then, oscillated between this desire to disconnect from the continual low-level absorption of social media and the unwilling sense of being pulled into a maelstrom of highly urgent, affecting, and stressful events. These explosions would have embodied effects: a shot of adrenaline, a quickening of the pulse.

The Taliban taking over Afghanistan, as noted earlier, was one such catalyst. Another such moment was when an accusation of rape in Australia's highest seat of power, Parliament House, became front-page news. Brittany Higgins, a young political staffer, had reported her alleged assault by a colleague to superiors, but damningly, it seemed no action had been taken. In the wake of other high-profile, long-term cases of sexual abuse and assault in Australian schools coming to light, spearheaded by young activists and victim-survivors Grace Tame and Chanel Contos, the absence of accountability in Higgins's case was explosive. This news event built feminist momentum, accumulating speed and force. It was everywhere on Instagram, Facebook, Twitter. It snowballed into numbers attending and protesting in the 2021 Women's Marches that took place across cities in Australia. But it also created highly fraught dynamics for participants for whom Higgins's experiences were all too close to their own. This was the case for Margot, a charming twenty-one-year-old self-identified Libra, a white heterosexual woman who never had trouble being the "center of attention" at parties in the privileged eastern suburbs of Sydney. News of Higgins's alleged rape created significant ripples in Margot's social circles, not dissimilar to the elite social strata of Parliament. The net effect of the news cycle streaming across social media feeds catalyzed "a lot of . . . conversations for girls in the east," because "a lot of the schools were private, old boys schools that are in the eastern suburbs or on the north shore. It kind of like started a lot of discussions or arguments . . . about like, you know, all private school boys in the east are rapists. And I was like, well, I actually have a lot of friends who were there at the same time. I was sexually assaulted in high school. So I really feel like, you know, I relate to these conversations."

For Margot herself, this was a highly emotional time. Not only did these events connect to her own sexual assault at school; they also forcefully brought it into the present. They led to heated arguments with her boyfriend about his entanglement in rape culture via his own social circles, and to consequences with her own friends, who were often the romantic interests and girlfriends of his friends:

> But I think like, you know, in his friendship group, there was a guy who raped a girl at a party. And while he's always like, "I've never been friends with him. I don't like that guy." [But] it's like, you still don't say anything when he's at parties or when he's around your friendship group. Also his good friends, the way that they speak about women. . . . I think I was just wanting him to question a lot of those things, but because it was his friends and him, it was really personal and that made it a really difficult conversation for us to have.

I first spoke to Margot about this six months after the story of Higgins's rape broke. It was clear that this constellation of circumstances had been highly distressing for her. With the momentum and affecting force of the news, her personal relations were transformed into a frontier of these contestations and desires for social justice, not simply for these high-profile victim-survivors but for herself as well. Prior to the public surfacing of these incidents, she hadn't realized she had such "intense" feelings about assault and rape culture. And her boyfriend's disavowing his social connections to the rapist wasn't good enough. Margot was angry and tearful: "It was such a passionate and close and personal topic that, you know, I probably took [a] very much, like, 'It's your fault and you need to fix it' approach. It was really hard, I think, for both of us, because a lot of his friends and, I think, he himself, like . . . wasn't really locating a lot of what was happening in his friendship group and like his role in it and like this complicitness [sic] to rape culture. And I really wanted to articulate that to him."

Pain, as Sara Ahmed (2004a) outlines, is about the intensification of the feeling of an impression. Like a shock to the heart, enlivened by the effect of numerous young women coming forward, it resuscitated embodied memories. Margot didn't want to hold this pain herself, but her boyfriend had difficulty holding it with her; he couldn't accept the magnitude and significance of the harm she sought to describe. She said her boyfriend was very "black-and-white," rational; he didn't want to bend. I was reminded of Ahmed's (2012) discussion of coming up against walls in the discussion of sexual assault: the wall of masculine rationality can feel like a grating, hard surface, a closed door. Margot became fatigued as the emotional momentum threatened to burn them out: "Like that was a massive point of contention between us. And every time we tried to talk about it, it would be like an issue. And I think . . . over time, [it] just dropped out of our conversations because it would be a heated discussion every time and we would just get into fights because of it. And it was just like . . . we were both defending ourselves and our friends. Yeah. Yeah. So it just kind of like, wasn't sustainable, almost." I noticed how Margot took care to lighten the accusation in acknowledging the force with which she spoke to him—that it was hard "for both of them" in her relationship. This acknowledgment of mutual difficulty became a valve through which the built-up pressures of conflict could be released. But it didn't resolve the obligation Margot implicitly felt, to still be "reasonable" in these arguments even as the resonant trauma of Higgins's rape reverberated with her.

A year later, the defamation case brought by Hollywood actor Johnny Depp similarly catalyzed widespread ripples in the personal and social fabric of my participants' lives. In May 2022, news that Depp was suing his ex-wife Amber Heard for defamation in relation to domestic abuse suddenly became widespread knowledge via social media. Live media coverage of proceedings in the courtroom streamed into television news and, most notably for my participants, on TikTok and Instagram. It was literally unavoidable for many. In my own highly insulated Instagram feed otherwise dominated by dogs and easy vegan recipes, I was buffeted by unwanted "humorous" content mocking Heard in the court proceedings. Unsurprisingly, the case spontaneously emerged in interviews as participants recounted the ways that it touched their lives. Margot recoiled at its presence on her "For You" page on Instagram: "I was like, I need to tune out. I completely swiped immediately as soon as I saw anything because there is so much backstory there. I [am] very much a believer of believe women, trust women with their stories. But there were so many sides to it and I was like, this is just too much. I don't want to engage in it, so I very actively disengaged from that."

Social media is synonymous with the affective impression of "so many sides"—a cacophony of voices that becomes confusing and overwhelming. Mark Andrejevic (2020) characterizes this as an aesthetic of "framelessness," in which social media becomes positioned as a sensorial web capturing ever more nodes of data across space in the race for a "complete" account of truth. In the register of the everyday, this dragnet is experienced as paralyzing. Margot did not want to be touched by the reach of this story; she actively put up a barrier, backgrounded it as much as possible. Fortunately for her, Margot was in a relative social bubble at the time: she was traveling overseas to see family at this time, had infrequent access to social media, and had only one social encounter in which she "had to shut down" the discussion of what was happening. But for others, it became part of the grind. Crystal, a history student who also worked as a server, told me that talk of the case was everywhere: "I'd be serving a customer and they, they would be talking about it. You know, I'm sitting there trying to serve them that lentil salad and you know, I'm having to hear this, but I can't say anything obviously. And obviously, you wouldn't . . . approach a stranger being like, 'You're wrong.' But like the things that I heard in the streets at uni . . . "

At the age of twenty-two, Crystal was already a survivor of domestic abuse from one romantic relationship, and, as a child, had also witnessed her mother go through abuse. A white working-class woman who was the first in her family to finish high school, then attend university, Crystal was unable to talk through much of her experience of gendered abuse with her mother and her family. Rather, she had managed to carve out a queer, feminist bubble through her university friends, all located in an inner urban neighborhood of Melbourne where they worked and lived. From within this bubble, the TikTok momentum that mobilized in favor of Depp and explicitly against Heard was deeply unsettling.

Indeed, what was particularly remarkable, besides the "live" nature of these legal proceedings, streamed on YouTube, was the infinite volume of social media commentary that transformed the proceedings into a ludic zone of combat, under the moniker of hashtags like #JusticeForJohnnyDepp. This hashtag reached ten billion views on TikTok (Watercutter 2022), while footage of Heard crying was ridiculed in humor videos by social media creators (Winter 2022). Notably this contest was far from evenly weighted; narratives of untruths and vindication, right and wrong, emerged along clearly gendered lines.

The emotional grip of the narrative portraying Depp as a wronged victim appeared to catalyze widespread, deep resentments in relation to the status of men in the aftermath of #MeToo. The force of feeling connected to the "bedrock of common sense," as Stuart Hall has described it, was incredibly powerful, galvanizing the seemingly apolitical. Suddenly, as Crystal described it, "people who, you know, that would be like, 'Oh, let's not talk politics at the table'... All of a sudden they're jumping in [with] their, you know, opinions on something and they don't even know what's going on."

What was most distressing for Crystal was not this story of abuse, in and of itself, but the widespread support an A-list Hollywood celebrity like Depp would attract locally, in preference to and in complete disregard of the national incidence of gendered abuse and partner violence that had been gaining some traction in headlines in past years: "And then all, then all of a sudden... they're the supporters of victims being on Johnny Depp's side, but then they aren't engaging with what's actually happening down the road from them. So, I think the more emotional side of it was being like... why is it every time I open my Instagram, there's a guy from my high school posting 'I stand with Johnny Depp' or, like TikToks that were compilations of Johnny Depp making jokes in court." For Crystal, the alacrity and energy with which this thinly veiled misogyny erupted was hard to stomach. Abruptly, her presumptions about the political status quo were punctured: "I think the hardest part was feeling like you're the minority.... Like constantly every day seeing this way of thinking, and me and my friend being like, how are we the only people in the whole—in our surroundings that are thinking this right now?"

For Katie, a white, twenty-eight-year-old administration professional who had similarly experienced partner violence and sexual assault as a child, the tremors of this social media upheaval had deeply felt embodied, and the social consequences. While the general response "wasn't necessarily surprising," she said, "I think what I found the most hurtful or triggering or upsetting was responses of people that I know, whether it's people that I'm close to and their take on that situation and the ease with which they raised that with me, but predominantly in places like the workplace conversations cropping up, and the statements that were made about it were definitely not wonderful to hear."

Katie's tactic for navigating the landscape was to be "intentional" and "conscious" in her engagement with the case; she would take a breath, "go in" and read the court transcripts in a way that wouldn't be "overwhelming" for her day, but otherwise shut off her social media feed. In spite of, or perhaps due to, the intense social reverberations of the case, Katie—bright, articulate, and curious—engaged in an analytical fashion with the general public's response: "The biggest thing that that trial and the public's response to that trial made me realize is that I don't think a lot of people have an understanding of what it's like to be a domestic violence survivor, and that perhaps survivors are not necessarily perfect in their own actions . . . obviously a fight response that can be triggered as well. And I think the notion that there was mutual abuse in that case and that sort of tending to be the main perception of those allegations was very interesting."

Katie's mother was an academic, but Katie's own life circumstances had meant she had never managed to finish more than a semester of study. Yet she was discerning in her analysis beyond the Manichean framing of the case, and associated liberal assumptions of power that enabled a characterization of the two actors to be "as bad as each other" and thus for their actions to "cancel each other out." This kind of critical position-taking was not available to all of my participants. One of my youngest participants, Sumaya, a nineteen-year-old Anglo-Singaporean woman, had earnestly started out "believing Amber Heard" but had come to the position that Depp was in the right: "I personally believe that Johnny Depp is the victim in the situation. Just even if we just forget about like how much we will love Johnny Depp in the movies, et cetera, et cetera. From a legal perspective, there was absolutely nothing backing up Amber's case like full stop. Like that should be enough. Like if we just want to think about this really objectively. So I do support Johnny Depp in this case."

In this formulation, Sumaya believed that Amber Heard herself was understood to "appropriate" victimhood, and militated against the broader feminist cause of elevating the voices of abuse victims: "Like I'm very much for women supporting women and I'm very much for women elevating voices, but the, the worst thing for feminism is women who exploit and take advantage of the good work that the women before them have done, to hurt the people around them basically. . . . Amber Heard has used the work that's gone into lessening that, but she's used it as an oppressor and used it to oppress the victim, which really frustrates me because like women should not be hindering other women." Further, Sumaya felt, those feminists who had been supporting Amber Heard couldn't "even acknowledge Johnny Depp because he's a man. And that is a patriarchal thing because men can definitely be . . . in domestic violence situations."

I was, truthfully, somewhat taken aback when I heard Sumaya—warm, kind, and thoughtful—take this position during the interview. She sensed this, and noted quickly she would welcome my own thoughts if I thought differently. In the moment, I felt conflicted. I didn't wish to debate her, particularly as I had avoided all social media discussion of the case. In the end I refrained from voicing my equivocation, just saying the phenomenon was very "big" and "messy."

But Sumaya's position was understandable. The online discourse was not only, as one *New Yorker* article termed it, "toxic" (Winter 2022). Compounding the concerted and intentional "firehose of falsehood" (Andrejevic 2013) generated by bots and right-wing social media activists about the trial, there was the general excess of information that is structurally embedded online. The immense volume and speed of details and hot takes that proliferated across social media invited a sense of the intricacy of the case but simultaneously the possibility of cutting through the complexity with clear divisions of "truth" and "lies," "right" and "wrong." The excess itself was influential in reestablishing a binary and unequal polarity as a means of parsing or, as Andrejevic puts it, "cutting through the glut."

Sumaya, like other middle-class young feminists, respected institutions such as the law. While feminist legal theorists have long been critical of the guise of legal neutrality, equality under the law, and singular truth (Davies 2008), Sumaya's respect for institutional systems of parsing social outcomes led her to conclude that the finding for Depp meant he was in the right; Heard, therefore, had to be wrong, and thus an enemy to other women. And, as many of my participants noted, the emotional fallout of this distant case that nonetheless felt so close was simply exhausting. Sumaya had been chatty with me throughout our interview, but she also didn't want to "talk about it anymore."

ON THE PULSE, ON THE CLOCK

Feminist thought has long highlighted the particularity of theory; thought is always generated in and by social contexts. This chapter has drawn attention to how the rules of online feminism cultures extracted personal attention, energy, and care from my young feminists. They felt obligated to let the outside in at all times, continually witnessing the stream of wrongs that circulated through their feeds, such that any form of respite was understood in terms of lack, of failing to be good, of relying on existing privilege. The temporality of online culture required immediate, authentic, but perfect reactions to events.

The emotional buffeting to which my participants were continually subject raises questions about what kinds of reflective possibilities were open to them. In the demands to continually be on the pulse, to be a master of the quick take, and to articulate the right position, while not being defeated by the reverberation of trauma that was all too close to home, my participants inhabited a precarious position. Taking emotional and intellectual time and space to be slightly removed from the direct reception of bad news was seen as an emergency measure rather than a norm. The social media "bedroom" was not a place of rest. No wonder, then, that my participants overwhelmingly found the interviews and workshops—spaces of slow deliberation and listening—so unusual as spaces of reflection, as I further discuss in chapter 6. On continuous standby, they normalized reactivism as a standard orientation to social media and to others. The everyday experience of online feminism, then, was one not of creating or negotiating space but of reacting to what was continually coming, of changing, of transforming. It left little room to breathe.

Lisa Baraitser and Laura Salisbury (2021) suggest that in pandemic times and beyond, the temporalities of care need to inform social organization. They suggest that this requires "waiting with" and "responding with." Importantly, the generation of thought should not simply "react" or "manage" but also "contain." Using the work of psychoanalyst Wilfred Bion, they suggest that political thinking "becomes a space of containment that allows the violence of the world to be taken into the self and digested over and through time, rather than unthinkingly expelled as invasive or intolerable. Such thinking, imagined according to the processes of a body able to digest rather than be torn open by explosive, incendiary 'thoughts,' produces a space and time where violence might be suspended, delayed and therefore thought about" (7).

This framework foregrounds a capacious holding, waiting, repetition, and enduring. Yet I think the challenges in doing so in the present conjuncture must be made explicit, as I have tried to do here. In significant ways, participants such as Marina, Margot, and Bernie held the violence of a social media information overload. Marina was compelled to hold space for it through her job; she could not simply tune out the voices and needs of her students. Others, like Sumaya, resorted to heuristics of right and wrong, legal and illegal to manage the messiness and volume of claims or, like Kristen, scrolled past and aimed to detox from the sensory excess. The pulse of a feminist social media feed plugged spectators into a continual aliveness to social wrongs. It produced temporalities and momentums in which my feminist participants were frequently filled to capacity as misogyny "pressed" upon them (Ahmed 2004a). They admired feminist influencers who refused to hold or digest misogyny, who expelled that violence through their reaction videos, even as they recirculated this violence in the world. To be on the pulse, to always be ready to respond, was highly valued; but a responsive heart tethered to the continuous circulation of feminist social media meant that it was almost impossible to carve out a reflective room of one's own.

2

IN YOUR LANE AND
KNOWING YOUR PLACE

I recall, during a gray wintery morning in 2021, the long conversation I had with my young participant Shae, as I curled up at my computer. Shae was a young white queer woman in her early twenties who was in the middle of her sociology degree at university. She lived with her parents, so she was speaking from the privacy of her bedroom. There was a quiet intimacy to this meeting. Shae and I, while living in different cities, were both in lockdown and this interview was our only social activity for the day. As requested, she shared numerous screengrabs from her recent feminist social media engagement with me. For her, this was all channeled through Tumblr. Tumblr was part of Shae's morning routine. She would wake up, scroll for fifteen minutes, then get on with her day.

Shae wasn't as obsessed with Tumblr as she used to be. Tumblr used to be one of the places on the Internet that afforded safe spaces for marginalized identities; providing "silo sociality" (Tiidenberg et al. 2021), it allowed people to navigate ideas in depth without having to save face based on social position, thanks to its anonymity. But since beginning sociology,

Shae's world was bigger; it had significantly opened up. According to Shae, Tumblr involved a lot of "shouting into the ether." She felt that intersectional feminism on Tumblr was "fairly single-minded if you know what I mean. . . . Like people get an idea in their heads and they stick to it." I asked her about one post she shared from her #IntersectionalFeminism feed. It read:

> The future isn't female. The future is nonbinary it's genderfluid it's queer and it's trans it's natives rising up against their colonizers it's sex workers getting coin it's gay it's bi it's pan it's ace it's ppl of color it's ppl w disabilities THE FUTURE IS INTERSECTIONAL.

I wondered as Shae read it out: Was this a future in which all these cited groups were seen as distinct and separate from the category of "female"—and how did this relate to Maria Lugones's (2003) insight that gender itself is not separable but a product of the colonial project? Was intersectionality the new better form of humanism ("I'm not a feminist, I'm intersectional?")? Or was I reading too much into it—perhaps what the writer really meant was that "the future isn't only female" or that "female" itself felt like an outdated referent in terms of gender?

What, I asked, did she think of this particular post—and the intersectional future it envisioned? She mused:

> What I noticed when I read that, it was like, they're saying that things aren't solidly a category—I mean—they're saying that, everyone has the right to exist, you know, no matter who you are, it's all the same. Like, you know, [a] "we're all in this together" type thing, but you're still very much using categories to, I guess, transmit your message.

She went on to observe:

> I think actually weirdly Tumblr is one of the few places that have— gotten on board with the idea that nothing is binary, if you know what I mean. . . . But the funny thing is, is, and I've noticed this for many, is Tumblr seems to be obsessed with like labels for everything, for absolutely everything. If you could think of something, it probably has a label and then a sub-label. So—for . . . a place that thinks, 'Oh, you know, it's all just shades of gray, it's all on a spectrum' . . . they do seem to love categorizing people, you know?

The central paradox of Tumblr intersectional feminism, then, was that it was a feminism that insisted on gray, and formally opposed labels that were black-and-white. However, as Shae noted, it was nonetheless bound up and entangled in categorization. This felt familiar to me—after all, narratives of the tensions between essentialism and fluidity have long been part of how feminist histories have been narrated in scholarship (Hemmings 2011).

But there seemed to be something more in the affecting pull to intersectionality that my participants described in their knowledge cultures. Looking at my transcripts after my interviews, I saw that "intersectionality" was mentioned over and over again. It was cited literally hundreds of times, and its emotional repercussions were marked across my cohort. Understanding intersectionality was often narrated as a rite of passage. It "fucking rocked my world," according to one white queer participant; "it was a complete theory . . . it was like a complete actual framework with which I could proceed," said a queer participant of color. It was also narrated in contradictory terms: as open, highly expansive—"THE FUTURE IS INTERSECTIONAL," as noted earlier—but also as something providing classifications, something that placed you or put you in your place.

It was important, then, to know about intersectionality. But its ubiquity could disorient. In another Zoom meeting that week, Ade, a woman of West African heritage brimming with ideas and theories on life, told me that reading different posts on intersectionality made her question herself:

Oh, this is a different thing to what I thought I knew it meant. And then I go back and make sure I go back to read the paper [by Kimberlé Crenshaw] and I'm like, did I read that correct? And like, definitely words evolve and like meanings change. So I'd really love to like, get an understanding of like, what is the understanding of intersectionality? 'Cause I think it's become such a big part of, like, online feminist discourse, but there's like so many—it's kind of been corrupted into so many different uses and it's like hard to keep up because it's quite alive and—a current thing.

For those who have critiqued the "travels" of intersectionality as a theory, Ade's question resonates. Intersectionality has been termed a "buzzword" (Davis 2008); the politics of its use have been keenly dissected in concert with the institutionalization of feminism (Nash 2019). As a term first primarily articulated within the academy (Crenshaw 1989), it now "parachutes" down into different contexts (Lewis 2013). In online culture, it is a crucial part of being fluent in social media feminism; it has become a means of currency on dating profiles; it is a neat encapsulation of one's political identity on Instagram. Everyone seems to "know" what intersectionality is. Indeed, the expectation of the rapid and natural-seeming mastery of knowledge is intensified in the so-called Information Age precisely when the capacity to Google any question seemingly opens up knowledge for all. Being in the know was evidently felt to be important by many of my young participants, and particularly my white participants in relation to understanding race. Some, shamefaced and tentative, confessed to me that they hadn't heard of intersectionality until a couple of years earlier. They felt naïve and often, sincerely, wanted to do better.

But this chapter is not a straightforward story of youth empowerment through access to online knowledge of marginalized others. I depart from the premise that claiming to be a knower is always political. As Lorraine Code (2006) argues, knowing and its association with mastery have been crucial to the legitimacy of colonial projects of "enlightenment" of those considered "closer to nature." For Ken Hillis Michael Petit, and Kylie Jarrett (2012), the very claims of "opening up" knowledge that are found in online culture resurrect older forms of authority and status. The participatory invitation of "access" and "search" constructs an ideal subject concomitant with the technologically idealist, corporate messianic vision of firms such as Google: an explorer of new worlds; a pioneer; a knowledge discoverer, transcending space. They are positioned as "latter-day Vasco da Gamas, Captain Cooks, and Neil Armstrongs navigating the proprietary intersection of the digital realm and bodies-as-information" (Hillis et al. 2012, 22). This colonial lexicon signals a highly gendered and racialized set of assumptions in relation to which certain bodies are figured as knowers, and in which other bodies feature as resources and information on that quest. Scholars of gender, race, and digital culture have long argued there are clear gendered and racialized ramifications to such practices (Bailey and Trudy 2018; Brock 2011; Gajjala 2001; Nakamura 2015; Noble and Tynes 2016; White 2006). As race and gender are transacted and decontextualized in the visual and textual cultures of the Internet, marginalized others risk the reinforcement of their status as objects to be circulated, interacted with, and shared.

This backdrop shapes how participants located themselves in relation to intersectionality as a concept, and how intersectionality spatialized their relations, to use Lugones's words, with respect to the asymmetries of power that constituted those relations. In Foucauldian terms, it was an ordering mechanism. For all participants, intersectionality was "useful" in that it provided certain orientations to the social world. But its uses were not the same for everyone; as Sara Ahmed (2019) explains, use differs in connection with what you are used to, and questions of use always implicate "forness." The use of a thing can tell us for whom it was intended; and how a thing comes to be used can tell us about the social conditions that make such use available. Ade's ambivalence, notably, indexed the cramped spatiality of being a non-white person positioned contingently on the boundaries of being seen as an expert and being seen as a knowledge object in and of oneself. The story I tell draws significantly on critical race and feminist scholars who have powerfully highlighted the highly personal and power-striated dynamics animating theory's effects; it also navigates away from an emphasis on "misreading" intersectionality to understand its personal uses in varied attempts to ethically navigate the social world. Taking this up, I go on to explore its performativity in everyday contexts and how intersectionality was used by my participants as an orienting and locating device for positioning themselves in relation to others.

MAPPING THE TERRITORY

To begin, it is important to note how intersectionality has expanded from its origins. In the academy, intersectionality's movement from margins to center has created concerns about its appropriation and misuse (Carastathis 2016; Carbado 2013; Cho et al. 2013). As Gail Lewis (2013, 871) notes, "Unexpected things can occur in the slipstream of travel when concepts and theories are on the move." Sumi Cho, Kimberlé Crenshaw, and Leslie McCall (2013), in commenting on this discursive expansion across sites and disciplines, highlight the political stakes, noting that "some of what circulates as critical debate" about intersectionality reflects a "lack of engagement with both originating and contemporary literatures" (788). Institutionally, Sara Ahmed (2012, 14) notes, intersectionality is frequently misunderstood as "diversity," a "happy" standard for institutions to achieve. This expansion, associated with its status as "the way to theorize the synthesis, co-constitution, or interactivity or 'race' and 'gender'"(Carastathis 2016, 1), has thus been met with significant ambivalence. Jennifer Nash (2019) describes the fallout in terms of the "intersectionality wars." For many Black feminist scholars, the mainstreaming of intersectionality incites its continuous reclaiming as "territory that must be guarded and protected through Black feminist vigilance, care and 'stewardship'" (4). But, as Nash argues, what is at stake is not simply an academically and historically "correct" use of intersectionality but battles over the place of Black women and the figure of the Black woman in the field's imaginary. Thus locating the political nature of this angst, Nash advocates for a movement beyond defensiveness—not because the stakes of intersectionality's use are only imaginary, but because of the way in which defensiveness and the corrective impulse lock Black feminist scholarship into place.

For my participants, the knowledge cultures I discuss here are connected to but also removed from the dynamics of scholarly use. In these everyday settings, intersectionality is taken, even more than in scholarly networks, as the central means of understanding overlapping and unequal differences as opposed to a situated theory developed in particular (geo)political and institutional contexts (King 2015). In these everyday settings, I argue, while intersectionality is technically understood as a theory, its imbrication in the interstices of online culture, popular culture, and institutional culture even further removes the distance between *self* and *theory* possible in scholarly contexts. Rather than constituting a perspective, a framework or a set of questions that opens particular paths, intersectionality becomes not simply "the framework" but the standard against which efforts, practices, and intentions are measured. But consequences depend on participants' own positions and accrued cultural capital.

To provide some context for this "standardization," Priscilla, a participant who worked in the nonprofit sector, noted that intersectionality is now codified in legislation in the Australian state where she lives. The legislation highlights the circulation of intersectionality as a form of measurement that is tenuously attached to its theoretical origins. In the tradition of law seeming to "descend from above" (Davies 2008), there is no reference to Crenshaw, nor to any other Black feminists who have been crucial in contributing such ideas—Patricia Hill Collins, the Combahee collective, Sojourner Truth—or even to Aboriginal feminists such as Aileen Moreton-Robinson (2000a, 2000b) who have long articulated similar ideas in Australia. The conditions of the law's construction are made invisible. On the website clarifying its interpretation in connection with the antidiscrimination legislation with which it is associated, it is made accessible as a nonexhaustive list of attributes "exposing [people] to overlapping forms of discrimination and marginalization." These aspects include Aboriginality, gender identity, sex, sexual orientation, ethnicity, color, nationality, language, migration status, religion, ability, age, mental health, housing status, geographic location, medical record, and criminal record, to name a few. Intersectionality, in its official form, looks dizzying and expansive.

The sprawling nature of intersectionality as a standard was managed differently by my participants. Priscilla, a twenty-five-year-old woman born of Taiwanese migrant parents, formerly a talented and ambitious student and now a talented and ambitious professional, was pragmatic and creative when it came to thinking intersectionality. In my notes, I have termed her a "professional feminist." Priscilla expanded her role in the organization where she works—initially entrusted with widening women's inclusion in leadership, she strategically carved out space in her portfolio to also attend to migrants of "culturally and linguistically diverse backgrounds" because of their lack of representation in leadership. Enterprisingly, she found funding to widen these possibilities and also develop a role in her organization for a First Nations liaison, because, as she noted, this was culturally specific and she wouldn't be able to do this work with her own background. Priscilla, then, was not daunted by what she termed the "mainstreaming" of intersectionality. For her, intersectionality was a "really useful way for people to understand that different people have different experiences and different needs," when delivering programs that aimed to benefit them. Buttressed by her own networks, cultural and social capital, and a boss who was white, middle-aged, and male but nonetheless highly supportive, Priscilla felt more than capable of using intersectionality as a tool.

For others, this mainstreamed openness of intersectionality—capturing any and all elements of significant identity difference—was harder to manage. The pragmatism Priscilla adopted—and the awareness of her limited position, experience, and knowledge—was not a position that was universally available. For younger participants, lacking the material resources and networks of a career in social justice, the stakes of intersectionality were more often affectively registered through anxieties about measuring up. With intersectionality translated as a standard, rather than as a framework, participants walked a precarious line between opposing binaries of being intersectional or failing to be inclusive. This was intensified for white middle-class participants for whom intersectionality was refracted through the lens of personal responsibility, linked both to the earnest desire to do good and to the implicit self-assurance that what they said and did mattered. In the context of online culture, the seemingly indefinite openness of intersectionality led to significant anxieties about checking all the boxes. This was stressful. Ollie, a twenty-two-year-old white nonbinary participant confided:

I definitely, I think that's even more kind of what I've experienced is, worrying that if I'm posting something, I'm leaving out part of the narrative, or like I'm not . . . like I'm not actually getting the information correct. You know? Or I feel like there's just so—we're so bombarded with information. Like there is just so much information. So if I make a post, there are always gonna be a thousand things that I'm leaving out. Like I can't, I can't put everything in one kind of thing. And I think that kind of stresses me out. That's something that overwhelms me . . . it's also why I'm hesitant to repost these things because it's like, yes, of course this is a good post that talks about a certain issue, but there's so many different sides of that issue.

Ollie wanted to do their best. At their elite high school, they and their peers had been positioned as activist future leaders. They and their friends were "frustrated and really passionate" about a number of issues and wanted to put "resources" out there. Remembering back to the resurgence of Black Lives Matter in the United States in 2020, and in the context of the pandemic in 2021, however, Ollie was overwhelmed by an "oversaturation" of information and resources, so much so that it was disorienting:

I wasn't sure exactly where to start and, you know, I'm—I'm trying to follow it and what's going to be the most valuable thing to share, but sometimes it's hard to sift through all of that stuff. That, and recently, in terms of vaccine stuff, you know, I've been trying to find resources that have good information about vaccines and about the risks and about why—why we need to be kind of getting vaccinated as quick as possible. . . . I want to put something online to continue on with that, but then . . . I can't necessarily find the right thing or I'm scared to say the wrong thing.

Ollie was, frankly, overwhelmed. They sincerely wanted to practice a social justice that was considerate, fair, and open. They had begun a psychology degree at university because of their desire to help others. But this version of intersectionality had so many sides. It asked for, in Lugones's (2003) terms, a God's-eye view of the world, beyond one's location on the map striated by power. Attaining an intersectional perspective, then, was about ticking all the boxes. It promised an idealized inclusivity where one could be across all kinds of different experiences; the diversity it opened was overwhelming. Intersectionality was emphatically not a framework, separate from the self, that could be used as a tool for seeing; it was something that had to be incorporated into the self.

As intersectionality emerged as an imperative and ever-expanding standard for acting inclusively, this continual stretching of the self exhausted even the most energetic of young activists. Bella, an ambitious, bubbly young white woman juggling paid work, study, and volunteering, gave a dizzying number of hours to her activist work every week. She had the benefit of undertaking much of her activism in a collective based at her university, where they shared the responsibility for updating social media and were able to run posts past each other. And yet this was a fraught exercise, because, according to Bella, "you need to post on everything. And if you—get to a point where if you don't post, people are going, Hmm, you haven't posted on this. Like we expect you to post on this." It would often be the case that you might not have expertise in a particular area—but in this conflation of intersectionality and inclusion, it would be important to not appear selective or partial with the issues they posted on. In 2021, this required understanding the history of Afghanistan's invasions and the colonial politics in Palestine with a spike in settler violence that year. And trying to post publicly on Palestine created drama, as Bella breathlessly recounted: "Obviously like the Palestine conflict and like all the big things that have been happening around that, we had, like, we posted some infographics and then we had someone say, oh, like, they interpreted that as antisemitic. And we were like, 'Ooh, sorry!' And then other people were like, no, by taking this down, you're not supporting, like Palestinians. And we were like, 'Ah, sorry again!'"

It was a rapid learning curve. Bella pondered what she had learned from all of this. Sometimes, she said, you would try to not be drawn into the pressure of "everyone posting on their socials" about these issues and wait—but then she would worry, "Would this be a less authentic strategy?" She tried to summarize her current position:

> I'll amplify the voices of others speaking on these other things. And—at least that's, I guess, what I try to do rather than . . . the big thing that's a big criticism, is like, don't center yourself in this movement, which is a very important point because if it's a Black Lives Matter issue, like I'm not, not at the front, this is not my time . . . but—when you've got issues that a lot of people are working on, there is constantly the—not, not the Oppression Olympics, but—how does everyone's experience

impact here and whose voices do we listen to? Maybe I'm just going down too much of a rabbit hole.

Intersectionality could indeed lead you down rabbit holes. The responsibility to be in the know literally disoriented young white feminists as they contorted themselves, stretching across issues to show they weren't biased, choosy, or exclusive in terms of the issues they cared about. The magnetism and anxieties posed by this translation of intersectionality were strongest for my white middle-class participants who had been most frequently addressed as potential leaders as well as immersed in middle-class discourses of feminine selflessness and care. Paradoxically, then, this responsibilization, as stressful and anxiety-inducing as it was, reinforced that it was the role of young white middle-class feminists to know, to provide a "universal," nonpartial perspective. Bella and Ollie, evidently, were struggling to uphold this responsibility. Terms such as *amplifying* and *platforming* helped to reassure them that this was not an effort in recentering the self but a means of highlighting other voices.

These practices were viewed as key to good leadership as opposed to "neoliberal white leadership" by Gabi, a chatty white queer woman who was often seen as a leader herself. But such contradictions had to be smoothed over verbally, as exemplified in Gabi's careful explanation of intersectional leadership. She began, "Leadership is like a support—is representing the marginal—" then corrected herself, "platforming, sorry, the marginalized voices you know, I'm making sure that everyone like has a seat pulled up at the table for them. I think intersectionality is kind of like what encompasses all those different ideas. And it's just super important that we are applying an intersectional lens to everything that we do; otherwise we're just going through the world catering for a certain kind of person."

Gabi self-consciously discarded the word *representing*, with its risky associations with an overstepping whiteness. Instead, *platforming*, like *amplifying*, felt supportive, behind the scenes, backstage. To platform was to be a good host(ess)—to ensure everyone had a seat at the table. The ascendance of the platform as a dominant cultural form, according to Rianka Singh (2018), has its own logics in the "elevating of some voices, and regulating of action." For Singh, it is a spatiality that thus reflects rather than questions white assumptions of individuality and voice. The ease with which platforming was condensed with understandings of good leadership showed that platforming could be flexibly used for those seeking to visibly do intersectionality. It could convey, modestly, a sense of background "support"; it could also recenter whiteness as a necessary arbiter of difference, selecting who was to be included at the feminist table.

A BIRD'S-EYE VIEW

Maria Lugones (2003) argues that to think critically through a spatiality of resistances and dominations requires the capacity to see one's relations in both a concrete and an abstract sense: "You are concrete. Your spatiality, constructed as an intersection following the designs of power, isn't. This discrepancy already tells you that you are more than one" (10). This doubleness of vision is required in order to place the self, because without it, to use Lugones's words, is to assume the "top position" of the map, a bird's-eye view that fails to consider one's own implication in power.

And yet the intersectional spatiality that was most available to most of my participants via their social media was one that tended to privilege a highly abstract rather than concrete view of power relations. This was exemplified in the US-centrism within which notions of intersectionality were entangled, directing attention to US dramas, problems, and oppressions as a spectacular but character-forming medium of witnessing. For many, intersectionality initially promised a thrilling expansion of the social worlds of these young people, particularly as many encountered these ideas in their teens. For numerous participants who had been or were highly active on Tumblr, which was dominated by American news, celebrity, and other content, this required being across issues that were only indirectly connected to their lives and yet felt extremely urgent and significant in terms of forging a sense of who they were. For example, Sumaya, who was finishing high school, was "passionate" about abortion rights, defining who she was as a feminist. However, she mostly referenced the importance of this debate within the highly charged terms of the Texas abortion criminalization in 2021 (this interview taking place before the overturning of *Roe v. Wade*), rather than in terms of local legislative changes in Australia that had occurred in recent years. Nina, who was two years older but who had the benefit of the intellectual distance afforded by her progression through a liberal arts university education, said that she had learned to take a "back step" away from the magnetism of the US news-celebrity cycle: "With the US presidential election in 2016, I sort of came away from the online cultures from that and realized that I didn't know a lot about what was happening in my own country. And I was focusing so much of my energies on staying on top of everything that I figured my efforts would be better spent on producing more active change offline as well."

The economies of online knowledge cultures, as with scholarly networks of knowledge, are transnational. They orbit particular metropolitan centers and recenter knowledges of the global north, in particular the United States. American news cultures—from the Texas abortion scandal to scandals at the Met Gala—were frequently cited as "common knowledge" in my group discussions and interviews.

What happened in the United States felt important, urgent; Australian culture was local and parochial by comparison. Such relations of center-periphery make sense in the history of Australia's own uncertain sense of white Westernness, reflected in sustained national foreign policies attaching Australia to the perceived greater powers of Britain or the United States. Ien Ang (2003) notes perceptively that feeling on the periphery produces desires to be recognized and seen in the terms of the Western "metropole." Nina's coming to terms with her own lack of knowledge indexed the paradox of this push to be "on top of" the news cycle as a form of intersectional vision. Intersectionality for my feminists both promised a bird's-eye view—seeing the "thousand things" of Ollie's imagining—and made such a view normative. While aspiring to a view from "nowhere," this translated into a singular lens prioritizing US-centered events and perspectives; it also translated into knowledge remaining curiously abstract. Staying on top of everything, attempting to keep a view from above, meant you couldn't orient yourself. You couldn't ground yourself in the pragmatic world of everyday interactions. Such a paradox, I suggest, arguably informed the unease of many of my non-white participants who felt that the racialized interactions of their everyday realities could not be seen even as intersectionality took on the heightened status as the social justice concept that could explain and document the complexity of lived experience. I suggest that its continuing salience in terms of ranking advantage and disadvantage needs to be understood in terms of how it becomes useful to those in everyday contexts. Middle-class whiteness or proximity to it lends itself to investments in the possibility of having "the complete picture," yet the pursuit of this and what this feels like in the context of the rapidity and overwhelm of online culture is registered as highly disorienting. Ranking, ordering, and categorizing felt like ways to ethically manage this infoglut and the dizzying array of perspectives one can encounter, even as such ranking may occur with the single-mindedness that Shae noted earlier.

This kind of ordering and categorization is reassuring, for some. But far from this producing a productive reflexivity, this fragility can limit how non-white others are relationally imagined and made visible. To give a concrete, if somewhat surreal, example of the historical centrality of the United States in defining race in the national imaginary, I refer to one of Ade's passing comments on how they were considered African American growing up, despite their Australian accent: "Particularly with the kind of popularization of American media and like a lot of African American personalities, people used to think I was African American growing up. I was like, I'm not African American, I'm African."

To return to the contemporary context, the pull of the United States in framing race as spectacle was ongoing. Indeed, a number of participants critiqued a hypocritical attention to Black Lives Matter in the United States in locating problems "elsewhere," echoing Nina's description of the overly "theoretical" nature of online social justice debates. In one group discussion, this came out as follows:

> **Speaker 1** It's really easy to like look at stuff far away and be like, oh, that's bad.
>
> **Speaker 2** Look at that problem!
>
> **Speaker 3** And then just kind of ignore everything else.
>
> **Speaker 1** It's very Australian as well, yeah.

However, prioritization of the race issues to be addressed through intersectional feminism at times relied on binary and universalized categories of what Blackness and whiteness meant. For example, the implicit imbalance in caring about a US-driven phenomenon that highlighted racism was felt to be addressed in caring about Indigenous issues, as Aboriginal people in Australia have adopted "Blak" as a specific form of identity in connection with white colonization. Indeed, many participants had noticed that Indigenous activists were outspoken in highlighting the need to pay attention to Australian race inequalities and already followed a number of activist groups on Facebook and Twitter prior to the most recent resurgence of Black Lives Matter. However, a neat translation of Black Lives Matter into Blak Lives Matter did not necessarily address the highly complicated experiences of race in the twenty-first century, particularly when framed by settler/Indigenous, Black/white, and white/multicultural binaries. When

I asked Ade if, as a Black person, they felt connected at all to Blak politics, they responded: "I think there's a lot of overlap . . . African immigrants here are settlers, of course. And I think there's a part [of us] that needs to be very cognizant of that. But at the same time, I think, and I think this is a bit that people don't often think about, is that lot of African immigrants are also here because of colonization. And particularly when you look at the African continent, that colonization is still ongoing."

This argument is not to deny that white participants cared about a range of issues to do with race, nor that they were unable to "see" it materializing. For example, during the pandemic in 2021, multiple interviewees grappled with the highly classed and racialized enclosure and surveillance of low-income housing tenants who were locked down in military fashion following COVID-19 outbreaks. Yet binary diagnostics—even when aiming to deploy intersectionality as a framework—continued to shape attention, priorities, and visibilities.

Historically, in Australian feminism, white women have been seen as intermediaries between Australia's colonial "past" (First Nations people) and its multicultural present (non-white migrants), positioning whiteness as the natural and legitimate arbiter of belonging (Hage 2000; Moreton-Robinson 2000a, 2000b). With whiteness as an invisible "middle," connections between ongoing Indigenous dispossession and non-white exclusion and exploitation were not obviously available to be made. This rendered intersectionality a tool that enabled the envisioning of particular experiences of race but continued to maintain a bird's-eye view—an implicitly white position from nowhere—as the central mode of seeing. This was quite different, however, for participants of color whom intersectionality had helped to place themselves on the map.

For example, intersectionality was grounding for my participant E. As a Black Nigerian trans masc person who had often been read over their lifetime as "intimidating," "although I'm just a big teddy bear," E stated, intersectionality had helped them to locate their experiences. In school, they were not included in discussions about feminism; conversations directed to them were more often about "Africa." Accordingly, encountering intersectionality as a concept was a transformative personalized political experience. This feeling of being marginalized centered their Blackness.

Bernie, a nonbinary Malaysian participant who migrated to a regional town in Australia when they were a child, similarly felt removed from discussions of feminism until they encountered intersectionality as a framework privileging the experience of race. While they felt they had "always been progressive," arty, creative, the one that did not fit into a conservative family, they did not feel addressed by the kinds of feminist discourse that were discussed by their mainly white, straight, and cis friends: "I felt like there was a detachment between the mainstream feminist discourse and my experiences. And it wasn't until I discovered intersectional feminism that I really began to like fully embody everything that, you know, they were talking about in that sphere and be able to really concretely apply like the feelings I had about injustice and the feelings I had about oppression into my life." The experience of encountering intersectional feminism as an idea was embodied but embodied differently than for my white participants. Far from originally being encountered as abstract, it provided something of a concrete structure through which Bernie's political feelings could be articulated; these feelings, not simply being personal, could now "go somewhere," they said. Going onto Tumblr and finding the perspectives of "fat feminists and Black feminists and First Nations feminists" helped Bernie to find new, orienting coalitions.

For E and Bernie, then, coming across intersectionality was key for them in being able to imagine themselves as subjects of feminism's address. Feminism did not otherwise resonate, but intersectionality was for them. It located them on the map, not necessarily "in" feminism but transversally in a place where they could feel that power produced them as "more than one" (Lugones 2003, 19).

WHO DESERVES ATTENTION IN AN INTERSECTIONAL HIERARCHY?

How, then, to analyze and use intersectionality, as it expanded across categories, and across differences, morphing into the thousand things that could be left out? One could argue that context mattered in what you selectively included and excluded in your post; you could blame the character limit in your tweet. More broadly, another principle came to implicitly determine how intersectionality in its infinite plurality was mobilized: who was most worth attention in the context of constantly competing claims to time and space in social media culture? Accordingly, intersectionality applied in this form was a moral equation, adding and subtracting privilege and disadvantage, calculating openness and closedness, in connection with particular identities.

This sense that disadvantage was relevant and held value in an economy of attention inflected my participants' negotiations in how they expressed and explained their identities to me. In the recruitment for this project, I had set up an expression-of-interest form. It asked for participants' emails, age, and how often they engaged with online feminist culture. It also asked for information in a "free response" format on participants' identities to ensure "a diversity of backgrounds," deliberately framed loosely so as to not foreclose on any form of participation. Sensing how this could be a complicated endeavor, however, and not wanting participants to spend too much time crafting a "perfect" response, I provided a brief sample description participants could follow: "Akane is a cisgender, heterosexual woman of Japanese descent."

Whiteness, heterosexuality, and cisgender status were not always marked by interested participants. However, descriptions of identity in connection with historical markers of disadvantage generally came readily. Participants of color noted their ethnicity; queer participants, their sexuality; trans and nonbinary participants, their gender diversity. There were also numerous identifications of chronic illness and neurodivergence in participant responses. Sometimes, these descriptions went further, noting a history of family violence, eating disorders, or sexual assault. Evidently, the young feminists who were interested in my project already brought a language of experience that they could use to describe themselves and their identities.

By the time it came to interviewing these participants, however, I was struck by the clear anxieties about the way in such "disadvantages" were articulated, even though they had been freely volunteered on the form. While participants evidently felt that these kinds of identities were relevant for a project on feminisms that sought "diversity," there were high stakes to claiming identities of marginalization and disadvantage. Many of my non-white participants felt uncertain about claiming "race." Maria, a young Filipina who had clearly experienced racism and racialization more broadly in Australia after migrating in her teens, said, tentatively, that she didn't know if Asians "counted" as people of color. Priscilla, my talented, ambitious NGO professional, said she wouldn't self-identify as a "person of color" in a context where others deserve the label "more." Marcela, a Latin American migrant, told me she was genuinely confused about how she could describe herself because so many white people told her she was "white"; therefore, it was difficult for her to discuss her feelings of dissonance in relation to the comfortable whiteness of Australian society, against which her family's experience of precarity, struggle, and professional devaluation seemed at odds.

Similarly, many participants who suffered chronic illness, sometimes in debilitating ways, and who had systematically been dismissed by medical institutions, took care to tell me they did not have a disability. Elise, a white queer writer, explained that they had talked to people who would "absolutely encourage me to identify as disabled by having my chronic illness [but] it just doesn't quite sit right with me . . . I think there's just a lot of ways in which I am still able to navigate the world. . . there are ways in which I am not disabled. Like . . . if we go with the social model, you know, I'm still able to work, I'm able to access spaces."

It was clear for Elise that, even in citing the social model of disability, in that disability is socially created through social barriers, assumptions, and practices, they were still not really disabled because others were certainly more disabled in terms of what they could not access. Similarly, Cathy, a white nonprofit professional, had noted on her sign-up form that she experienced chronic illness , but when I came to ask her about it, she was clear to minimize the structural disadvantage of her condition: "[My] chronic illness does not cause me to suffer barriers to social life or employment or anything that I would consider to be making a disability . . . and I mean, I would never question anyone with a chronic illness saying they had a disability, like, you know, totally whatever people want to define it for themselves, but . . . it's also kind of a recent thing for me to recognize how gendered, because it's gynecological, how gendered the health system is."

Cathy felt that this condition was socially significant because it indexed the gendered nature of credibility in the health system; and yet it was not significantly serious enough in terms of barriers or disadvantage for it to be called a disability. In puzzling out the sensitive politics of priority here, Cathy retreated, however, to a position of "no judgment," as disability was an individual matter, something that could be defined and decided by anyone for themselves.

This form of being alive to multiple levels of disadvantage was also, I note, a means of registering care. Jillian, a white trans poet, spoke passionately about witnessing one of her close friends struggle every day with the health system: "[She] is disabled, chronically ill, Black, and a woman and queer and the, the insane levels of exhaustion. She's also a single mother, the insane levels of exhaustion that she deals with, just trying to succeed past one of the intersections that has disadvantaged her in life." While all of these forms of life experience would be experienced simultaneously, Jillian's enunciation of all of them, and the difficulty of succeeding past "one," was a way of emphasizing the fatigue and exhaustion that her friend struggled through every day.

This worried preoccupation with those that were worse off, in order to not encroach on their "lane," however, meant that intersectionality paradoxically could not offer a mirror to whiteness or privilege, a phenomenon that has also been described by Emma Dabiri (2021) and Olúfẹ́mi O. Táíwò (2022). While the language of privilege saturated my participants' perspectives, it usually was expressed in terms of turn-taking, letting others "take the mic." Intersectionality, in short, was used mainly by participants to see multiple forms of disadvantage. It was described, for example, by white queer participants in primarily explaining the connections between holding the identities of queer and woman together, rather than whiteness, queer, and woman together. In explaining how they come to understand intersectionality, Jean, a highly driven and passionate manager of a small social justice collective, noted: "Since I'm queer, I already had the two identities thing to consider just in myself, like working out my own identity. And so I think it was seeking out the kinds of websites that were catering to queer women, so often there's discussions of that intersection."

As is so often noted in the critical race literature, whiteness remained invisible. Evidently, Jean "knew" she was white. Yet this knowledge was not readily at hand in terms of thinking through what was offered by intersectionality, a framework that was widely understood to centrally address issues of race. This inability to see race except in terms of lack was irritating for others. Lakshmi, a Sydney-based events coordinator of Pakistani heritage who worked in a human rights organization, expressed significant frustration with this:

> I don't make all the decisions at the organization [I work at], but I feel certainly some of the others in our organization, they are always looking at those points of disadvantage, and challenge. And I feel that's not the way we should always approach things . . . if you go on Twitter, you'll see it . . . and that I see that whole intersectionality framework and debate as part of that. . . . There's that whole thinking that you've just got to assume that there's a challenge that needs to be overcome. I think that's not the way I like to look at things.

Lakshmi was in the awkward position of being one of the few non-white people in a human rights organization centered on helping non-white people. She felt quite distanced from what she called the "eagerness" of colleagues and others in the NGO sector to embrace intersectionality as "a huge buzzword . . . I'm not an expert . . . but I find that maybe it's a bit hyped up." Lakshmi said she preferred a "strength-based approach," one in which the constituents of her organization were seen to have agency, ideas, their own means of maneuvering. Nadia, a middle-class South Asian migrant who had moved to Australia for her research career, spoke similarly. Nadia felt that intersectionality was useful not simply for understanding disadvantage but also for understanding "complicity" as well as marginalized groups' agency. In relation to what she called "two-thirds world women," she stated simply, "Women have resources. Women can fight for themselves. It's just that you don't have to contribute to the further oppression."

It is well noted by scholars that intersectionality is often framed predominantly in terms of compounded disadvantage (Luft and Ward 2009), although the accuracy of the reading is indeed disputed in the literature (Carbado 2013; Collins 2015). I suggest that its continuing salience in terms of ranking advantage and disadvantage needs to be understood not in terms of misreading but in terms of how it becomes useful. Middle-class whiteness or proximity to it lent itself to investments in being "good"; an ocular preoccupation with disadvantage made it more comfortable to inhabit whiteness, eliteness, and class privilege, or at least to not look at it all the time. Additionally, this counting and ranking of disadvantage made it feel possible to have the full picture in a way that felt manageable, beyond the "thousand things" that you could leave out of a situation, as Ollie mentioned earlier.

STAYING IN YOUR LANE

This intersectional equation may have felt useful in giving a complete picture, or at least of validating the multiple disadvantages of a person. But because of the overarching sense that disadvantage was a scarce resource in the moral economy of attention, it worked in tandem with a prohibition on speaking to an identity-based disadvantage unless you experienced it yourself. This was online etiquette that in some ways was a practical form of holding space for others. Yet, as I explore in more detail in chapter 3, it still did not effectively counter the power dynamics of who was understood as a "storyteller" and who was understood as a "story"; more problematically, this didactic prohibition reinforced proprietary understandings of identity that hampered, rather than fostered, the possibilities of reflection in knowledge sharing.

For example, I turn to the agonizings of Nina, a highly articulate, erudite young feminist in my cohort whom we met earlier, to illustrate how these prohibitions produced walls around legitimate knowledge. In the first year of my project, Nina was a twenty-one-year-old university student; she was white and middle-class with "supportive parents," smart, humorous, and open with her insecurities and perceived flaws. We talked about how her status as a gender studies major shaped how discussions about feminism took place in her social circles. Compared with most of her peers, who principally derived their knowledge through social media circulation, Nina reflected that she didn't want to "sound too narcissistic" but went on to say, "I tend to think I'm better at arguing for the points of feminism from gender theory, because I've had to really examine the sort of claims that feminism makes, really deeply. Not only because it gets interrogated whenever I mentioned that I'm studying it, but also because that's part of the degree, we have to learn about how the feminist movements came about, why they came about, critiques of them, who was left out from each movement and where we're going."

Nina had a critical sensibility. In school, she hadn't been "cool," but she had always been outspoken and indeed, she had been known for being so. Nina used to regularly post her views on abortion, US filibusters, and other political issues across social media ranging from Facebook and Tumblr. More recently, Nina used Instagram more often—she had a public account focusing on chronic illness and disability based on her own experience. She started it in her teens in her search for community and sharing of experience and advice by those with chronic illness; but recently, unusually, the normally loquacious Nina had little to say. This was because she was now largely "well" and able to manage day to day, thanks to a new device, a J pouch, that had been inserted into her colon. She now was almost never in the hospital, and so:

> I always feel like I have nothing to talk about and it almost feels insulting to come on to that platform where I have more followers than I have on anything else—and share like, "Oh my God, I'm doing so great. Like . . . my life feels so normal" when most of the other people that are both following me and that I follow are not doing so great . . . it feels like really rude to come on and be like, I'm doing great, especially cause my, my J pouch is not something that a lot of people have.

Nina still had a wealth of knowledge about her condition and chronic illness; further, her gender theory background arguably furnished her with the capacity to comment on a larger context in thinking through gender and disability. She was well aware that knowledge did not come only from direct experience. But with these norms of who could know, and who could speak, she rarely posted. She did not want to be "rude"; she did not want to flaunt her newly gained bodily privileges in front of her audience. More profoundly, in the normative tethering of personal experience to knowledge claims, she felt like she was now an "imposter" in this space. Indeed, Nina was afraid of being perceived as uncaring, and fake: "I think about [how I am perceived] probably more than anything else in my day-to-day life . . . I am frequently guilty of doing that thing where you look at your social media platforms and you think about what they look like to someone who doesn't know you. Like it's terrible. But I think about that all the time. And I would hate to come off as someone who is insensitive, or wrong, or taking up space when they shouldn't be taking up space . . . I think about it—a crippling amount—which is terrible."

There was perhaps an irony in Nina's description of this anxiety as "crippling," a term with palpable medicalized, ableist connotations, in her very wrestling with questions of how to make a nondisabled claim to linger in a social media space of chronic illness and disability. What Nina was trying to articulate, I felt, was the sense that this fear of the potentially hostile outside gaze literally reduced her own capacities, and closed down possibilities.

My argument is not that Nina should have had, or was even asking for, the same attention from her chronically ill audience as her body and everyday life changed. Rather, my discussion here is to indicate that the "nichification" of community necessary to manage the general overwhelm of online feminist culture often reinforces a static view of identity, one that relies on sameness to shelter from the outside world (see also Kanai and McGrane 2021). As one's identity could and did change, in real terms, this kind of contingent community could be experienced as profoundly isolating. Attempts at connection in this context could mean an overreach that could be construed as both politically and morally wrong. Nina went on to say, "I'm an ex-perfectionist. . . . And I guess there is the element of not wanting to say the wrong thing, of not wanting to get things wrong. So yeah, it's, it's hard sometimes."

I personally doubted that Nina was an "ex" perfectionist; in any case, "ex" or not, the fears of "getting it wrong" (Gill 2023) were continually registered. Indeed, Nina's seemingly confident self-expression was bounded by rules about how to use your voice. A sense of broader social responsibility was paired with the lurking worry of individually failing to live up to acquitting it in the right way.

This sense of limited license to speak was particularly strong for Nina, as her domain of public voice was also uniquely an online space. For those with chronic illnesses, as my participants told me, unsurprisingly, online public spaces could often be easier to access than physical public ones. Nina had built up this account through her own personal experience of chronic illness, and was connected to similar accounts; she was not otherwise connected to organizations or institutions working in chronic illness or disability, which may have created at least a sense of being part of a collective entity beyond that of yourself.

But I observed on her Instagram feed that Nina was now actually much more expressive in relation to workers' rights because of her ongoing experience volunteering at a nonprofit workers' advocacy center. She shared posts on their reports, on current statistics of exploitation of women hospitality workers, and more. She felt strongly about the need for funding for such centers, pointing to the independent recommendation following the high-profile accusation of rape in Parliament House mentioned in the previous chapter, that more centers were needed: "We need them all over the country and every state, every territory for people to have access to and they need to be government-funded, they need to have adequate funds and resources to support the workers there." More broadly, her experience volunteering at a workers' center enabled her to participate in discussion about Brittany Higgins's case from a perspective that was not only based on the experience of sexual assault and rape but also expressed in terms of structural change: "A lot of people who talked about it online and . . . it resonated with me . . . I could connect it back to the center, as an example for anyone experiencing any kind of similar experiences."

Further, when an acquaintance tried to disagree with her on the basis of a convoluted argument that feminism was "problematic," her feminist perspective and the legitimacy of her knowledge remained bolstered by the collective weight of the center's work. Nina decided to unfollow this acquaintance because his argument was, as she put it, based on hypothetical counterclaims, rather than the reality of women's experiences at work:

> It was another case of a white man that I knew feeling like he needed to add his two cents in. . . . And it's not that white men don't deserve platforms for speaking about this, but at the same time, I don't need them to say that this doesn't happen when I know that it does.

She went on to explain how this high-profile case was merely the tip of an iceberg:

> It just confirmed a lot of exhaustion that women go through every single day. We're not all going to get raped every single day. That's a very outlandish statement, but we all experience . . . not being believed or belittlement of dealing with bureaucracies that don't actually care about us, whether we've experienced rape like Brittany Higgins unfortunately went through, or just mere microaggressions. And I was tired. I was really tired of having to say, hey—we shouldn't have to go through this.

As a young person, Nina had a short history of being a paid worker. But being part of this group was invigorating for her. Speaking from the knowledge base of personal experience could be lonely, but even as an unpaid volunteer, the sense of being part of a collective, and being privy to knowledge that had been developed through a professional mandate, through helping a constituency beyond herself, afforded a sense of legitimate knowledge, questioning, and reflection that was difficult to sustain on her own.

MOVING "OFF THE LINE"

Alison Kafer (2013) notes the complicated politics of articulating belonging to an identity when that identity spans highly differentiated, unequal experiences of the world. In connection to "crip," she suggests that while offering an expansive view, it may "run the risk of appropriation . . . [but crip politics] also offer a vital refusal of simplistic binaries like disabled/nondisabled and sick/healthy. Claiming crip . . . can be a way of acknowledging that we all have bodies and minds with shifting abilities, and wrestling with the political meanings and histories of such shifts" (8). In doing so, Kafer holds to the importance of a hopeful but critical politics that constructs the "notion of 'we' as more promise than fact" (8), being open to potential coalitions, while attending to inequalities in the terms of openness and closure of such identities. This emphasis on the potential for "we," I think, indicates precisely what was absent from Nina's anxious imagining of her online chronically ill and disabled audience, and the limitations of social collectivity across lines of difference in these online imagined communities. To step outside of one's own corner on the intersectional grid was translated into "taking up space." With the backdrop of this gamified, but not playful, conception of identity, the multifaceted nature of one's identity could be registered only in terms of the ranking of disadvantage, and "match" with others in terms of identity categories. You could be contingently accepted, but only if you stayed "in your spot." As such, the norms of the intersectional grid contrast with the "spot" that Lugones (2003) imagines, a spot that illustrates the crisscrossing, overlay, and simultaneity of logics of domination and resistance.

If the "future is intersectional," as the passionate Tumblr user whom we met at the beginning of this chapter argued, what could that mean? As I have tried to show, intersectionality organized everyday relations in the disorienting knowledge cultures of online feminism. Pressured to stay on the pulse, and to always have the right reactions, my young feminists found that intersectionality became a moral standard through which they could parse the deservingness of attention as the currency of payment in online culture, applied both to their own experiences and to those of others. However, in promising a lens seeing "a thousand" perspectives, it was necessarily boiled down to the counting of disadvantages tied to identities to be manageable.

A focus on cumulative oppressions thus helped participants to prioritize what to look at, and what to see, in the constant stream of social media; but this microscopic scrutiny of oppression blurred and backgrounded practices of whiteness, eliteness, and class privilege in particular. This additive intersectional equation also had the paradoxical effect of portraying traumatic experiences and forms of oppression as blocks that stacked rather than intersected. Such an imagining reinforced the competitive, proprietary, and market-based nature of communication online: you had to "stay in your lane" in exploiting only your own experience for the public. Such harsh and contradictory parameters created real struggles and anguish for my cohort as they aimed to do good, find community, and relate across the linear imagining of unbreachable differences.

PART II

Moving Upward, but Not Taking Up Space

3

LEADERSHIP JOURNEYS AND INTERSECTIONAL RESOURCES

In chapter 2 I outlined how, in online feminist knowledge cultures, intersectionality was translated as an ordering device, simplifying and plotting identities along axes of privilege and disadvantage. This was a grid that essentialized the relation between knowledge and experience, in order to judge the deservingness of attention in the dense and fast-moving economies of social media content. Such knowledge cultures thus translated oppression into a practical measure suited to social media attention economies: the more legible the disadvantage, the more attention. My participants navigated their emplacement on such a grid, being both highly cognizant of how their lives corresponded to this taxonomy of marginalization and highly cautious in noting relative privilege. As I explore in this chapter, this produced inherent tensions for my participants, overwhelmingly women and gender-diverse people, in how they could relate to each other, and men were, for the most part, left off the intersectional grid I have described. This further reinforced the magnification and objectification of racialized and trans experience, understood as "the most" oppressed identities in this inward-looking republic. It also implicitly positioned white women as leaders, who had the duty to act on the basis of privilege but who, in this essentialized knowledge-experience equation, could "not know" the real oppressions at stake.

This chapter traces how an intersectional grid produced templates of feminist relationality along restricted lines of movement. To practice intersectional feminism was to see from a detached vantage point, to embark on a leadership journey, and to bring others up with you. This "inclusive" leadership rebranded what has historically been understood as women's work: the work of looking out for others, ensuring others' safety and comfort. And yet, like women's work in "always on" convergence culture, it was often undervalued in practice (Jarrett 2015; Ouellette and Wilson 2011). Leadership was articulated abstractly in terms of project management, in corralling expertise. It had to be aspired to, but paradoxically had to be told in terms of the loving ignorance critiqued by Mariana Ortega (2006): confessing *you could never know* what it was like to have someone's (oppressed) experience, but still would like to legitimate their experience by including them on your journey. The spatiality of this intersectional grid thus mobilized a linear, "upward" journey by two mutually dependent subjects: the feminist leader and the included, disadvantaged other(s). It positioned the leader as invulnerable but selfless, and the disadvantaged other as a storytelling resource.

And yet leadership held broad appeal for participants across class backgrounds and ethnicities. A pervasive awareness of deep levels of social injustice made leadership feel mandatory *now and in the future*. Beginning as I did with questions around family, childhood, and schooling, in order to understand participants' social histories, I was struck by the commonality of references to leadership—often situated in positions at school, at university, at work, and in their organizing and extracurricular work. For my participants, institutions such as schools and universities operated as leadership dream machines, producing both linear trajectories of achievement and modes of telling the self, in terms of "confidence" journeys and ongoing development. Leadership was a seemingly ecumenical discourse, addressed to all, and available to all. But in the rigid allocations of "privilege" and "disadvantage," it could also mean a disorienting shock when you had been addressed as a leader but realized in fact you were a leadership resource for others' journeys. And once you were a leader—you could be quickly burned out as your lack of actual resources to continue doing the feminist work you sought to do became quickly apparent.

As young people (and I've spoken to other young people) there is this feeling that we need to do everything now—and younger than anyone can, and better than anyone can. There is this weird cultural obsession with people doing things young and really well and really brave and like, "Oh, I wish I was like you when I was younger, that sort of mentality." It is also a lot of pressure and we put that on ourselves, and each other.

Bella, age twenty-two

It is important to first establish that leadership journeys were not simply mediated discourses that could be selectively taken up or left to one side. They normalized a competitive relation with the self and with others as *required* to remedy the mistakes of the past. Student leader Bella had been seen as a leader since childhood, and explained it concisely: social justice leadership felt urgent and it felt as though it had to be done yesterday. For young people, particularly young women, discourses of upward trajectories in "representing the change you wanted to see" were embedded not only culturally but also institutionally in post–girl power Australia (Dobson and Harris 2015). For those with existing material privileges, expectations of leadership began early and were experienced as natural. For example, white middle-class Gabi, in her own words, was the kind of person that tended to "float" into leadership positions. Her mom was a white-collar worker, specializing in managing people at a large professional services firm, and her vocality and her ambition had been encouraged at home. "I'm like very loud," she said, and "being at the forefront really comes naturally to me." When she was in high school, she said, "it seemed like, every time I was in a group project, people would kind of look to me to kind of take charge and delegate and bring everyone together. I suppose that's just where it [the leadership] started. Maybe being an older sibling too?" Gabi had attended a private school for girls and credited this environment for fostering a feminist sensibility. She had been immersed in an educational institution that privileged girls' and women's ideas, "probably not to the extent that they could have," she said, but "we learned about Malala (Yousafzai) . . . and the importance of women's education. . . . So I think those ideas were kind of instilled in me from a very young age."

The language of leadership in university marketing material and in the curriculum of certain undergraduate degrees thus directly appealed to a student like Gabi. After school, Gabi chose to undertake a degree promising a focus on both international social justice and leadership, two of her interests that had been encouraged at school: "Like the whole premise is like being a leader for social change." The university where she chose to study was located not far from her childhood home in the comfortable eastern suburbs of the city. Gabi's leadership felt normal for her; her family, peers, and institutions all seemed to acknowledge and legitimate her leadership potential.

Like Gabi, white middle-class Bella had been marked out as a leader since school due to her exuberance, energy, and desire to make change. Bella sat on her local council as a youth representative and, like Gabi, chose her university because it promised structured pathways to leadership: "I always had it strategically planned out because I also do part of my degree as a global leadership program. And it allows you to get points for involvement with certain things."

Making the most of every opportunity meant that Bella had applied and been accepted into numerous youth leadership and ambassadorship programs—ranging from being a social justice ambassador for a leading streetwear brand to being a youth advocate for an international charity with offices in Australia, which had led to other speaking commitments for brands seeking to align their mission with feminist values. But her chief activist leadership role was in a student collective, and this dominated her free time.

Siblings Ollie and Margot had been addressed not only as leaders but as international leaders from a young age. Of French/English heritage, they had attended an elite boarding school overseas, and at this school, there were expectations that they would be the "green leaders of tomorrow." The school emphasized young people's responsibility not only to care for the environment but also to actively promote and advance practices of sustainability in the communities in which they were situated. Activism and leadership, then, were conflated for the privileged students of this school. These expectations of high-flying achievement were so ingrained that it felt almost shameful to settle back in Australia. To enroll in an undergraduate degree at a nonprestigious domestic university seemed inadequate in relation to their potential: "It's like you've gone to an international school. . . . And it was almost like this shameful thing to go back to where you like, where you used to live and just do the normal things like go on a gap year and then to do just do, a you know, an arts degree and then get a job."

In Anglo-American discourses of youth potential of the last few decades, young people's activism has become synonymous with young people's "leadership." These discourses intervene in and intensify existing pressures on girls to achieve, represent, and transcend the inequalities of capitalism in the capacity cultures of popular feminism (Banet-Weiser 2018). In Angela McRobbie's (2009) well-known formulation, gender is a key mechanism through which neoliberalism renews its hegemony as "top girls" become the meritocratic face of capitalism. While disputing the generalizability of Anthony Giddens's theory of individualization positing the increasing mobility and choice available to increasingly "disembedded" young people, McRobbie (2015) highlights the prevalence of this emphasis on "achievement" and "advancement" for young people regardless of class background and material, social, and cultural resources.

However, the emphasis on career advancement in leadership was inflected differently according to social context. Sara was a twenty-two-year-old from a large Italian family spread across a regional town not far from Melbourne, and, in contrast to her metropolitan peers above, this regional location shaped a focus on leadership as building capacity in her local community. Sara had had a comfortable upbringing; her mother was a primary school teacher and her father, an engineer. She said she had been taught from a young age to be "grateful" for what she had, and to "give back" to the community. Her parents had always engaged in community activities, ranging from helping at the school canteen and serving on the parents and teachers committee to volunteering for the local football team. Sara herself had accordingly engaged in programs for tutoring disadvantaged children and fundraising for local schools, and had performed leadership roles at her own school as part of this service. At the local university, she had also taken on a role as an ambassador encouraging student participation in extracurricular activities. For Sara, directly "bettering the lives of others" in the local community was a key motivation of hers; she wanted "younger children to have the life I've had."

Julie was another young leader who gave significant amounts of her personal time to others. Of South Asian and white British heritage, Julie did not hesitate to explain one of her driving motivations in life: "I like helping people. I know it's such a generic answer, but it's honestly the core of where I'm at. Like, I would literally set myself on fire for someone else to be warm. It's just something that has always been taught to me, like kindness and empathy and respect for others. And so I just want to like promote that in the world and be able to help others see their own potential." Part of Julie's desires to help stemmed from her own experiences of marginalization. Her schooling experience differed significantly from that of Bella, Sara, Ollie, and Margot: as a child, she experienced intense bullying based on her weight and her brownness. Julie's working-class parents were loving and supportive but weren't in a position to make demands on teachers in relation to their daughter's treatment, or to move her to another school. But in high school Julie had flourished. Her teachers saw her potential and encouraged her. She made lots of friends. She was active on the student representative committee and took this interest in leadership to university. Julie was now popular—she had been elected women's representative for three years in a row: "I was successful . . . I've been very lucky in all three elections I've run in. So I'm very grateful. I'm hoping that that's a testament to my work and to my rapport around uni, I'm hoping people aren't just voting for me cause I'm like, oh, this [sur]name looks cool. But yeah, I was very lucky to be women's officer for 2020."

When I met Julie in 2021, she brimmed with enthusiasm as she told me of the initiatives she was trying to implement to make campus safer for women and gender-diverse people. This was a continuing uphill battle. The collective she directed received no funding and was repeatedly under attack from conservative student groups. However, the university as an institution still provided fertile conditions for leadership: it offered a structure in which students were made aware of each other as citizens with interests, vulnerabilities, and rights. The normalization of student groups provided rich opportunities for students to collectivize and lead. In this context, leadership discourses were pervasive in addressing my young participants, providing a language and imaginary for changemaking.

For young people, being a leader was held out as desirable but also as necessary in creating social change through school—across those of varying class backgrounds and school experiences—and university. Outside mass educational environments, leadership programs, training, and discourses also abounded. Maria, a Filipina migrant who did not hold Australian citizenship and who had thus been effectively excluded from university due to the costs of studying as an international student, was now involved in programs in which she was positioned as a youth leader, delivering youth leadership programs for others. These spanned several community initiatives, including working with a local multicultural youth program. "I had the opportunity to co-deliver a young women's leadership program with them, which was really cool," she said. "This was the year before the pandemic, and yeah [I also got involved with] leadership sort of things like public speaking, but it's a blur right now . . . I also volunteered with [a] creative kids magazine, like basically just facilitating the group of young editors who are twelve, thirteen years old, and supporting them to make a magazine. But yeah, those areas . . . youth, CALD, and like women's empowerment type things."

The acronym CALD, standing for "culturally and linguistically diverse," is often used in Australian government- and council-sponsored programs. Maria confided that she had "never heard of CALD" before being employed by her local council. Indeed, she felt she had a tenuous grip on the relationship between terms such as *people of color* and CALD and her own ethnicity, being from the Philippines. Online, she had observed that people often didn't know that Filipinos were Asian "because they spoke English so well"; and they disputed that Asians were POC, leading to her own confusion. But Maria had learned that there was a need to deliver leadership opportunities to young people; and that to be "CALD" deepened that need. This then created employment opportunities for her, based on her own designation as "diverse," to also help a cohort of younger CALD people.

As a young progressive person, or as a girl or a woman, to accept one's coding as (culturally) diverse could render you legible and eligible for certain leadership pathways. Such pathways or journeys involved understanding the self as a subject of ongoing improvement and development, professionally, ethically, and attitudinally. This was experienced differently across my cohort. Confident, popular Gabi was delighted by the longitudinal aspect of my project; the prospect of two personal interviews, undertaken a year apart, was interpreted by her as an ideal means of charting her personal growth. But this understanding of the self as a subject of ongoing development on a journey of empowerment was used even by participants whose lives did not straightforwardly correspond to such descriptions.

Take for instance my participant Sonya, who had grown up in a white working-class family in Melbourne. When I met her, she was twenty-eight and pursuing a postgraduate degree in psychology, mainly online, while living in rural Australia with her partner. While Sonya had developed a professional vocabulary around trauma and stigma, much more magnetic to her in an everyday sense were discourses of personal growth that repositioned her life in terms of confidence accumulation and development. She experienced these discourses, in her words, as "feminist." In her midtwenties she had first started engaging seriously with such discourses in therapeutic feminist accounts such as The Sweet Feminist on Instagram, an account that posted images of cakes with slogans like "feminist as f***" and "abortion pills forever," together with reassuring messages frosted onto them, such as "You're doing great" (figure 3.1).

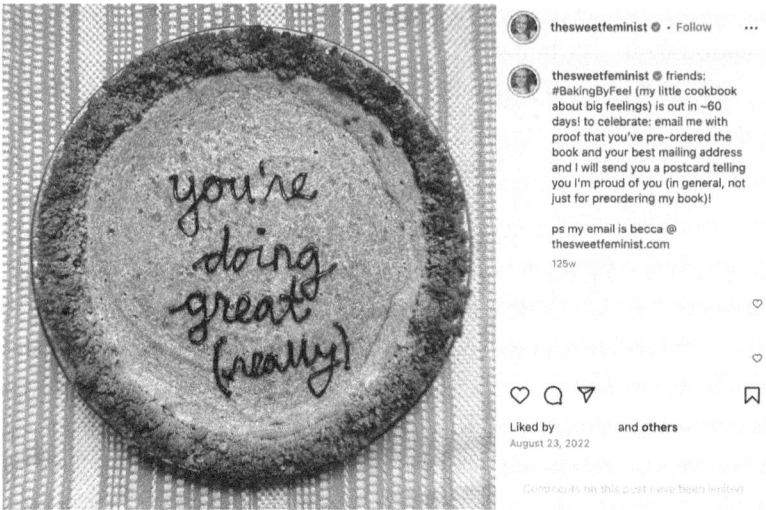

3.1 The Sweet Feminist, "You're doing great (really)." Instagram post, August 23, 2022. Screenshot by author.

These breezy messages of "female empowerment" gave her "enough self-confidence" to end a relationship with a long-term boyfriend, which was a "really big outcome," in her words. She had begun to flood her own feed with such encouragement: "One message is one thing, but when your feed is full of it, that has an impact. So, that's when I go, hey, the algorithm can be really good, because, if I'm liking an empowering message, then I'm going to see more empowering messages, and that—when the algorithm fills my feed with all the empowering messages, that can definitely take you from picking up your phone because you're in a bad place . . . and then, after you've scrolled through, you're feeling a bit better."

But it wasn't enough to have an empowered "present." This present state was a markable point in her journey from a promising past to an even more empowered future. In fact, Sonya also used this language of empowerment to evoke an inner defiance since childhood. This was articulated in terms of "proving people wrong": "Since very, very young, I wanted to prove people wrong . . . I want to prove your stereotype or your assumption of me incorrect. So it was like, this is where the boys are playing in this primary schoolyard. And I was like, no, I'm going to go play there. And I'm going to prove to you that the girls can actually join in. And I may have been the only girl, but I'm going to prove to you that I'm going to be here." Proving people wrong was a form of demonstrating capacity as a girl in different forms, such as being able to play soccer (football): "I remember when I was young . . . suddenly the Matildas [Australian national women's soccer team] kind of started getting known about, and I was just out there and I was like, 'You think we're different to the boys? And I'm going to prove you wrong.' And I loved going to soccer because I could prove everyone wrong from the assumptions that they had about me or not, not necessarily assumptions I had about me, just assumptions they would have about me because I'm a girl with a sister."

Shani Orgad and Rosalind Gill (2021) have observed how the discourses of self-belief have saturated Western media culture for the past few decades; they often position a state of resistance, but it is often unclear against what. The very indeterminacy of this empowered disposition of "proving people wrong," together with a clear directionality in the narrative of gradual confidence accumulation, made it useful for Sonya. It could be used to give a resistant veneer to a child wanting to belong in the playground and to feminine girls (girls with sisters) playing sport. It took the feeling of lack that accompanied the indignities of being a poor kid not having nice clothes to wear at school on non-uniform days, but articulated the lack as to do with *confidence*, and girls being sidelined from playing sport, things that were much more sayable, and less mortifying. More generally, Sonya could chart her life in terms of upward growth in confidence in myriad ways: negotiating pocket money from her dad in exchange for good grades; living abroad with a boyfriend for a number of years; breaking up with this boyfriend; finding Instagram feminism; and now, spreading confidence as an online feminist citizen: "I like and save and comment with different posts as a way to show support to whoever's creating it. So, it's strategic. I'm going to engage in this as a way to power you up and show you that you are supported." Confidence was a language and a framework that enabled Sonya to also give back, and allowed her to focus on the positives of her position as a now highly educated young woman. Such a vocabulary also reorganized Sonya's life along a linear journey of accumulation: from a childhood where she had proved she could play with the boys to a present where she herself could spread confidence as a commodity, empowering others who needed it, not herself. Struck out from this line were the feelings of embarrassment, vulnerability, and fear from growing up with few material resources as well as the continuing financial and emotional insecurity and isolation accompanying the sparse offline social networks Sonya could call on while living rurally.

Other working-class participants who had more access to offline feminist social circles, in contrast, voiced suspicions about such leadership ideals for women. Hayley, raised by a single mother in rural Australia, and now a reproductive health researcher in a significantly larger regional town, was highly ambivalent about the abounding professional leadership discourses of "women in STEM" (science, technology, engineering, mathematics) that she regularly encountered. For Hayley, who had been working to support her family since she was a teenager, "women in STEM" indexed a highly individualized, middle-class version of feminist aspiration:

> I kind of get a little bit tired of the whole "women in STEM" thing . . . I just feel like so many people, it's like their entry-level feminism, they've never been discriminated against in their life, and then they're like, "Wait a minute. Being a woman is a disadvantage. Like it's going to give me a disadvantage in this job when I've never felt I had one in my life before." And I just think that a lot of women in STEM circles is all about, "This is my problem. This is what I did with it" instead of being like, "We are working in a system that, you know, systematically disadvantages us and people do nothing about it."

Hayley was critical of this approach, which distilled oppression into individual problems and then required problems to always already be solved: "This is what I did with it." In short, it required the disavowal of lack; to be empowered meant you helped others—you gave back rather than seek connections across shared needs that were still not met. It replicated racialized, gendered, and classed ideals of being a good white feminist host, purporting to serve others while negating the self.

INTERSECTIONAL RESOURCES

An upward journey for a feminist restricted my participants to a linear path: empowering others, leading social change. But movement on this line required others to be led. Based on their own experiences, this dyadic relationship was observed ambivalently by a number of my young feminists, for whom new claims to intersectional leadership felt like a shrinking of space. For E, intersectionality was "definitely different" now, compared with when they were a teenager in school. Now, they stated, "It's very popular to be like, like an intersectional environmentalist and intersectional XYZ. And actually everybody just overuses 'intersectional' in my opinion. And it has become a bit of a buzzword and I'm very—I'm very of two minds about it."

Intersectionality was now a popular adjective to append to professions: environmentalist, leader, and so on. As an object, it had become proximate enough for many to grasp and display as part of their identity. E was deeply ambivalent about this. When intersectionality was a buzzword, it was harder to defend and to control its responsible use: as Sara Ahmed (2019) argues, when something is "overused," it can be "used up." While it had helped E to orient themselves when they discovered it as a teenager, the popular embrace of intersectionality changed the spatiality of these dynamics. "This is really silly," E confided, "but on Tinder you'd see people be like 'intersectional feminist,' like, and they'll put it in the Instagram bios, and like, on their Hinge profiles. And sometimes it can be a kind of a weird red flag."

As a young "ethnic person," E was continually alive to red flags that indicated you could not take for granted smooth travel, and that you had to be on guard. Implicit in this caution was the awareness that intersectionality could be used for others to expand into space, in the vein of the "loving," "ignorant" inclusion Ortega (2006) has famously observed of white feminism. This kind of inclusion is pleasurable, Ortega elucidates, because the white feminist "sees herself as someone who really understands women of color, who is putting the voices of these women on the map, who is 'giving' them a voice'" (62). Drawing on the work of philosopher Marilyn Frye on loving perception, Ortega argues that the loving, ignorant white feminist perception of women of color continues to homogenize the experience of race and fails to reflexively and critically locate the deep desire "to be respected in a field that claims to care about women of color and their thought" (62).

The newfound openness of intersectionality thus did not necessarily radically alter everyday relationality but rather sharpened its contradictions with the pressures of leadership. While "it's very much a point in time with the Internet where it's kind of cool to be a Black woman," as my participant Ade noted, this new "coolness" was intermeshed with demands on access and desires for contact: interlopers sliding into her DMs (private messaging on social media platforms) to ask questions about Black Lives Matter, people "dumping their deepest emotional traumas" on Ade in the smokers' section at queer bars. While race and gender might be "hot commodities" (Nash 2019), the desires for contact in everyday incidents, such as Ade's colleagues attempting to prove they knew about BLM, were wearing.

In these everyday worlds, intermeshed but also removed from the scholarly worldmaking discussed by Ortega, the anxiety of such whiteness was more visible. In the compulsoriness of better seeing and knowing from this bird's-eye view, and thus transforming one's subjectivity, its very impossibility was registered in the fragility and insecurity of the kinds of demonstrative relationality discussed by Ade and E.

Such anxiety increased the demands of reassurance on my non-white participants, both heightening and narrowing expectations of their knowledge. I return to Ade's irritation in relation to the assumption that she "would know" or have access to some transcendental truth on BLM: "I personally feel like Black women on [the] Internet aren't always given a lot of space to be problematic or to fuck up or make mistakes or just be like regular people, like other people. Like, I feel like we're held to a higher standard."

Ade sensed there was a closing down of space; the higher standard afforded less room to move. Further, the presumption that she would know was a highly objectified position—as if she herself were becoming an intersectional resource. Other participants of color also noted the subtle and incessant feeling that they had to fulfill the desires for knowledge of white people, desires that positioned participants of color as providing a type of knowledge that could be accessed. Positioned as providing a type of knowledge, usually involving direct experience, could mean conflating highly different experiences. Filipina participant Maria, for example, who often took on speaking engagements as part of her work, felt the brunt of this when she was asked to speak on refugee experience during Harmony Week. This week, notably, already registered the whitening effects of happy "diversity" discourse: Harmony Day, then Harmony Week, was the conservative Howard government's translation of the International Day of Elimination of Racial Discrimination into a celebration of multicultural diversity in the 1990s. But, as Maria explained, she is a migrant, not a refugee:

> And I feel like as women and people of color, we can be tokenized in that way. Like people assuming that, you know, oh yeah, this person is this race or this gender. Like, they will surely know all the answers to these questions, but it's a lot to carry.... I made it very clear in my biography that I'm not a refugee and I really can't speak about that. So I think... it's just—be respectful when you ask questions, keep in mind that like, you know, the other person is a human being too, you know—don't, don't be weird.

Here, Maria registered the pressure on her to be useful in particular ways. To be useful, as Sara Ahmed (2019) argues, is to be useful for someone or something; your use means you become part of another journey, a bigger apparatus. Your (non-white) race and (nondominant) gender mean you could "unlock" particular experiences for others that wouldn't otherwise be accessible.

Desires for knowledge are never innocent, nor are they neutral. This is particularly so in relation to theory that purports to open understandings of the marginalized. Highlighting the unequal human geopolitics of the academy, frameworks such as two-thirds world feminism and theories of difference, according to Chandra Talpade Mohanty (2003, 2013), do not simply "travel": they are trafficked. Following the cross-border movement of her germinal essay "Under Western Eyes," Mohanty (2013) argues that "hegemonic feminist knowledge production traffics antiracist feminist scholarship across borders, domesticating women-of-color epistemology in ways that either erase or assimilate it into a Eurocentric feminist globality" (981). Accordingly, notions of difference that originate from two-thirds world scholarship may be cited, highlighted, and celebrated but resituated within what is ultimately a uniform notion of difference and sameness. Lorraine Code (2006) terms these knowledge "monocultures," structured by practices of purposive knowledge production such as specialization, categorization, and classification. In such contexts, as your race becomes a type of experience that could constitute knowledge for others, you could become an object of interest. People could "become weird," according to Maria, in their desires for the incorporation of this type of knowledge into their repertoire.

Experiences of disadvantage could thus hold a certain magnetism in social media economies. Indeed, a number of my tertiary-educated participants noted that social media was useful, more so than academic work they had encountered, because it gave access to experience, not theory. But the promise of immediacy and access of social media culture—along with its overwhelming provision of (re)sources—could intensify expectations of always getting a response to your question, that simple answers could be found in connection with complex problems, that another's experience could simply be "learnable." This was not a problem only in connection to race. I return to Ollie, who discussed the ambivalence they felt around the transformation of their identity into another's "education": "It can be pretty exhausting to be like for a lot of people, the only queer person, trans person that they know in their lives. So . . . I like it when people ask questions, I like when people just want to know, but then . . . it can be definitely exhausting to kind of like rip my heart and soul out and give you my whole like identity and my struggle in my story. And then, you know . . . it's just like used for your education in a way." Preserving the self in such circumstances was a balancing act. Ollie "liked it" when people showed curiosity, but the border between dialogue and the risk of being consumed was a fine and ambiguous line. In the imperative to better educate the self and to better know, there was also a corresponding hunger—a "great wanting," as Ortega (2006, 62) notes—to do so.

When you became a resource, visible connections with you could also become valuable. Ollie spoke of these dynamics when raising money for top surgery on GoFundMe, a crowdfunding platform. GoFundMe has been critiqued for its reinforcement of the hierarchies of deservingness of GoFundMe recipients (Campeau and Thao 2022), and its intensification of existing inequities, in best serving those already connected with privileged networks (Berliner and Kenworthy 2017). Ollie's significant cultural and social capital placed them in an ideal position to turn to crowdfunding for their medical need that wasn't caught by a social safety set. However, they felt the ambivalence of such visibility and the unwanted connection it invited: "I'm not complaining about the fact that people are sharing it. Like, that's amazing. And I'm so, so grateful, but it's like . . . people that I know, when it comes down to it, on supporting trans lives, they aren't doing it. It was just like either they know me personally, so they're willing to do it for me or they saw other people doing it. But then, I don't know, don't message me about it."

Ollie felt the desires of others to extend their political subjectivities, not only through publicly visible support on social media but also through direct contact with them. Ollie did not welcome this incursion. They did not want to feel like a "half-subject" (Ortega 2006) whose citizenship was completed by others in the act of contributing to their fund. Ollie then apologetically suppressed their annoyance, saying, "I'm making it about me," and reiterating they weren't going to complain about the very acts of sharing and donation on which successful crowdfunding depended. However, it was clear that they felt ambivalent about how their need for surgery could be converted into others' performance of a generous and inclusive identity via the demonstration of their proximity to, and funding of, Ollie.

Being a resource led to demands. The pressure to "resource" others—and to make them better resourced in their intersectional feminist or other leadership journeys—could not always be resisted, even if it was exhausting to do so or they knew they were being pulled into the same pattern of response. Leila, whose parents had migrated from West Asia, showed me a social media post that summed it up for her, as the "Middle Eastern correspondent" for her friends: "I am not exotic, I am exhausted." In our interview, Leila spoke in such a way as to denaturalize the term *Middle Eastern*, given its orientalist associations. Bernie, a nonbinary person of color, said that in large and only lightly moderated social media groups, they would regularly jump in, particularly if it involved standing up for others: "For me it's always worth it because you never know like what background someone is from and these kinds of ideas . . . it's like the bystander effect, right? Like even if there's no one there to be harmed by it, that [could] also be like an idea that just shouldn't go, but should, that should just go on its merry way and not be challenged. I think it's always worth it."

But sometimes boundaries on access needed to be drawn. Now in her late twenties, white working-class Liz noted that at first she was excited to be invited to speak about disability for nonprofit organizations. These invitations accrued as her Instagram profile and thoughts on social justice snowballed and found bigger audiences. Over time, however, she decided to systematically decline these unpaid invitations. She no longer wanted to give these organizations the knowledge and time they were asking for, particularly when she had been living below the poverty line on disability payments for some time: "Now I'm more jaded and more cranky and I'm still disabled. And I don't want to be giving people who are paid to work with people like me, paid to work with chronically ill and disabled women, my labor for free."

The question of compensation for labor is a complex one in feminist theorization, where the valuing of labor solely through pay has been critiqued (Federici 2020; Jarrett 2015). This may also speak to the proprietary transformation of identity knowledge in online feminist knowledge cultures that I addressed in chapter 2. But what I want to underline here is Liz's understanding that the benefit of knowledge does not necessarily uplift evenly. While some, employed in the field of social justice, could further extend claims to expertise and potentially further their career trajectory, Liz did not necessarily move from her spot on the map. She was still jaded, still disabled. More broadly, my participants' accounts showed the potential to be frozen into place—to become a knowable type of disadvantage—even as others ascended the heights of becoming better leaders, better knowers and seers. As opposed to prompting an awareness of "partial perspective," as Donna Haraway (1988) puts it, theories of difference, in particular conditions, could be incorporated into belief in and desire for a "conquering gaze from nowhere" (Haraway 1988, 581).

CONFIDENT, CAPABLE, AND BURNT OUT

The upward journey of intersectional leadership did not, however, necessarily correspond to the conditions in which my young feminists worked, often involving different kinds of reproductive labor that was rarely recognized and not compensated. Indeed, as sociologists of employment have long observed, "soft skills" associated with femininity do not necessarily benefit women as they move into professional work, presumed as they are to be "natural" to women (Adkins and Lury 1999; McDowell 1997). Entering the world of professional work made it clear that young people might be discursively positioned as leaders, but this usually meant leadership in a deferred sense, as in the leaders of tomorrow but not today. For Bella, who had devoted her study time, work time, and spare time to social justice leadership while at university, this was experienced as deflating. When I interviewed her the second time, she had finished university and had commenced working at a sexual health charity with a youth-directed program. Though she said she did feel valued in the work she was doing, at her workplace, being a young person now felt more like a tick box than a platform to be heard. As she described it, "When we've done youth projects, it's been like, reminder: I am a young person, you hired me because of that. They're talking about youth advisory councils and I'm like, as someone who's been on them, please listen." She had been trying to educate people with initiatives such as buying pronoun and ally pins, but the human resources department hadn't been willing to distribute them; similarly, she had posted about IDAHOBIT (International Day Against Homophobia, Biphobia and Transphobia) on the internal online noticeboard but had attracted little interest.

To be positioned as a feminist leader was often a shiny institutional badge but often meant that you, in turn, were used up as you became a useful resource. For example, Hayley, who was highly cynical about "women in STEM" leadership discourses, nevertheless gave a substantial amount of her time to advocating for others. She sat as a representative on an early career researcher committee, where she tried to campaign for measures that would help postgraduate parents through gender-related equity measures. She noted a substantial gap between the institutional fondness for such gendered leadership discourses and the resources, human or otherwise, actually provided to enable systemic change: "They slap an Athena Swan medal ranking on the uni, have a committee that deals with something, they have no powers and no budget and [are] typically run by people who are discriminated against and actually taken out of their time [to do their own work]."

Hayley persevered but was keenly aware of the limits of such institutional leadership. Julie, similarly, had reached somewhat of an impasse in her leadership by the time of her second interview, in 2022. As a young working-class woman who had always taken on significant amounts of paid work during her studies, she had taken on the role of a youth support worker between her interviews in 2021 and 2022. While Julie had the instinct that this would be aligned with her desires to "help people" in her career trajectory, the minimally trained and supported position drained her of her resilience and time during her final year of university.

Julie's experience exemplified the contradiction between discourses of leadership that extolled inclusion, and the day-to-day, grinding work of care. Her main charge as a support worker was an often violent seventeen-year-old boy that other colleagues had refused to work with: "I had shifts where I'd just come home crying. . . . They would sometimes be sixteen-hour shifts, because I'd be starting at 3:15 in the afternoon, going to bed at 11 at his house, staying there and then waking up and leaving at 7 a.m. in the morning. . . . So, it was just extended periods of time . . . it used to be two people on a shift, and then it went down to one for sixteen hours. So it's—I did the best with what I could." Julie was simultaneously trying to keep the women's collective going, but many members had lost steam following the pandemic-related fatigue of 2021. At the age of twenty-two, she felt the pressure of needing financial security because she was engaged to her boyfriend, an apprentice butcher. They wanted to find a place where they could move in together. She wanted to spend time on her studies, and had begun a final-year research project as a gateway to postgraduate study. But she felt that she just couldn't let go of the hours she spent doing paid work, in order to devote time to the project. Julie was still cheerful, but her material circumstances and the time and energy she freely gave to others militated against the upward linear progression that had been ingrained as the norm for someone with her passion and social justice politics.

For other participants with impressive career accomplishments, leading was not simply the "happy" endpoint of an upward line. Take Kelly, who, at twenty-five, was already something of a corporate leader: white, middle-class, and private-school-educated, she embodied the confidence that Sonya so often cited. She spoke with aplomb and did not hesitate to introduce her professional credentials and feminist activities in her group workshop. She was on the board of several nonprofit women's organizations, and in her postworkshop interview, I learned that she had won several awards for her work outside work, organizing events, campaigns, and activities promoting women's success in the IT sector where she worked.

And yet this journey had felt almost compulsory for Kelly in the responsibility she felt to look out for others, against an everyday backdrop of harassment and abuse. In Kelly's journey, workplace harassment had been a recurring feature of her life since she was a junior employee. On the service desk where she had started at the age of eighteen, her colleagues were about 90 percent men, and she and the other few (young) women were regularly harassed by male coworkers. Sometimes this harassment was just mean, the kind of harassment that occurs when men compete with each other to make the weakest link the butt of a joke—the POC, the queer, the gender-diverse person, the woman. Sometimes this harassment was sexual, such as at Christmas parties, when some had too much to drink. Now, Kelly had the power to call this out and did not hesitate to prosecute abuse. She said, "I really don't care. Like I'll sit with you and talk about exactly what made me feel uncomfortable to your face and—I don't want an apology. I just want to tell you what you're doing, to fix it." And beyond face-to-face confrontation, Kelly was fully prepared to wield her authority as a manager: "I don't care. I will take your job. Like, you just, you don't do that stuff anymore. This is 2021. Like I find it hard to deal with anyone that's just not on that level now. And then I'll just prepare to get rid of them."

At work, Kelly felt—and was—capable. She was able to act on her intentions and was unintimidated by the gendered power dynamics she faced. In some ways, this self-possession and ability to advocate for herself and others had symbolic value. As a young woman working in corporate, it could be read as a mode of operating in the world connected with ambition and success: go-getting; being a straight shooter. Kelly was aware of her worth, having worked her way through the ranks and moved companies in this process: "I came to this organization for the culture. So if you're not giving me the culture, why am I here, to be as blunt as that?" By the "culture," Kelly meant a professional working environment that was, at a minimum, harassment-free, and she understood that top employers sought to keep talent like her.

And yet this self-advocacy was far from a simple building block in a journey of upward ascent; it was an embodied defense that Kelly had developed in order to not be crushed, a response to an ongoing sense of potential onslaught from all directions. Beyond the workplace harassment that she had endured, she had also seen abuse on a familial level. At the age of sixteen, she had learned that her mother had been sexually abused on a long-term basis by Kelly's grandfather, who had lived with them off and on when Kelly was a child. Kelly became protective of her mother but also of friends and colleagues who could face the possibility of violence. She was sensitized to the pervasive possibility of abuse; whenever she heard friends say things that were "borderline," her "ears perked up"; she was immediately ready to have necessary conversations. She was an abuse detector, in her friendships, for her family, and in her position of authority at work, even though, she acknowledged, it was not good "for my own mental health to continually be able to look out for that kind of stuff."

For another of my professional feminists, Priscilla, cool confidence was the visible, presentable facade of long-standing personal struggles. A second-generation migrant and a talented professional in the nonprofit sector, Priscilla had a knack for argument, such that her teachers and parents "thought she should go into law." She was academically brilliant. She had participated in an accelerated program at high school and began university early. She had also moved away from home early, at the age of eighteen, and so she began professional work early on in her undergraduate degree, amassing a portfolio of work that had led to her career strides after graduation.

But this confidence and independence were in fact the traces of a hard-fought survival. Priscilla's tools of argument had long been considered assets for her, and since a young age these had been signifiers of a go-getting, ambitious young woman. But she had realized that these dispositions had been sharpened by a violent patriarchal household: "I didn't respect him in the way that he expected me to. Like I used to always be willing to get into arguments and things. I think that was a big part of it. . . . I guess that's probably also colored the way that I do my feminism now." Priscilla reflected, however, that such proclivities for argument were self-destructive:

> Having arguments in that way, getting really angry and really feeling it . . . it's really not good for me. That adrenaline that comes in is permanently damaging. And it's the same sort of thing as when, you know, I was having arguments in a bad way with my dad . . . I think that it's almost in some ways like PTSD. So I don't really like to engage in that, in that level of like back-and-forth argumentative sort of style anymore.

Similarly, she said, frankly, that while moving out early on could be narrated as "precocious," it had more to do with desperation. Home "wasn't a situation that I could stay in . . . if I'd stayed at home, but I probably also wouldn't be alive," she told me in her interview.

It was not hard for Priscilla to advocate for herself, to speak up when things seemed wrong. Rather, she needed to teach herself to pause, to hold back, to not engage. Priscilla's visible confident shell was what remained of her individual struggle for survival. Kelly, similarly, during my project, had realized she needed to hold back. The continual onslaught of national news in 2021 and 2022 about high-profile rape and abuse victims who had been ignored, discounted, and vilified in the court of public opinion was too much for her. When I spoke to Kelly in 2022, she had largely removed herself from her social media; she was trying to create some space in her life that didn't make her feel as though she had to be permanently vigilant, always ready for a fight.

AT THE END OF THE LINE

In some ways, Kelly's feminism was indeed driven by being at the end of a (family) line. The trauma of the women in her family drove her feminist leadership, organizing, and activity: "[My mum] didn't have the opportunity to, and neither did my grandma because she had the exact same experience as my mum. And I'm sure it goes back and back and back. So I find that almost as the driver with everything that I do, I do because they couldn't." And yet, due to the trauma experienced by her mother and her lack of a paid career, Kelly felt unable to discuss her activities with her. She didn't want to rub her success "in her face." She noted that her mother was "very proud of everything that I do, but some of it, I don't think she 100 percent understands."

The cultural template of feminist leadership I have discussed faced founding contradictions. It emphasized individuals standing out, but by unobtrusively elevating the voices of others. This inadvertently positioned leadership as an exceptional altruism, a disinterested, self-negating service, where you became a flat shape uplifting others, a *platform*. Of course, such negation was nigh impossible in the promotional discursive conditions of social media, or the broader imperatives of youth achievement, resulting in the particular objectification of racialized and gender nonnormative experiences as they became valuable plot points in the story of a leader that could see the full picture. For, while different experiences were understood as deeply personal and irreducible, they also held exchange value in their telling if they could place their subject on a line of progressive development. The fears—and acts—of "appropriating" experience spoke not just to the implicit identification of the norms of recognition on social media but also to the fact that experience was already conceived of as intellectual property, to own, show, and tell.

Such an individualized, proprietary understanding reinforced the notion of knowledge as ultimately individually derived rather than collectively theorized, flowing in a linear, predictable fashion from direct experience only. To borrow from Taina Bucher's (2018) if-then formulation of algorithmic reasoning, if I am "XYZ," then I know "ABC." But this linearity meant the potentially messy, affecting resonances of different experiences could not be embraced. This left only the purportedly empowered, strong feminist as a viable space of dwelling: a lonely position, where you ended up frozen in place. It could give a vantage point to see harm and abuse everywhere, without seeing what you yourself had undergone, as some traumatic experiences could not be easily told and packaged into "resources." I have suggested that this linear spatiality of self-development and leadership is a dominant way in which intersectional feminism is taken up. It is one that is so normatively embedded in cultures of youth education and sociality that it is difficult to refuse. But it contradicts the enmeshment, the collectivity, and the messiness of identities and power that intersectionality, as a theory, aimed to explain.

The "popular intersectionality," as Katrin Schindel (2024) terms it, of online feminist knowledge cultures sought to capture then mobilize the oppressions of the world. All you had to do, as a young person, was lead, and uplift and empower others with you. Individual aspiration, confidence, and inclusiveness are understood to be the antidote to generational and historical inequalities. Yet the neat linearity of intersectional journeys, requiring some to harness others' resources, and others to self-exploit their own, showed how curtailed and isolated such movement can be. As you had to always be in a position of becoming empowered, there was little room to articulate ongoing disadvantage. As Kelly confided, being in a position to empower others was translated as helping others further up the line, not yourself. Good feminist leaders helped others. They were shiny, luminous, but they didn't take up space.

4

DON'T BE THAT GIRL

When Gabi was in high school, she aspired to work for UN Women, "but not so much anymore," she says. At the time of our interview, she didn't feel she could align herself with its politics any longer. She still followed them on X, however, and included a tweet to show me during our first interview as an example of her feminist social media feed. In this tweet, UN Women combines the words "THROW / THEM / OUT" in connection with an image of numerous colorful trash bins, each bin representing a form of sexism such as "unequal pay," "sexual harassment," and "gender stereotypes" (figure 4.1).

Gabi shared this tweet with me in order to express her critique of it. She felt this tweet demonstrated that UN Women was, "to be honest," a bit too "girlboss." Girlboss is not something you want to be. According to Gabi, "I feel like, yeah, this is very like neoliberal white feminism from memory. Like yeah . . . a lot of what white feminism loves to focus on is like the gender pay gap, which is obviously a big issue. But then there are things like, just how different women of color versus white women are treated when

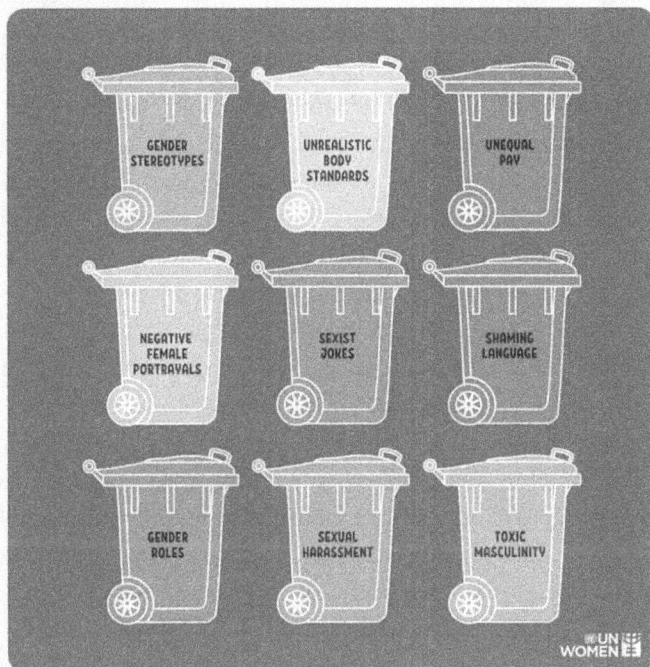

4.1 UN Women, "THROW THEM OUT." Twitter post, August 15, 2021. Screenshot by author.

they go to the doctors and stuff like that." While Gabi spoke of UN Women, and white feminism, her words evoked a distinct personality. According to her, white feminism "loved" to dwell on surface-level problems, the gender pay gap seemingly a "single lens" issue, while ignoring the everyday problems of women of color. She acknowledged that, yes, "there's only so much you can put in 140 characters or in an infographic," but it could have been more "nuanced," with some of the issues "only concerning a certain type of woman."

I highlight Gabi's comments not to dispute or back up her claims in relation to UN Women. I begin with her critique in order to highlight how the proving of intersectional feminist credentials required defensive moves. In online knowledge cultures, to be in the know, certain forms of feminism, and indeed, certain kinds of women, had to be continually put under the microscope and, if necessary, repudiated. In the main, this type of woman was white, sometimes wealthy, and identified as always at risk of problematic behaviors such as narcissism, ignorance, and not knowing her place. Gabi herself was also white and middle-class, a correspondence that, I suggest, heightened the urge for dissociation with such feminist "types," particularly against a backdrop of social justice imperatives to disconnect, dissociate, and refuse complicity.

In this chapter, I argue that the impulse to distance the self from a "certain type of woman," and to beat others to the critique of her, has become central to claims of being a "good feminist" and doing "good feminism" in the speedy cultures of social media. This intensified self-scrutiny, and scrutiny of everyday acts of problematic femininity as performed by women, involved copious amounts of energy. Such an inward focus corresponds to a broader "turn to character" (Bull and Allen 2018) in which neoliberal projects aim to distill good politics into problems of personality within one's individual control. These practices were exemplified in modes of making sense of the celebrity cultures that streamed through my young feminists' social media. It was necessary to be continuously aware of problematic positions, statements, and absences in celebrity behavior, speech, and cultural artifacts, and thus always be poised to critique. This anxious performance of critique, what Sara Ahmed (2004b) might call a "declaration" of intersectional feminism, was both offensive and defensive. In cultures of ongoing, minute, lateral surveillance, it could throw the spotlight on another's faults, shielding the self from interrogation. It was connected to the culture of knowing and judgment that Mark Andrejevic (2013) and Jack Bratich (2010) have observed in interactive surveillance cultures spanning social media and reality TV: you are invited to critique, and in the act of critiquing, indicate your immunity to the problematic element you have identified.

What was notable was how the fear of being made a lesson for others permeated broadly into everyday practices for my participants. In social media cultures of lateral surveillance, critique was applied as a general lens to celebrities or microcelebrities but was always linked to the possibility of being the object of critique. Not in intention but in effect, the anticipation and execution of critique could thus replicate misogynistic practices of "sacrificing Britney to save America," to quote Anna Watkins Fisher (2011), whereby the ridicule of celebrity women is used to punish women's behavior that is out of bounds. At the same time that participants lauded the very emergence of redemptive documentaries about Britney Spears and other maligned celebrity women of the early 2000s, it was striking how the figure of the failing, "cringe" female celebrity who made mistakes about what she wore and how she spoke loomed as large in the feminist social media attention economy as men who practiced extreme violence and misogyny, such as Andrew Tate. There was often a slippage between the stern identification of supposedly neoliberal feminism and the relief of pinpointing someone else, another woman, "getting it wrong."

GIRLBOSSES AND NEOLIBERAL WOMEN

Girlboss was one of the recurring terms used by my participants to describe the kind of feminist girl you did not want to be (although as you read this, I note that there will certainly already be another girl figure to take her place). Girlboss could be evoked not simply by explicit self-representations or statements but, as with brands, by aesthetics, "vibes," and associations. As with many terms on social media, the current significance of *girlboss* had traveled some distance from its original referent. It was at first predominantly associated with success in business, following the publication of the 2014 memoir *Girlboss* by Sophia Amoruso, a young Californian entrepreneur who had experienced rapid success as a fashion retailer. *Girlboss* entered the Western cultural lexicon the same year that Beyoncé performed at the American VMAs (Video Music Awards) backlit by a glowing "FEMINIST" sign several feet high. This was a time of feminist renewal, a feminism associated with individual success, positive ambition, and visibility, building on the discursive presence of "girlpower" from the 1990s onward.

By 2021, *girlboss* was still in the spotlight but very much already done, over, passé as an ideal, when I spoke to my participants. On TikTok, the hashtag #GaslightGatekeepGirlboss, while often hazy in its exact signification, demonstrated that #Girlboss was now associated with an unsavory image. At the beginning of January 2022, cult British fashion magazine ID asked, "Does the downfall of high-profile girlbosses mean we're no longer falling for it?" *Girlboss* was now connected with fraudulence, unbridled ambition, and the criminality of personalities such as Elizabeth Holmes, an entrepreneur who had run a high-profile multibillion-dollar Silicon Valley con. Amoruso had also declined in popularity, having gone from the heady visibility connected to a Netflix series based on her life to filing for bankruptcy and dodging allegations of discriminatory and abusive behavior at her fashion startup (Mull 2020). More broadly, however, *girlboss* evoked a mainstream feminism that had now reached saturation point in the social justice market. It was no longer done to brand the self as a girlboss; rather, one had to avoid being branded as one. Bella, a student activist, explained to me, "We were trying to create some, like, hoodies and shirts for our collective. And we specifically had conversations. Like, we don't want it to look like, girlboss-y, Cotton On feminist. Like, that's like an aesthetic now, right? Feminist T-shirts and tote bags and mugs, like girlboss mugs. . . . We specifically realized that we didn't want our image connected with that . . . even in terms of how we design a T-shirt, can impact how people see our values."

Being situated in a circuit of feminist networks necessitated the appropriate response to a constant stream of possible connections and associations. As popularities waxed and waned, it was sometimes necessary to dissociate so that one's own image was not tainted by the fallout connected with other high-profile feminist brands, not just by personalities like Amoruso or Holmes, but by brands like Cotton On, a fast-fashion retailer. In the visual culture of social media, this involved particular aesthetics and language. For example, certain phrases ("Hey angel, Hey babe," according to Bella) could sound "girlbossy." Bella breathlessly explained, "I even have a T-shirt that's—do you remember when the 'Future Is Female' [T-shirt] came out?" "The Future Is Female," a slogan originally coined in the 1970s, had exploded in circulation in 2017 on T-shirts and in online selfies coinciding with Hillary Clinton's ultimately unsuccessful US presidential campaign. Bella went on, "And then there was all the subsequent shirts like, no, 'The future is like disabled women, Indigenous women' . . . Like even, even that now just feels . . . half of it feels outdated, but then it also feels like virtue signaling, and like, 'Here's how to include all the things' and because that has been co-opted by your fast-fashion brands, it no longer feels genuine."

Staying on top of the pulse in responding to feminist cycles required distinguishing the self from the "feminist commodity activism" (Repo 2020) and commercial feminist influencing (Scharff 2023b) that Bella and other participants disdained. It demanded efforts to protect one's own feminist image, particularly in making any kinds of claims to speak or represent feminism in any way. This image should not feel "dated"; even more importantly, it should not just be but feel genuine, requiring anticipation, effort, and thought. Authenticity, as Sarah Banet-Weiser (2012) has commented, despite or perhaps indeed due to widespread critiques of the "fakeness" of social media, has continued to hold even more significance on social media in terms of women's self-representation. Caught in an infinite feedback loop, authenticity requires labor to show the right attunements, feelings, vulnerabilities; paradoxically, the more labor invested, the less authentic the presentation.

Authenticity, for Bella, required dissociation from cringe, commercial iterations of feminism such as *girlboss*. Being an authentic intersectional feminist required positioning the self in distinction to girlboss, as I learned from Gabi: "I feel like girlboss feminism, which I feel like you could almost equate to neoliberal feminism . . . it's maybe a little cringe, but then it's just because I feel like the people that tend to like use those girlboss catchphrases and those ideas tend to be like white middle-class women. It's all about promoting your own voice I suppose. And not bringing on all perspectives." *Girlboss* was self-promotional. This was bad, although it seemed to be a logical outcome in an age where young people were so heavily addressed as potential leaders. It was also to be potentially ignorant of your own limitations; but the obverse of *girlboss*, to bring on all perspectives, was seen as somehow doable despite the anguish voiced by many of my young feminists about inadvertently leaving voices out.

Gabi, as I mentioned, was a white middle-class woman. Yet presumably the cringe was due to the term being used by other white middle-class women, those from whom Gabi needed to differentiate herself. As with Amoruso and Holmes, *girlboss* evoked a white feminism indelibly connected with traits like narcissism and avarice. Rather than "white" being a descriptor of a structural position to which Gabi also, unavoidably, belonged, it was a marker of feminist identity that implicitly could be eschewed through the articulation of one's own politics. Indeed, the main way to avoid girlboss feminism and, indeed, one of Gabi's main justifications to leadership, was squarely connected with her claim to lead intersectionally: "Intersectionality has made the biggest impact on like my feminism, my life, how I like yeah, go about through discourse and like yeah my opinions and beliefs."

The desire for intersectionality was intertwined with the desire to avoid being seen as a girlboss and a white feminist: a selfish, bad hostess who was ignorant to boot. Such desires dovetailed with white middle-class desires for "perfect" feminism (Kanai 2020), and arguably also the conviction that whiteness was something that could be left behind, as the political problems of whiteness were projected onto high-profile, problematic others. Underpinning these practices of dissociation and aspiration were deeply ingrained cultural beliefs in personal agency and choice. That is, one could choose to leave behind whiteness, to reject complicity; it was simply a matter of willpower and commitment to self-improvement that certain famous others did not have.

WOMEN GETTING IT WRONG

In the online knowledge cultures in which my participants were situated, terms such as *intersectional feminist* and *white feminist* would circulate as means of classifying behavior deemed ideal or problematic. These were terms that became more salient when one's self-representations became more visible in the push to be future leaders. The weight of visibility was indeed significant for those who sought to take a position in the generalized injunctions to responsibly exercise one's political voice. In the cycles of social media, this opened up an availability to be critiqued as personal feminist views were read, in Bella's words, as one's "image," or brand. Putting forward any kind of message circulating via social media invited ready critique of what it failed to include or consider, with cascading moral ramifications. Thus UN Women as a clunky, complex transnational institution could be attributed the personality of being a girlboss. To be visible as any kind of feminist representative online was to have one's identity textualized and individualized. But the kind of reading practices that predominated were not oriented to positioning the person-as-text within culture. More often, "reading" a person hinged on exposure: detecting clues that revealed a fundamental identity problem. This kind of paranoid reading (Sedgwick 1997) usually positioned the textual production of a person as the tip of the iceberg, the visible minutiae revealing something potentially massive and suspect underneath.

This genre of critique was frequently in play on social media, catalyzed by continually breaking stories of famous individuals, usually women, going awry in their feminist journey. Wayward (mis)steps would become controversies to be routinely and ritually dissected, evaluated, and discussed. The online discussion of the couture worn by Latinx American politician Alexandria Ocasio-Cortez ("AOC") and queer white British supermodel Cara Delevingne at the 2021 Met Gala was one such site of critique that overtook the usual discussion of aesthetics at this event:

Akane So . . . did you see a lot of Met Gala in your feed this week?

Holly Oh my gosh. So much. It was everywhere, specifically Cara and AOC.

My participant Holly described the antagonistic environment of critique connected to the two women, both displaying conspicuous slogans on their attire at the Met Gala. For AOC, much centered on questioning the political work effected by the capitalized words "TAX THE RICH" on the back of her dress, from the bodice to the skirt. According to Holly, "When I was on Twitter, I saw a lot of 'isn't taxing the rich your job,' like, 'Go do that.' And then on Instagram it was a lot of, 'Oh my God. Yes, tell all those rich people haha,' like, just eating it up. And yeah. I mean, I found it cringy and not actually that effective, but also everyone talking about it all the time got really annoying."

A young white queer woman with a long-term chronic illness, Holly had a social life that was mainly online. She generally needed to be immersed in online life to feel connected to the feminist current, even as she was irritated by the unnecessary "noise." Like Gabi, she felt that failing to hit the right political note was "cringy." Cringe indexed an earnest attempt to raise one's political voice that nevertheless flopped; it was naïve; it wasn't cool. But at the same time, Holly didn't feel that this purported failure merited the amount of criticism she saw; the effect of the obsessive chatter and criticism of the authenticity of AOC was fatiguing. Notably, critiques of the Met Gala itself, the clout, wealth, and inequality that underpinned the Metropolitan Museum of Art, and associated industries of celebrity manufacture were less easy to come by.

Delevingne was heavily dissected online for wearing a corset emblazoned with the words "PEG THE PATRIARCHY," with the gravity of her missing the mark registering as something more than "cringe" for many spectators. According to Jillian, a queer white and disabled trans woman, "She's a very famous queer woman who can do absolutely anything she wants. And what she chose to do was—steal a phrase of a Black creator and not credit her and then be still a phrase that was problematic as hell. I feel like in her position, she can really be doing more than that, as you know, as a supermodel." Jillian, like Holly, was smart, sensitive, and well-read. Living in a small regional town far from other young queer people, and with a disability that made it difficult to find sustainable work, online culture was also important for her participation in a sense of shared feminist and queer social life. Jillian attributed full agency to Cara Delevingne in this decision; she ought to have known that this was a phrase originally created by a queer POC creator and trademarked in 2015, and so wearing this corset was not a decision to be taken lightly.

Holly had similarly sent me an example of a critical tweet she had seen, which argued that Delevingne in fact was upholding the patriarchy with her corset's message (figure 4.2). The tweet itself focused on the potential feelings ascribed to "pegging": shame, humiliation, and so on, and thus denounced Delevingne's attire. This notably contrasted with the meaning attributed to it by its trademarked creator, Luna Matatas, who argued the slogan was meant to be "playful" and not about "anal sex or men" but subversion (Moss 2021). But what was more at play was the analysis of Delevingne's identity in and of itself, as Holly reported: "I mean, people were . . . very critical of it. Like the tweet I sent [suggesting] that it's, you know, kind of homophobic, but other people were saying, 'Yeah, it's performative, but it's not that bad. I mean, she's a queer woman.' And then people were saying, 'Well, her dad or grandpa or someone is really, really rich.' But I don't know. Everyone's just so annoying."

Critique, then, didn't necessarily turn on the semiotics of *pegging* and *patriarchy* but on Delevingne's own identity traits—her wealth, her queerness—in determining her responsibility or excusability for this faux pas. As with intersectionality as a framework, addition and subtraction of forms of identity, translated as ranking levels of disadvantage and privilege, were operative here. Delevingne was queer, thus removing her from the heat of allegations of problematic positioning, while her economic capital reinforced the blameworthy nature of her messaging. Having a rich father or grandfather highlighted the gap in what she should have known before such messages were circulated on social media: she should have known more, known better, and known in advance.

Such additive and subtractive dynamics worked to occasionally shield some figures from critique. For example, while a number of white participants were particularly critical of *girlboss* and *leaning in*, they followed and openly admired high-profile women of color who advocated views that demonstrably overlapped with the kinds of girlboss feminism they otherwise eschewed. One prominent example was Ghanaian Australian influencer and entrepreneur Flex Mami, a microcelebrity increasingly featured in national design and fashion outlets for her bold style. Flex was openly individualistic, pragmatic, and career-oriented in the advice she gave for

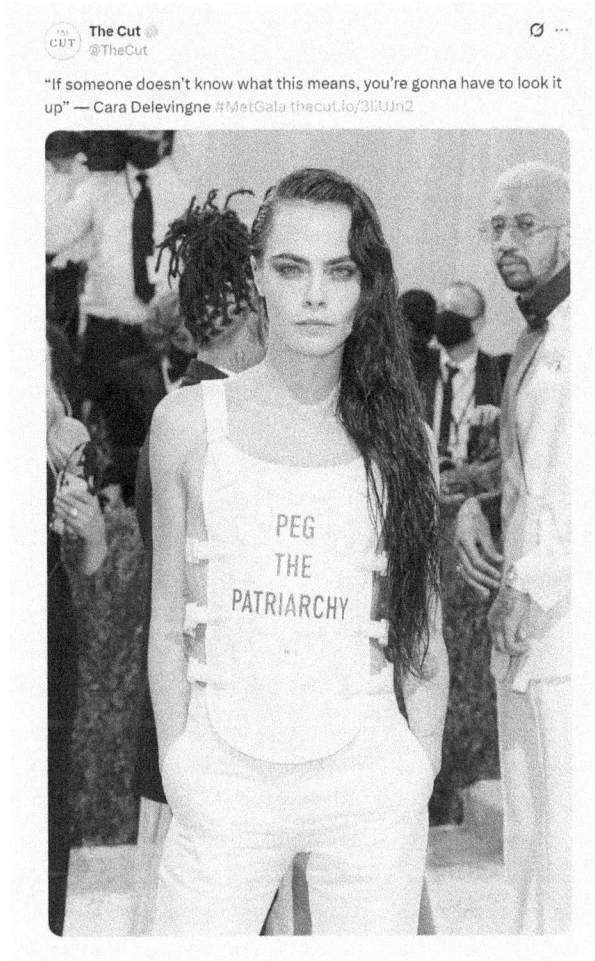

The Cut ◎
@TheCut

"If someone doesn't know what this means, you're gonna have to look it
up" — Cara Delevingne #MetGala thecut.io/3liUJn2

4.2 Cara Delevingne at the 2021 Met Gala. Twitter post by
The Cut, September 15, 2021. Screenshot by author.

getting ahead: she advocated for drawing boundaries, setting intentions, and refusing guilt about being selective with how she gave her time to others, including friends, particularly as a woman of color. This message notably seemed to resonate most with white middle-class participants who clearly held leadership aspirations. For example, Gabi favorably commented on Flex's conceptualization of one's activism as a "pie chart"—rather than spreading oneself too thin by giving to too many causes, she noted the importance of specializing and managing one's time.

As discussed previously, however, the legitimacy of visibility for women of color was precarious. Jillian went on in her interview to discuss one of her heroines she followed on social media, Munroe Bergdorf, a Black British trans woman and activist who was gaining significant celebrity in the worlds of popular culture and fashion. Jillian loved "the way she thinks about things" and "the way she interacts with the community." But what most awed her about Bergdorf was her sunniness and her sheer power to get things right: "I know she's a big famous trans woman, and . . . for the power that she now has, she hasn't, she literally hasn't fucked up once and that I cannot believe. Like I'm just . . . like the fact that she has managed, she must put in so much effort to be so good for so, so many people . . . I feel like I'm a bit in awe of her." Bergdorf was able to express meaningful, intersectional intellectual contributions as an activist that rang true for many different identities without "fucking up once." Jillian was visibly blown away by Bergdorf's ability to "be so good for so, so many people." This indicated that getting it wrong was actually an expected, though not necessarily forgivable, part of being a famous person and that getting it right was actually, in practice, a nigh impossible standard that was demanded not just of one's practices but of one's image as circulated on social media.

Yet perhaps Bergdorf's track record as a highly visible Black woman was unsurprising, as Ade observed of the heightened regulation of Black women's conduct in politicized spaces: "I think this is the phenomenon where Black women are not allowed to be or not, are not expected to be regular Black women on the Internet. [They] always [have to be] like popping, these Queens, like Black girl magic. Like I love it, don't get me wrong, I love Black girl magic, but at the same time, it's like, you know, like when can we be mediocre? . . . Like, I feel like we're held to a higher standard of like, 'Oh my gosh, how dare you say this?'"

This had particular ramifications for the forms of critical insight that could be demonstrated by Ade. While often positioned as an intersectional "resource" at work, she noted she had to bend over backward, be "super polite, super friendly," to avoid any imputation of aggression. For example, at work, Ade recounted a situation where she sought to provide feedback in the course of a discussion: "Someone wants to tell me, 'Oh, let's not call people out. Let's call people in.' Like, I'm sorry, this isn't a callout. If this was a callout, I would have told you and let you know, 'Hey, this is a callout and I'm calling you out.' This is a professional conversation and some feedback that I'm providing to you." Ade noted that she had to tread particularly carefully to not be read as overstepping, aggressive; her "feedback" was more susceptible to being read as an ungenerous "callout." Thus, returning to the example of Munroe Bergdorf, for Jillian her being "so good" was perhaps unsurprising for a Black woman of Bergdorf's stature. As observed by many (Kanai and Gill 2020; Sobande et al. 2022; Sobande 2019), a culture of "woke" capitalism has propelled some Black and nonwhite people into the spotlight, particularly as representatives of a more meritocratic capitalism, but without necessarily leaving the space for them to deviate from an outward brightness and positivity.

PREDICTING THE PROBLEMATIC

This culture of critique tended to divide feminists into binary positions—being visible or invisible, and getting it "right" or getting it "wrong." In an age of too much information, people need, and take, shortcuts. As I discussed in chapter 2, this meant that intersectionality was translated into a mechanism for ordering and classification. But there were other analytical shortcuts that operated in order to evaluate the practices and positions that streamed across the social media news cycle. In such knowledge cultures, it was not enough to ascertain the causes of what might be problematic; one also had to predict it in advance. Certain identities had bigger red flags in terms of being potentially problematic. For example, for white women who attracted significant visibility and who purported to be feminist, like Delevingne, audiences were poised and ready to denounce potential pitfalls. It was too easy to get it wrong because standards were high: being seen to practice intersectionality required the deployment of a sophisticated language around inclusion, but also being a likeable woman: not immodest, not overreaching. It was risky to call for the "pegging" of the patriarchy; it did not "include all perspectives" and it didn't feel nice.

Overall, identities in themselves raised risk factors in terms of association and dissociation. Online, or even in your offline life, you did not want to follow the wrong person. I return to the conversation in chapter 2

I had with Shae, who had signaled the paradox of how, on Tumblr, people were "obsessed" with categories as they proliferated in attempts to understand the world. Shae explained that singular categories, in and of themselves, were associated with being more "gray" or open and inclusive than others, which were more likely to trigger a sense of risk or a red flag. For example, when I asked her how comfortable she felt on Tumblr in terms of her sexuality, she responded that bisexuality, like pansexuality, was highly accepted on Tumblr because

> sexuality is a spectrum and bisexuality, because you're going on both ends of that spectrum, it is the spectrum if you know what I mean? It's like being pansexual, you know, it's, it's kind of like the ultimate ... and—I don't believe this, but this is what I get from Tumblr—it's like the ultimate sexuality, you know, it's like, oh, you're attracted to everyone. . . . It's the same with nonbinary people I've noticed as well ... I mean, I think nonbinary is technically no gender, but also if people are all genders, that's a bit of a lean toward, you can just be anything.

Shae was speaking from her own observation of norms on Tumblr; evidently, this feeling of being the "ultimate" sexuality or gender was definitely not always personally experienced by other bisexual participants, who told me of feelings of bi erasure and the anxiety of potentially taking up space in queer online circles when in long-term relationships with men. But against the background of the broader context of online "infoglut" (Andrejevic 2013) I explored earlier, Shae's comments indicated how identities took on certain preemptive classifications: analytical shortcuts that helped to flag whether certain people were safe to handle. Identities that were typified as more open, conveyed through the feeling of "grayness," were less risky to deal with. Accordingly, while bisexuality and pansexuality were types of sexuality, they didn't feel like categories because they felt inclusive, extending to both ends of the spectrum. Similarly, nonbinary did not feel like a foreclosed category but like a possibility: "You can just be anything." This was a significant expression of agency—to be anything—and it also conveyed a radical political openness. This feeling of "openness" could be presumed to lower the risk of an identity that was "complicit" with varying structural oppressions spanning patriarchy, racism, and capitalism.

Conversely, a presumed "closedness" of a particular identity was used to predict problematic behavior or political complicity, according to Liz, another queer participant who had spent most of her youth on Tumblr. Liz explained, for example, that in online feminist spaces on Tumblr, lesbians were seen as having increasingly "risky" identities. A lesbian woman was seen, in particular, as a red flag for closedness and transmisogyny, sensitizing some in feminist spaces to jump immediately to intervention: "One thing that I have found challenging in feminist spaces over the last five to ten years is a real kind of ostracization that's occurring against lesbians in our, in community and in feminist spaces. There are some women who immediately equate the word *lesbian* with TERFs. [They follow with] the interrogation and questioning of lesbian sexuality, with questions like, 'Well, would you sleep with a trans woman?'"

The acronym TERF (Trans Exclusionary Radical Feminist) was first used online by activist blogger Viv Smythe (2018), but as she notes, the term ultimately became notable not for its originality but for its useful shorthand in describing the trans-hostile rhetoric that trans activists had been resisting for some time. As for Liz, she was all too aware that this kind of interrogation on behalf of trans women reflected the presence of everyday transphobia, and especially the intensification of extreme transmisogyny in recent years that was visible in far-right protests in Australia (Lee et al. 2023) and in the "moral panic" of policies and legislative rollbacks in the United Kingdom and in the United States (Stryker and Chaudhry 2022). She suspected a general lack of cisgender sexual openness to trans people and hazarded that this could be all the more embittering if it came from queer circles too. As Jack Halberstam (2018) argues, the legacy of trans women's decades-long exclusion from the Michigan Womyn's Music Festival, along with the emergence of white feminist texts in the 1970s insisting on "women-born women," casts a long shadow, both producing trans as an identity that can be debated and excluded and engendering a constant vigilance in countering anti-transgender feminism.

At the same time, there were several layers in this experience recounted by Liz. She paused and reflected that, in such feminist circles, being "closed" and "open" was seen to be much more of an individual moral responsibility for women than for men: "I think that kind of interrogation is way more prevalent than would happen to straight men or gay men. . . . I'm not saying that anyone should sleep with any particular person here, I'm not questioning anyone's identity, but I am making a comment that lesbians, in particular, get these pointed questions that seem to want to goad us into an argument." Liz's observations indexed not only a reality of rising transphobia but also increasing and injurious slippages between "feminists," "lesbians," and "TERFs" that positioned feminists and lesbians both as anachronistic (Rogers 2023). Indeed, in the presumptions against cisgender lesbian sexuality Liz described, there were arguably resonances with other, older struggles over the claiming of the position of feminist "heroine" in stories of feminism's history. Clare Hemmings (2011) notes the "ambivalent position of lesbian feminism" (31) in Western stories of feminist progress, loss, and return told by feminist scholars. As queer theory ascends in visibility, Hemmings argues, "lesbian feminist engagements become firmly identified with the past, become anachronistic, as do their presumed subjects" (6). While cisgender lesbian sexuality is not formally connected to these institutional disciplinary movements in gender studies, the presumption that it is always already oriented against trans from its point of departure also implicitly located this sexuality in the past.

Positioning progressive cisgender politics in terms of sexual partnership can also be fraught. Cameron Awkward-Rich and Hil Malatino (2022) pertinently remind cisgender scholars that for trans people, partnering—platonic, erotic, familial—does not necessarily have to include cisgender people, or be oriented toward them. They note, while trans-for-trans (t4t) sexuality is complex in its practices and meaning, "many of us are (and have been) t4t. But if you derive your sense of trans worlds from academic writing and/or popular culture, this would be easy enough to not know, fixated as these genres tend to be on the dramas of trans people negotiating cis worlds of sense" (1). Awkward-Rich and Malatino subtly highlight how there can be a visible fixation on the dramas of trans people in worlds made for cis people, crisscrossing with a broader fixation on experiences deemed "intersectional," open, marginalized. In feminist cultures seeking intersectional resources, *trans* can thus be simplified and objectified into simply meaning a signifier of feminist practice: a totem for the open, or good, feminist, a red flag for a bad one.

The question remained of what to do with your risk assessment, once you saw a red flag. Jillian didn't agree with "canceling" per se, because she felt people needed to change, and canceling didn't necessarily have that effect. Despite an implicit omniscient standard required of prominent figures such as Delevingne, Jillian personally noted that she didn't have huge expectations of celebrities—what could they know? For example, she said, "I don't even really have a problem with people like [supermodel] Kendall Jenner, trying to do, you know, that whole crowd trying to do kind of lefty things. I don't mind when they try." What became clear, however, was that while participants had varying positions and perspectives on such online cultures of observation, dissection, and analysis, the ritual of critique still appeared central to the cultures in which they participated. It was impossible to avoid.

For sophisticated white participants such as Bella, the anticipation of being called out as a girlboss was thus heightened. They also didn't want to be guilty of a "basic" version of Instagram feminism. If you leaned too much into being a "nice," inoffensive girl, your feminism could be seen as "more appropriate for twelve- to fifteen-year-olds," as one of my highly perceptive working-class participants pointed out. My young feminists were also anxious to ensure that they were not "silent" and thus ready to critique what could be diagnosed as others' problematic, or "performative," behavior. This produced repetitive circulations of paranoia: by not calling out, one could be complicit, but if one called out, it could be read as performative in the sense of being inauthentic. Holly put it in this way in her interview: "I saw a meme that actually—I might get that up because I feel like I've got it on my phone. . . . It's just a meme that says 'AOC's dress is performative, criticizing the dress is also performative. Everything's performative, we're all performing, welcome to clown school.' And then that kind of sums it up." Twenty-one-year-old Margot, back in Sydney after attending a prestigious international high school, also reflected with incredulity on the "performative" or ostentatious cultures of judgment she observed. While she didn't want to "sound like a boomer," she told me,

> My qualms with TikTok, it's like a battlefield on there. No one can do anything correctly . . . everyone has such insane amounts of access to everything and has such intense opinions on things. . . . The comment section on TikTok is hectic . . . I think there's become a huge thing with buzzwords as well. People using certain terminologies to get their points across and then it all becomes meaningless because so many words are thrown out there.

She observed,

> There's a joke now with the term "gatekeep, girlboss, gaslight," that kind of thing. I think that came from people using these buzzwords so often that it became irrelevant and meaningless and a joke almost.

These sentiments were echoed by others using a variety of platforms, including Instagram, Facebook, and Twitter. Jenny, a twenty-one-year-old white working-class social worker, also highlighted her fatigue with what she called "angry white Twitter feminism," "where it's like, 'Your friend says this, don't be friends with them anymore, dump them, call out these people, don't put up with this shit anymore.' And it's just like, yeah, I love the attitude but . . . in real life, it doesn't work. Like you actually have to be patient with people and generous with your time and understand that people aren't going to get [it] straightaway or they're not going to listen to you the first time."

As Maivân Clech Lâm (1994) observes, the feeling of authority in relation to the critique of oppression remains "attached to white persons, white theories, and white languages" (872); white Western feminists, she argues, manifest the "authority to enunciate rules" (972). Many participants were notably disaffected with such cultures of critical classification. Yet this disaffection did not necessarily detract from the centrality of such critique to belonging in online feminist culture. Even as both Holly and Jillian explicitly noted their ambivalence in connection with the antagonism underpinning the dissection of highly visible figures, they also remained highly informed as to what the critiques were in order to take a position on them. They were cognizant of the rules of engagement.

BALANCING RISK AND ASPIRATION

The affective repudiation attached to modes of getting it wrong, such as embodying girlboss behavior, was notable, but it is relevant to note that *girlboss* was not always such a bad object. Rather, *girlboss* emerged in the backdrop of continuing cycles of idealized forms of feminine capacity that promised possibilities of agency and success under capitalism. Against the longer-term trend of telling girls and young people they should be leaders — to be the feminist change they want to see — what my participants reported were continuing shorter-term social media trends that showcased different kinds of "girl" to embrace, before they had to be discarded. These were notably more compelling for my women participants, more so than for my nonbinary participants. For example, Pippa, a quiet white middle-class woman in her midtwenties, spoke of the emergence of "that girl": "I think now that's called being 'that girl' . . . I guess maybe a few years ago it would have been called a girlboss thing and it's just kind of had all these iterations. And I think this most recent iteration probably started on TikTok, but has now made its way everywhere. It's about like girls waking up. . . . Like they look so pretty, they're skinny. They have this perfect life and . . . it's really like this 'women having it all' kind of vibe."

That girl was the new *girlboss*, but she hadn't yet lost her shine. Serene and productive, that girl documented waking up at 6 a.m. to walk her dog, enjoying a nutritious smoothie at 7 a.m., working on a laptop, making a delicious dinner, then sleeping in a perfectly made bed with mood lighting at 11 p.m. Pippa's description captured how these girl "types" seemingly projected ever-changing variations on a theme of feminine success, capacity, and achievement. She also noted a new temporality that circulated in tandem with *that girl*. This involved a rejection of the significance of the mainstream work identity of grinding from nine to five every day for a more enlightened "five to nine." Like the immaterial labor critiques celebrating the "outside" of the factory as generating potential for creative work (Hardt and Negri, 2000, 2004), showing what one did between five and nine was purportedly more telling of a creative, spontaneous laboring identity. Pippa described this phenomenon on TikTok:

> So this was people who showed what they do either from 5 a.m. to 9 a.m. or from 5 a.m. to 9 p.m. I get the premise of that. Like yeah, you have an identity outside of your work, but this is just like more forms of labor outside [of it]. And it was like people going to the gym and it was so connected to people who were like productive or people with social lives and you know, it was still very glamorized. . . . Like now we're productive from 5 a.m. to 9:00 p.m. And also just like the idea of like videoing yourself every day. And having to document [it]. Like, there's no waste of time.

Pippa thus demonstrated a critical sensibility in terms of analyzing the personal ramifications of the five-to-nine trend. Yet, unlike other white middle-class participants who explicitly disavowed the *girlboss*, Pippa confided the connections she felt and the hopes *that girl* inspired.

Pippa had significant insight into her own habits and understood that this content exacerbated her own desires for self-control and infinite self-improvement in ways that could push her over the edge. A history of disordered eating beginning from early adolescence haunted her every day; and while she told me she was generally "healthy" now, she had a highly conflicted relation to the promise of control and "managing" that seemed ever-present in the kinds of everyday "girl" content on TikTok and Instagram that crept into her feed. She was continually drawn to the intermeshing of discipline and dreaminess in the *that girl* content she saw: "I do set a lot of tasks for myself in the day I, I quite naturally feel like, 'Oh, I really should be doing that.' And I guess like that's where the comparison stuff starts to come in where you feel like you're not good enough because you're not doing all this stuff and you're not having, you know, the most amazing day just because you don't wake up at six and have like a million things done." Such dreams, she knew, required ever more control and monitoring of her time, body, and schedule. This was a kind of cruel optimism (Berlant 2011) — of being attached to an object that did not work toward your flourishing. But the possible dream of practically achieving this remained compelling: "It's like the idea that if you just woke up a little bit earlier, you would have the best life, or if you just did a workout every day, you'd be so happy."

Margot also separately admitted the magnetism of the aspirational pull of particular forms of idealized womanhood. This had been particularly significant for her as a teen, growing up on Tumblr:

And then Tumblr was like the first time I kind of really saw like eating disorders, glorified. . . . [And] things about like women being, you know, independent and like cool and you know, smoking and drinking and like being rebellious. Tumblr was a really massive part of like forging what was like an ideal woman . . . Tumblr just feels like a favorite dream.

She elaborated:

It was just like kind of mental all over the shop, but yeah, definitely forged what I, what my adolescence thought an ideal woman was. . . . Like all through high school, I was striving to be this cool girl kind of thing. Like that did not stop until, probably even so when I was back in Australia, for sure [after finishing school].

The "cool girl," however, had morphed for Margot. As a high-achieving university student, the allure of "having it all" remained: "I think at the moment, I'd probably be like, wanting to be a well-rounded balanced woman who can do like social life, who can flourish at uni, has a boyfriend, who has friends. . . . Yeah. I like want to be, you know, social and have fun and like go drink cocktails and then work, just effortlessness I think is what I want to be as a woman." She noted, reflectively, "Which I guess is also just maybe like an older version of that cool girl that I want it to be."

I was struck by the similarity of Margot's aspirations to a *Sex and the City* lifestyle of the mid-2000s. Such dreams of effortlessness were notable, particularly given Margot's continual anxieties about managing her time: "I'm not gonna have enough time to study. I'm not going to have enough time to relax. I'm not going to have enough time to do X, Y, Z, which makes me very anxious. Yeah. And I like structure, which does not fit with the carefree effortless woman."

It was understandable how effortlessness was so desirable, when all parts of your identity and your politics required work and were thus continually put under the microscope. Pippa, for example, agonized over her desires to work in fashion, a domain in which "top girls" have historically been illuminated (McRobbie 2007, 2009). She lived in a mid-sized town in which opportunities for such a career were limited. But she wondered if her desire to always do more, to move to larger cities like Sydney and Melbourne or abroad, was another manifestation of the internalization of girlboss logics: "I think just the nature of being in your early twenties, it's really hard to not fall into that, you know, must have a job. Must, must move cities, must be in the big fashion capitals, when, really like what's wrong with [staying put]... I guess I'm finding it more and more to question those norms that, that capitalism or just social norms that kind of placed on young women or young people." The *girlboss* and *that girl*, then, were not simply empty and flexible mechanisms of critique, distancing, and differentiation. They also at particular times promised the possibility of thriving under capitalism. Both a carrot and a stick, these luminous figures held out the promise of a serene life connected to the ever more careful segmentation and control of one's time, one's labor, and oneself. They held an ongoing allure, a promise of feminine capacity, of self-management, a dream of future, better, uncomplicated selves.

Pippa and Margot were much more explicitly vulnerable about their struggles to be certain women than other similarly positioned participants. But what perhaps connected them to other participants was the sense of compulsory expansion: constantly pushed to achieve, to exceed, to transcend as an intoxicating promise of future agency, but through the continual monitoring of self, and careful distancing from variations on ideal femininity that would become illuminated for a time, then fall out of favor. Differing only slightly in tone and aesthetic, such girl "types" blended feminist-feeling ideals such as "go-getting" and "achievement" and gestured to leadership in seemingly practicable ways before they again had to be passed on, let go, repudiated.

GIRL PROBLEMS

I hope it has been clear that the aim of this chapter has not been to "call out" any of my participants, thereby entering into the same dynamics of diagnosing "good" and "bad" feminisms that were endemic to the cultures they described. Rather, I have aimed to show how the cultural contraction of feminist ideas to problems of personality narrows the space of maneuver in the everyday. In this chapter, I have suggested that in the normalization of ongoing, lateral surveillance in social media, and in the popularization of feminism and of intersectionality, feminism is both broadened and narrowed. It is broadened to encompass a minute scrutiny of everyday behavior, not simply of celebrities but of everyday participants in social media culture. It is narrowed to mean an evaluation of feminism along the lines of "good" and "bad"; and in the conflation of feminism with "women's capacity" (Banet-Weiser 2018), it is further narrowed to not only but *primarily* judge women's performance of feminism, and women-as-feminists. In this way, public women became prime targets for scrutiny, as seen in everyday rituals of celebrity critique. This affected all my participants in some way. But it particularly affected the women participants who were the majority of my cohort, with some, like Alice, whom we met at the beginning of the book, feeling "overwhelmed by her womanhood" amid consternation about reproducing capitalist-patriarchy in her career, cohabiting, and making everyday consumption choices. As their identities became texts to be potentially narrowly and critically read, such cultures of critique could narrow relational possibilities — inviting hypervigilance in relation to avoiding connection with being the "wrong" girl type or otherwise being complicit with patriarchy. But this anxiety could have effects beyond one's own insecurities; it could also rebound into enforcing a rigid set of feminist "standards" that were ever evolving, cutting off space to move on the map.

PART III

Lowering the Stakes

.

5

QUIET PUBLICS AND
LOWERCASE FEMINISM

My project began in 2021, the second year of the COVID-19 pandemic and associated strict lockdowns in Australia. All of my initial workshops and first interviews took place over Zoom, largely in participants' bedrooms on the other end. A sense of melancholy infused the backdrop of our conversations, but for my participants, none of whom were frontline workers, these interviews also felt intimate, and structured by quiet. Similarly to the young people in Rosalind Gill's online beauty cultures project, undertaken at a similar time, the pandemic provided some with the option to "press pause" (2023, 84), allowing the vigilance associated with feminist online identity to loosen and slacken. But by 2022, the overriding imperative of the "return to normal" punctured this delicate suspension of time. The return to normal renewed the sense of stretching thin my participants' time and energy; and for some, the cautious optimism of what life would be like once the state of emergency ended turned into overwhelm. Marina, the high school teacher I introduced in chapter 1, confided, "I'm dreading going to work sometimes. Yeah. So . . . that's gotta change. I've only been a teacher for four years. I can't already be this burnt out. I can't already be this done with it. You know what I mean?"

Like Marina, who was now, officially, at a dead end, other feminists similarly felt surrounded on all sides. In chapter 1, I discussed how in online feminist cultures, practices of activism as well as *reactivism* were held out as the gold standard of contemporary feminism. And yet this acting against the grain, in structures hostile to feminist politics, soon became "hitting walls" (Ahmed 2012). Not only did the new normal feel like a reintensification of everyday surveillance in presenting an invulnerable facade to the world; there was a reinvigorated misogyny that had now moved front and center in social media popular culture. The intellectual and emotional space my young feminists occupied was cramped by the extreme cis- and transmisogyny that social media made so easy to witness and encounter: the spectacular, misogynistic public trial of Amber Heard; the rise of men's rights activist and influencer Andrew Tate; in the United States, the overturning of *Roe v. Wade* rendering abortion even more inaccessible; the continuing news of sexual assault in Australian schools; and in public offline space, anti-trans protests that included neo-Nazis in their ranks (Lee et al. 2023).

Against these movements, this chapter explores the grounding spaces and temporalities that created affective-discursive possibilities helping my young feminists to endure, both emotionally and intellectually. Noting Chris Bobel's (2007) identification of how the "perfect standard" of activism places it always out of reach, for the most part, I highlight "quiet publics": spatiotemporalities outside of formal protests, organizing, and activism that sustained my participants. I say "quiet," as these were spaces where the "noise" of constant, immediate reaction and the fast flow of news could be muffled. Such spaces felt slightly removed from the feminist pulse, not squarely *within* or *on it*—more feminist-adjacent than directly oppositional. Traversing online and offline, these were bounded spaces of limited duration that allowed a diffuse sense of attention to experience, and social recognition, without scrutiny. The university classroom could constitute such a space; more modestly, the feeling of copresence in feminist podcasts, or even participating in the conversations of my own research workshops, helped to suspend the imperative to hover, think, act, and declare simultaneously. In the contemporary polarized, spectacular mediated landscape, and in a world of increasingly privatized space, such spaces of low-stakes conversations with strangers were vital but often ephemeral.

It is important to clarify, first, that while I devote this chapter to spaces "off" the feminist pulse, I do not discount the political or personal importance of organized activism. This chapter aims to say "and," not "instead of." My participants all registered protest as important to feminism in different ways. Some participants, particularly those in collectives at universities, such as Bella and Shona, did regularly attend and organize actions, and this was woven into their routines as part of their feminist work. Over 2021–22, as I have discussed earlier, many took care to support proabortion or anti–sexual assault campaigns that coincided with the production of images, slogans, and photographs that were designed to be shared online to amplify physical, in-person protests.

And yet I would like to draw attention to how offline feminist protests often remained intertwined with the pulse of media "events" and thus were not always easily disentangled from the pressures of the reactivism that I described in chapter 1. Thea, a thoughtful Torres Strait Islander woman who had worked in reproductive justice for some time, explained this dynamic when *Roe v. Wade* was overturned by the US Supreme Court in 2022, upending abortion rights. This created a wave of media coverage internationally, and particularly in Australia, where Thea's workplace was suddenly inundated with media requests. On the upside, her organization suddenly received a wave of donations, but this sudden urge to respond was "very emotional" and "stressful" because anyone providing reproductive health services was already "quite burnt out." Burnout, according to Hannah Proctor (2024), is an emotional state registering political defeat. Thea nevertheless took on this challenge.

An infrequent participant at rallies and protests, Thea told me of how she had accepted an invitation to speak at a local *Roe v. Wade* rally in 2022, organized in solidarity with those protesting in the United States. This involved multiple, messy stages of anticipating, worrying, and preparing: "To be honest, it felt very overwhelming because I was conscious that I was in a large crowd and I hadn't really been in a massive crowd in a long time. So one, I was worried about getting COVID, and I hadn't had COVID yet. And two, I feel like I'm the kind of person that does a lot of [emotional] buildup to something." Thea poured her energy into writing and delivering her three-minute speech, in which she wanted to foreground community and solidarity, rather than "rights" as a Western individualistic paradigm. After speaking, she was just too fatigued to participate further in the rally:

"I just got a bubble tea and then I didn't march, I was too tired to march. So we went and got dumplings in Chinatown and then that was enough for me . . . it's funny how much work goes into writing, like a three-minute sort of speech. And . . . you have so many people around you and you can just kind of feel like their energy too. I think it was a bit draining to be honest."

Protests created a spike of activity that was both enlivening and draining. But it was important to keep in mind that the issues to which they spoke were ongoing and enduring. As Thea pointed out, *Roe v. Wade* sanctioned "the bare minimum of what people wanted for access and it was insufficient to begin with anyway"; therefore, for anyone already working in reproductive justice, this was "pretty much just an ongoing part of advocating for rights and access." Accordingly, Thea strategically prioritized her self-care: "I, I have to put, put my energy more into thinking, what can I do and how can I take care of myself because everyone is so burnt out in this space." For this reason, it is important to not straightforwardly understand the "offline" as regenerative, in contrast to social media, or indeed as neatly separable from the online in the day-to-day. Practices that could, through one lens, be seen as exemplary of collective action could still feel part of the reactive churn.

For others, while there was relief at the change in national government after conservative reign for three long terms, the general move back to "normal" in the aftermath of the pandemic did not feel relieving. Also facing burnout was Marina, who returned to face-to-face teaching at the private boys' school where she was employed in 2022. Marina had been living defensively: she was worn down by the repetition of trying and trying and trying to inject "diversity education" into school. Indeed, she had had to quit:

> I feel I was just sort of hitting walls with like the behavior management and some of the attitudes from the kids. I think I came in it from a, "Yeah, I'm gonna, you know, educate and change the world and not just like in a literal sense, but in like . . . life lessons." And part of me was like . . . I didn't want to give up, if that makes sense. Like, "No, if I stick with it, it'll be fine." And it just wasn't getting better and I was, you know, coming home miserable.

In boys' schools across the country throughout 2021–22, news reports circulated of burgeoning actively misogynistic cultures, the denial of sexual assault, and the popularity of men's rights activists. Sexism was not new in such contexts. In 2021, as I discussed in chapter 1, Margot expressed disgust at the reports of sexual assault in private schools in the eastern suburbs of Sydney; she herself was very conscious of the sexist dynamics that permeated her social circles, which were composed of young people from single-sex schools, and was continually fighting with her boyfriend about their involvement in these dynamics. Australian boys' schools, as overwhelmingly private, rather than public, educational institutions, had long sought to concentrate traditional lines of privilege from father to son. But now they were sites of new generations growing up with the increasing centrality of extreme misogyny to social media popular culture (see also Haslop et al. 2024; Roberts and Elliott 2020).

In Marina's case, she was confronted not only by explicit support for the men's rights activist Andrew Tate but also by the active negation of her concerns about Tate's misogyny as being "unfounded." As discussed earlier, her refusal to watch Tate's videos was exploited by her young students, who had already learned to adopt the techniques of bad-faith argument. How could she say he was a misogynist when she didn't keep up to date with his content? On an everyday level, the line between information and disinformation blurred as the endless supply of potential "sources" of online information could be easily wielded to dispute any claim she made. At the level of nation-states, such bad-faith techniques have been termed "firehose of falsehood" campaigns (Paul and Matthews 2016) aimed at destroying the common ground needed for social debate. At the individual level, this was experienced as an onslaught to which Marina could emotionally respond only through closure: literally, all she could do was "shut it down." Doing the routinely expected "diversity work" (Ahmed 2012) to "educate" the misogyny out of her young charges was a Sisyphean task: "I guess, when I started, that was kind of what I wanted to do. Like I was willing to have those discussions and willing to change some minds and open some doors and things like that. And then I think . . . the more I did it, the more I felt I wasn't getting anywhere with it."

Marina had hit a wall; she was stopped. She wasn't getting anywhere. This sense of a dead end was not simply about individual students, school policies, or colleagues. It was about the sense of futility in throwing her emotional striving against the ever-mutating, boundless surface of online misogyny that would emerge through different public figures and scandals, translated and articulated through her students. Online misogyny was "always on" in its endless, "fresh" proliferation of content.

In her first interview during lockdown, Crystal, a white working-class queer student, spoke in an upbeat fashion about wanting to communicate her feminist ideas and historical research through a public TikTok account.

Only twenty-two, she had already lived through intimate partner and family violence, and felt it was important to connect to others who had similar experiences. But in 2022, by the time of her second interview, she felt worn down by the emergence of figures such as Andrew Tate, together with the explosive public defamation case interrogating the relationship between American actors Johnny Depp and Amber Heard. She was concerned and overwhelmed, and, as discussed in chapter 1, these sentiments were intensified by feeling "in the minority," being ambushed on all sides. Crystal spoke of her incredulity at seeing high school acquaintances on Instagram who had hitherto never expressed any political opinions "come out" to champion Johnny Depp as a victim of Amber Heard. From what she had described as her "queer, feminist bubble," this felt like an onslaught: "I just don't know how to think because I'm trying to block it out. I'm just not engaging with it. I just don't want to, it makes me upset. It's emotional labor being constantly—I'm really busy, I'm like, I can't add in any more. Me and my girlfriends, we talk, we're talking about it in our personal lives, but on social media, I'm trying to really just block it out."

More profoundly, Crystal's admission—not simply of trying to "block out" but of not being able to "add in"—was telling. The expansive logic of social media—the continual imperative to incorporate awareness into an all-knowing, agentic self—was now being rejected on a gut level by Crystal. She was at her limit; she couldn't take in any more. Once positioned as a knowing (intersectional) feminist, one was presumed invulnerable to injury. The continued opening of wounds through engagement with online political culture, and the possibility of setback, was sidelined by this normative line to follow: wound–growth–action–leadership.

"Bubbles" on social media are often denigrated; they are seen as for those who aren't resilient enough to engage in true politics (see, e.g., Pariser 2011; Kanai and McGrane 2021). Even my young feminists often framed bubbles in these ways, feeling an obligation to defensively justify their "self-care." Understandably, there has been much skepticism in feminist scholarship about the overuse of the therapeutic as a replacement of politics. "Self-care," addressed to women by the global pharmaco-beauty complex, conveniently marries consumption and politics in ways that shore up existing inequalities in the movement of capital (Elias et al. 2017). But as social media aims to cover the landscape and drive the sense of what is happening, online and offline spaces in which harsh realities were not forgotten but suspended in their impacts were a vital means of endurance, persisting, and going on. The accessibility of increasingly extreme mediated misogyny and transmisogyny did not provide more space in the "middle"; instead, in the suspicious, classificatory cultures of social media, proving that one's feminist identity did not come with a red flag became more onerous. These bubbles, from which little bridges could be built to others, were all the more important for my participants as young, politically aware people, against the backdrop of the increasing hostility and polarization that compressed the space to maneuver in everyday online feminist cultures.

BUILDING "LITTLE BRIDGES"

Crystal was surviving, she told me, through heavy reliance on her queer feminist circle, and "finding the quiet" by not extending herself to give provocative online acquaintances the benefit of the doubt. She had been going out less frequently to the usual queer bars she hung out in, because she was so busy working; at these bars, the violence of misogyny was, she noted, not entirely absent but much less striking for her. Jillian, the poet we met in chapter 4, was one of the most active in "finding community" as a possibility for sustaining herself, living in a regional town where most "youth" initiatives and particularly "queer youth" initiatives stopped at age twenty-five. The spaces she was most involved in were, in fact, related to sports, because she "had always played sports." She played cricket at a local trans-inclusive club, and although she was unemployed, whenever she did have spare cash, she donated funds to a local charity called Proud to Play, which supported trans people, particularly trans women, playing sports. She was also part of a queer support group for an Australian Football League team (figure 5.1). Of this support group, the Ruby Demons, she explained,

> They don't think of themselves as doing feminist action, but they really are ... they're not just working in the women's game, they're working for queer inclusion and queer safety at men's matches, which is important. And, you know, going to cheer squad, going to the games as the cheer squad and waving huge trans flags behind the goals on TV, they don't think about it, but it makes a huge difference for inclusion and for people at the club. And we currently have the female CEO [of the team]. So there's a lot of work going into trying to get as much done as we can while she's in charge. And a lot of that starts at that community supporter level.

5.1 The Ruby Demons' Instagram profile, February 20, 2025. Screenshot by author.

This work of visibility was to ensure a sense of safety and community at events. Jillian added, "Even if they rock up in [another AFL team's] jersey, it's fine. Because what we're doing is making sure that when our team plays here, queer people can see other queer people at the game."

Here, Jillian refused to draw neat lines between "queer" and "feminist," online and offline, formal and informal feminist work. This was not activism with a "capital A," she noted. "You know, it's not like, the best, strongest feminist work ever, it's not solving huge problems"; but on an everyday level it was about relationally producing community and possible outward connections through presence. This presence was active; presence was not simply existence but about bringing certain publics into possibility. This did not require an explicit branding as "feminist" or "activist"; indeed, it allowed for quieter forms of endurance. Similarly, in her poetry, Jillian eschewed the label of "political" or "activisty":

> I do want it to be doing feminist work, but I don't think it needs to be part of a, explicit kind of trending movement. I'm fine if it's part of a movement because it's part of community that makes sense. But I don't want it to be turned into some kind of talisman necessarily.

She said, drily,

> Look, if Dymocks [a large Australian bookseller] were going to put me in every bookstore and pay my bills, I would cop it. But in terms of the origin of the art, it's not coming from a place of [that] . . . I don't think I'm a leader type person . . . I do think, I also think living trans lives is feminist work in and of itself sometimes.

Everyday life, as Jillian stated, was work. She was nervous about her safety day to day. For example, getting most directly to her home via public transport required walking by a large highway that was shaded by trees. She often took the long way around, through a local lit commercial shopping complex, in order to protect herself. She got her groceries delivered rather than going to the supermarket. As a visibly trans person, being trans was something that preceded her as she moved around in her everyday life. Thus, where she dwelled, whether in physical public space or online, and the kinds of relationality she created as she moved in space were always politicized acts. As she summarized it in relation to her poetry, "I want to be building little bridges and wires between external landscapes and emotional [ones] . . . cultural external landscapes and kind of eco poetic, external landscapes as well."

For many participants, it was heartening to hear that attending university and engaging in its structures of sociality could also facilitate these connections. For Shona, a white working-class queer woman who had joined a women's collective at her university in Perth from a rural mining town, being the collective's "social officer" gave her a sense of solidity and purpose, as she described in her workshop: "When I sought out the women's collective actually, it probably wasn't really like to learn about feminism or anything like that. It was more just to like throw myself in a social situation because I hadn't been doing very well with my mental health and sort of needed [to] make those connections, especially after the year we had with COVID." Shona distinguished between "learning" about feminism and the sociality that underpinned the activities of the collective. In this way, in her role in the collective, she sought to socialize what was seen to be largely a solo, online intellectual activity: "If you want to learn about feminism, you really have to do it yourself, unfortunately, which can be quite like hard to navigate and you type 'feminism' into Google. You get quite varied results. And a lot of people are just like, 'Oh, too hard basket.' Like, whereas we . . . make social spaces where we can actually talk about it."

These social spaces were often simply activities that had low barriers to entry, eschewing the hierarchies that underpinned online feminist knowledge cultures. These activities created temporalities where women's collective members could, like Jillian in the queer football support group, be present for each other without having to account for themselves via a formula of privilege, marginalization, and knowledge. This relationality enabled members to do things together in public spaces that they couldn't do alone:

Like we've started playing pool [billiards] in one of the bars and we'd book out the bar for, say, one night every two weeks. And a lot of women wouldn't have that opportunity or don't even know how to play pool and would never try because when they do, they get approached by men who'll be like, 'Oh, sweetie, like, let me teach you how to play.' Or . . . come up behind you and be like 'That's not how you do it.' So giving women those opportunities to actually experience things and learn about things that they probably wouldn't otherwise.

Shona herself benefited from the open invitation to participate in such activities, and the organization of them. As a child, she had felt a great urgency to make change and "do something" with her life, but on moving to a larger city, felt like a "fish out of water" in the elite culture of the undergraduate law cohort to which she belonged. She often felt angry, knowing the casual reliance of other students on their parents' social capital for entry-level career opportunities during their studies. In this cohort, her lack of social capital was made clear to her. But the collective itself was a place of social richness for her: it allowed her the dignity of doing work for others and herself, in a loose coalition of interest (Dabiri 2021).

In the same workshop, Bella also noted the importance of the accessibility of events in terms of knowledge. In the leadership committee for a women's collective at another university, she noted that explicit, specific political terms did not necessarily "perform" the inclusive work they purported to do. In her experience, for events to feel like open invitations for all, "that also means sometimes—I wouldn't say dialing down, but like reducing the political discussions that we have—so that we can get people in on a social level. And then they feel willing to grow from there. And they don't feel like they have to know everything straightaway. So that's definitely like where the inclusion comes in . . . we've got to be inclusive, but we've actually got to be not too specific in what our like inclusion means. It's just like, 'Hey, everyone's welcome.'"

For Olúfẹ́mi O. Táíwò (2022) the shortcomings of the inclusive project are that it concentrates attention on the "room you're in," mistaking your own circle for the world. Such a focus gives rise to a narrow, self-focused deference politics, but at worst, it obscures a larger vision of what elite rooms you yourself are excluded from. On an everyday level, however, I suggest that the "inclusive" sentiments discussed here are, in practical terms, distinguishable from the "inclusive" weaponization of attention Táíwò critiques and the dynamics I have noted in the intersectional grid of online feminist knowledge cultures. The activities and events organized by Shona and by Bella aimed to bring people together in a simultaneity rather than "seriality" (Hands 2019). Moving away from the exhaustive ("taking everyone into account") and the sequential ("passing the mic"), these limited temporalities of simultaneous copresence—playing pool, hanging out—enabled the building of "little bridges" of Jillian's imagining.

My young feminists also found connective feminist copresence in spaces formally devoted to learning, such as in the university classroom itself. Harriet, who was twenty at the beginning of the project, had not in fact encountered feminism through her own social media feed, or through her own social circle. Rather, she had been introduced to it via an introductory unit called "Sex and Gender" at university: "Every week we'd have a reading and it would relate to *This Bridge*—*This Bridge Called My Back*. And that was, I don't know if you know it, but it's written by women, Black, sorry, women of color. And it's just like really interesting since it's their take on feminism as being women of color. And yeah, we did like, would do poetry as well, or songs every week, then we'd have to present one that stood out to us."

Young, white, and from an ethnically homogeneous country town, Harriet spoke of the wonder she felt in encountering these histories of feminism, and their crossover with queer, gay, and trans lines of thought. She had subsequently become immersed in feminist social media cultures, posting regularly on Instagram to give summaries of relevant news. At the time of the workshop, she was assiduously posting three times a week during Pride Month (June in the annual calendar). And yet, when I asked about spaces where she had had beneficial experiences of having dialogue and disagreement in relation to feminism, she answered, "Probably just that uni class. Just because I feel also like in social media, some of the groups that I'm in, I feel like they're very—just directing what they want to put out there, and that's it." Harriet prized the conversational elements of this class. Connected to others' art, music, poetry, and writing, there was a movement between personal perspective and other lenses and experiences. She felt that other students were "likeminded" in the purpose for their presence, and in sharing their own perspectives they created an interdependence in the classroom enabling an opening to the world.

For other beleaguered educators reading this, I am aware that Harriet's perspective does not always correspond to the reality of the classroom, as Marina's example at the beginning of this chapter shows all too well. Tiffany Lethabo King's (2015) analysis of academia notably observes how the everyday conditions of the neoliberal university curtail such possibilities. Classroom and academic spaces may indeed function similarly to the "winner takes all" social media dynamics Harriet noted. The speed of published thought and contingency of labor in the university produces anxieties about always needing to move on, to not linger. Such anxieties, heightened through the publish-or-perish mandate, foreclose on the importance of slow, thoughtful tarrying with a diverse corpus of work. But Harriet was not an academic; she was a young woman, still only twenty, who, prior to studies, had accepted the social norm that feminism was "excessive." And unlike some of my other professional, slightly older participants, there was no other obvious pathway for her into a social circle where feminist issues could be freely and respectfully discussed. She certainly couldn't discuss them with her immediate and extended family; she noted awkward family gatherings at Christmas and other occasions where it was clear she was the "killjoy" (Ahmed 2006). In this context, there was incredible *richness* available in the university classroom. The purposive simultaneity of the university classroom structured by the aim of learning, based on set readings completed by all members of the classroom, concretely provided a socially sustaining space for encountering and dwelling in difference.

POLYPHONY, NOT WHITE NOISE

I have thus far focused on relatively organized social structures like clubs, and universities, in providing important offline spaces of copresence. I now consider what kinds of holding places were offered in online culture. For the most part, they were "social" but not necessarily "social media" in the conventional sense. For many of my participants, feminist podcasts offered these possibilities of reassuring copresence and recognition. Podcasts were bubbles of time and space, where participants would selectively choose to tune into a polyphony of embodied voices, and simultaneously tune out the "white noise" of being online. Syed (2012) describes white noise as

> a noise containing many frequencies with equal intensity
> background sounds, meant to detract from distracting and undesirable noises
> a meaningless or distracting commotion or chatter that masks or obliterates underlying information. (1)

While it would not be accurate to describe participants' feminist social media feeds as "meaningless," particularly in relation to Syed's focus on the everyday chatter and noise of racism, I think it useful to borrow this sense of "noise" in its effects of disorientation, as several frequencies are incorporated into the one "stream" of information. Jasmine Rault (2017), building on Syed, suggests that white noise works as a "continuous indistinct noise" (586), which saturates a field of sensation (587). In contrast, the podcast medium allowed the luxury of being embedded ambiently into a single conversation, making it possible to *just listen*.

These podcast spaces of "tuning in" could be described as "publics" in the sense that Michael Warner (2002) evokes, brought into being through the reflexive circulation of discourse. But as much digital media scholarship has sought to use the term *public* to describe actively, self-consciously resistant spaces and connections—for example, in "hashtag publics" or "feminist publics" (Rambukkana 2015; Mendes et al. 2019)—I want to highlight the original, playful address to a lone reader in Warner's (2002) essay: "If you are reading (or hearing) this, you are part of its public. So first let me say: Welcome. Of course, you might stop reading (or leave the room), and someone else might start (or enter). Would the public of this essay therefore be different? Would it ever be possible to know anything about the public to which, I hope, you still belong?" (49).

For my participants there was something readerly about listening to podcasts. Listening to podcasts felt secret—*secret*, as Natasha Zeng (2024) describes it, denoting something private but not shameful. While many of these podcasters were popular, they were not famous enough to warrant certainty that "everyone" would know who they were. As such, their profiles did not feel *visible*; and listening to them in your own time felt like sensory seclusion. Podcast consumption differed from the kind of radio that you heard in cabs, in hair salons, or on construction sites. Because of their mainly prerecorded nature, podcasts did not carry a sense of "synchronous temporality" or that listeners were part of a crowd that tuned in at the same time (Spinelli and Dann 2019). Being part of these podcast listening publics, for my participants, involved quiet acts of imagining together. Thus, they offered a different form of "liveness" in connecting listeners, hosts, and podcast participants (Euritt 2022, 267). They combined the "listening in" and "listening out" described by Kate Lacey (2011): actively listening "out" to come across the not so ordinary and the less familiar, but also listening "in" by carving out a protective sensory sphere around the self.

Listening to others' voices for an extended but finite duration set a measured tempo beyond the frenetic or distracted scroll. My participants favored podcasts with two or more cohosts that often had a "deep dive" on a particular topic. Sometimes these were considered, critical, and humorous takes on popular culture trends, and redemptive analyses of celebrities, often women, who had been wronged in the past, such as *You're Wrong About*, an American podcast run by two journalists critiquing past fads, and *Shameless*, an Australian popular culture podcast for, according to its tagline, "smart people who like dumb stuff."

At other times, podcasts brought to the surface moments of personal experience, usually intersecting with the coming and going of cultural trends. These podcasts included *I Weigh*, a body-positive podcast hosted by British actor-activist Jameela Jamil; *After Work Drinks*, by two Australian women journalists, on pop culture; *Bobo and Flex* (now defunct), involving the humorous philosophizing of long-distance friends Bobo Matjila and Flex Mami, two influencers located in the United States and Australia; and *It's a Lot* by Australian feminist influencer and "chronic oversharer" Abbie Chatfield (Listnr 2021). These feminist public figures made their lives accessible through their overlapping circulation on Instagram and through their podcasts.

My participants recounted their enjoyment of the friendships audible in the playful dialogue between cohosts; for example, on Bobo and Flex, twenty-one-year-old Jenny loved the rapid-fire back-and-forth: "They would sort of talk about things happening right now, sort of popular culture topics or, yeah, just the dynamic. I just really loved it." More broadly, participants were attracted by the sense of embodied friendliness and lack of formality of the spoken word. With Abbie Chatfield, for example, it was noted by Jenny that she was "very outspoken" but "she doesn't tear down other women," which she emphasized several times was "nice" and "nice to hear." Chatfield was also "very, very casual," similar to "how I would talk about it with my friends." This sense of casualness and warmth allowed an open point of entry that, indeed, was sometimes not necessarily felt with formally activist or feminist posts that had to "tick all the boxes."

My participants also sought out podcasts that traded directly in experiences they had not personally dealt with—the minutiae of the everyday, as I discussed in the previous chapter. These included the recounting of challenges faced by women in their lives or chosen fields of work. For example, Greta, who was nineteen, was directly seeking advice on the paths that lay open in her life. She had decided to study science at university, with a view to potentially progressing to studying medicine afterward. She told me she had listened to an episode of popular Australian women's podcast *Mamamia*, titled "The Baby Catcher," on the recommendation of her mother. The host, Mia Freedman, interviewed a woman, now a successful obstetrician, who had been prevented in the 1970s from studying her field at university. Not only was this "really interesting," but Greta was actively seeking other stories like this that could provide an orientation point in her life and emotionally anchor where she was going. She knew she was young; she also felt young in her wealthy white family, where she was the "baby."

She also felt much younger than her confident coworkers at a bar who were in their late twenties, doing things like "living in their own apartment" and "having long-term relationships." She sought out podcasts to eavesdrop on conversations between late twentysomething women on things they viewed as normal. In another podcast, she said, "They talk more about, they're a bit younger than the women that do the *Mamamia* podcasts. So they are, they can talk more about like dating and I guess like boy things and, you know, like living alone for the first time. So it's, I guess maybe a bit more like closer to what I'm going to have to deal with . . . I think it's just, again, it's like really good to have opinions and perspectives of other people that are a bit older in different circumstances and yeah."

Greta had barely dated but had an embodied awareness of the sexism of boys from the parties she had attended with friends, made up of students from elite private schools in Melbourne. She had already begun to learn a critical approach to the sexist, sexualized language boys used for weighing up the girls they encountered. Therefore, podcasts for her involved reassurance and learning from women who were often just slightly older. While not laying out a direct path for her, their manner of talking, relating, and explaining their perspectives embodied her hoped-for near future as a confident, articulate woman. Their plurality of voices also allowed, to some extent, the trying out of different positions and differences of opinion. Greta described why she liked one podcast to which she regularly listened:

> I personally really enjoy it because the three ladies are older . . . it's less common for me to get those kinds of older, more mature perspectives of mums and, you know, people in their mid-thirties, you know, I don't get that every day. So I really, I find that . . . I wanna say rewarding, I guess, I just find it really interesting. And, and often they'll say something that I'm like, wow, I didn't even, I wouldn't have even thought about it in that perspective. And they're very, like, feminist podcasts, you know? So I've, I've really found that interesting to hear different points of view from what I can sort of get every day. I really, I really enjoy that.

I have kept the length of this passage to show how important indeed this was for Greta—listening to these moms and millennials and "trying out" their perspectives was "really interesting," "really enjoyable," "really rewarding." The duration allowed presence and lingering in the slower temporality of the flow of words and music, providing space for a commingling of listener and recorded voices. While podcasts could, of course, be listened to at one-and-a-half speed, they still did not feel like the churn of scrolling through visual texts, a second here, a few seconds there.

In Louise Rosenblatt's (1994) book *The Reader, The Text, The Poem*, she outlines how a text is never simply words on a page, or here, sounds in a recording; it is a social mechanism that allows the reader's imagination and that of the author to merge. Reading, then, is always a social "event," and the text is thus never separate from the reader. Yet, as social media scrolling abbreviates the reading time of posts to a shorter and shorter duration, its sociality can feel rapid-fire. Listening to a podcast could feel relatively luxurious, allowing such social merging without necessarily having to visibly react, raise awareness, or "take anything anyway." With episodes often posted weekly, their structured occurrence felt like part of a familiar routine. The duration of the podcast allowed a sense that dwelling and lingering were valuable and permitted. In short, for my participants, feminist podcasts, even if listening to them in a distracted fashion, while preparing lunch or during one's commute, were often the most accessible, conversational forms of mass online culture available. This "background listening," as Kate Crawford (2009) has termed it, allowed the pleasure of entering a bubble of time that nonetheless felt socially connected. The podcasts were "poetic" (Warner 2002) in that they allowed imagining the self in a shared world with strangers. But the improvisational dialogical style, framed as between friends, dialed down the intensity of the address to the listening subject, as though they were only incidentally there.

Another example of conversational oral culture was the "corner" of TikTok where my participant E had found a home, listening and commenting on others' TikToks as well as creating their own. TikTok was mostly described by my young feminists as "addictive," "toxic," or sometimes an "escape," if they managed to fine-tune their algorithmically suggested content away from political concerns. E's experience was distinctive in that the corner of TikTok they had found fostered a highly intellectual, queer, anti-colonial Black African culture made by Africans in Africa as well as in the West. Passionate about decolonization and re-Indigenization, they had a "whole political education folder on TikTok," and stated that "so many of the realizations I've had in those realms [have] been through TikTok." Tik-Tokers on E's feed deconstructed Western presumptions of homonation-alism (Puar 2007) and problematized cultural sophistication as a measure of being a "good queer" and "good feminist." They spoke to experiences such as E's frustration with everyday encounters with white South Africans claiming equivalence with Black Africans, or when "people often use like conversations around like neopronouns and such to like derail . . . people who are racialized under the current systems, like when they're trying to like express a really valid emotion that maybe they don't have the like perfect words for."

E showed me one of the TikTokers on their feed who studied languages in precolonial Africa, illustrating how African languages often had genderless pronouns, obviating the need for neopronouns (new gender pronouns beyond the binary of "he" and "she"). E had commented on their TikTok that it was the same in Yoruba, the language of their Nigerian heritage: "We don't have gendered pronouns, we have age pronouns. You speak to your age mates one way and you speak to your elders another way. And . . . a lot of people like chime in, like from across the world, like so many different continents, about like how their languages didn't have gendered pronouns and how like their, like how all of our parents always mix [them] up." In a choir of other comments discussing similarities in other languages across the world, this sense of commonality helped E to articulate a righteous anger against this broader white articulation of goodness and authority in the judgment of older non-Western people, and in offers to "introduce you to neopronouns":

> I'm like, you know what? I should be the one introducing you to neopronouns. . . . like white queers often will position themselves as authorities. Like, "No, you are not a lesbian because you use he/ him pronouns." "No, you cannot call yourself a trans woman because you, you're not on hormones." And it's like, God—who made you the authority? And it's literally like that right. It's the, the inability to see how they're making themselves, as the white queers, they naturally think of themselves as a standard, as the rule to follow.

The essence of the richness E experienced was in the intellectual conversations they were able to have, "in real time," with Africans across the world:

> It's videos where it's like . . . only three hundred views. But there's like really rich conversation happening in those comments sections, because it's person-to-person. Like I really am talking to another person and they're like, "No, yeah, you're right because like 'da da da'—ten comments." And then I'm like, "Oh my gosh, well you just made me

think about 'da da da,' and I left another five [comments]." You know, it's like you're actually having conversations with people, and there are people pushing back or "Oh, let me add to that," or "Have you thought about it like this?"

E's exuberance tumbled out in their words as they recounted the sharing of ideas and viewpoints. For example, they mentioned the possibility of conversational back-and-forth in the form of "stitching" videos, whereby another TikToker would begin with "cutting in" another person's TikTok and then "pasting in" their own response. But overall, just being in the comment space still felt like "chatting." For E, it felt like you were talking "person-to-person" rather than in carefully crafted statements of position in argument. Such person-to-person sociality was enabled by copresence in a relatively niche space, indicated by the low count of views on the videos E showed me. This social space, not routinely accessible algorithmically to others on TikTok, felt expansive. In material terms, they often felt like they knew "all the West Africans in Australia"; in comparison with other English-dominated multicultural societies such as the United Kingdom, Canada, and the United States, the "new African diaspora" forms a relatively small part of the national population (Hiruy and Hutton 2020).

Consequently TikTok, for E, was world-building. This in turn had encouraged them to post their own TikToks more often with their own takes on life. Comments and reactions to their own videos felt not like an onslaught, as many participants experienced, but like being situated in an enlivening stream of social consciousness, to which they could optionally respond: "Everyone's just like shooting up their thoughts like, into the air. And then the thoughts are like coming past me, and then I might just like grab one." Like catching a shooting star, such a description resonated with the "polyphony" Joss Hands (2019) describes as part of resonant collectivities. Life moments were described; similar perspectives were voiced but they were not homogeneous; there was a sense of contributing one's own distinctive experience as part of a greater whole.

E's experience, as I have sought to stress, was not the "general" one of TikTok reported across my cohort. It was highly determined by being part of a small niche produced by the boundary of TikTok's "scarily accurate" algorithmic sorting (see also Tompkins and Guajardo 2024). But it illustrates how profoundly energizing and sustaining a vernacular culture may be. It afforded E a tremendously important space of endurance in an outside world where they were always a minority, in almost every space they moved through. Such cultures cannot necessarily produce such qualities at scale: indeed, the feminist Facebook groups with memberships of thousands of participants were almost always panned in strong terms by my young feminists as "toxic" spaces. Therefore, I have lingered on E's account to indicate how, in looking for possibilities of persistence and perseverance, it is important to look below the level of platform governance, and below the level of formal or "official" feminist, queer, or race politics. Spaces of endurance could be found in unexpected places, but each was unique; they were not necessarily replicable, and if they involved active conversation between strangers, as in E's corner of queer, anticolonial TikTok, they could not be manufactured en masse.

AN EVERYDAY VIEW OF COLLECTIVITY

The question of collectives, or how to make them, has underpinned analysis of social media for some time. Social media, or in the older vernacular, "Web 2.0," has been defined by its communicative capacity for "everyday sharing," in its early days, generating significant excitement about its ability to mobilize crowds for political purposes through "group intelligence" (Jenkins 2006). Later accounts questioned how the "social" nature of such media was built through private structures of appropriation and value extraction (Andrejevic 2013; Fuchs 2015; Zuboff 2019). They also added more pessimistic accounts of the "dark" side of the mob, in popular books such as *So You've Been Publicly Shamed* (Ronson 2015) and now in everyday commentary of "call out" culture (Sobande et al. 2022). Across these accounts, we see broader concerns about sociality and how people can come together for sustained political ends. These concerns about the feasibility of collective politics were, notably, also shared by my young feminists.

In the first two parts of this book, I have traced how the most taken-for-granted imagination of collectivity, under the rubric of "intersectionality," in fact sorted identities in terms of worthiness of attention. This atomized version of care thus set in place a competitive and objectifying practice of ranking that paradoxically turned attention away from the nonidentical but repetitive elements of personal experience that enable feminist collectivity to occur. This left little space for my participants to conceptualize themselves as potential beneficiaries of a collective feminism. Instead, imagined as a mission to serve, while the everyday operation of privilege was itself not always visibly analyzed, personal benefit from feminism was normatively deferred and deferred.

This chapter, in the final part of this book, has thus focused on what kinds of spatiotemporalities enabled my young feminists to endure. In contrast to the instinct often held by my own participants that a feminist identity meant an invulnerability to sexism and to other intertwined forces, or that dwelling too long on one's own personal experience was self-centered and sometimes "neoliberal," I have sought to linger on the question of what kinds of everyday mechanisms enabled them to get by—in short, what benefited them. This chapter has indicated that, in the everyday, it is often minor encounters, spaces, and temporalities, adjacent to and not necessarily Feminist with a capital F, that can be sustaining for young feminists and people affected by misogyny. These were most often "quiet publics" of collective imagining, co-dwelling, often not needing explicit interaction unless a high degree of commonality already existed. The young feminists I spoke to needed low-stakes and accessible but not arresting conversations, in bounded spaces where they could be present, absent from demands to stretch across multiple demands, all urgent, all at once. These included social clubs that enabled slow movements and participation in public space, listening without speaking, and lingering without surveillance. Besides the podcast format, such spaces are not generalizable or scalable, but this does not make them unimportant. The spaces I discuss here find their very efficacy in their limitations and exclusions: moments in time, rooms limited by a purpose. What I want to emphasize is that in the everyday, these forms of outward-facing copresence afforded the breathing room and the quiet in order to endure, to go on, to persist.

6

REGISTERING EXPERIENCE

Moving Between, but Not Moving On

I have thus far described how online feminist knowledge cultures could be lonely places to dwell, without trustful and generous encounters. This loneliness in the middle of seeming connectedness and inclusiveness was most sharply present when living an intersectional feminist life was translated into a series of abstract, generic calculations and risk assessments. The classificatory dynamics of social media translated suffering, trauma, and oppression into individualized cache, denoting worthiness of attention and right to speak, rather than as a beginning point for *knowing others* and building coalitions. The question remains: How then, if at all, could such online knowledge cultures speak to my feminists' circumstances and lived experience in more profound ways than simply denoting their place within a nebulous, yet highly bounded feminist (re)public?

Situating feminism in a long lineage of attempts to see and experience the world differently—this chapter explores how such knowledge cultures could rearticulate experience in ways that could be used to grapple with the structural inequalities as they appeared in my young feminists' lives.

How could experience be used not to delimit the boundaries of expertise but to foster politicized shared vulnerabilities? And how did these online feminist knowledge cultures also allow the recasting of themselves not simply as a group of individuals that "protected" the boundaries of feminism but as part of a collective that could benefit from its plural, nonidentical iterations? How did it help them persist, to keep going, in the face of what seemed to be ongoing crises of resurgent misogyny, lethal racism and settler colonialism, and transphobia?

In arguing against disconnected forms of identity politics that homogenize social groupings and categories, intersectionality theorist Nira Yuval-Davis (2023, 12) underlines the importance of a "dialogical epistemological approach" that "encompasses particular situated intersectional gazes on the one hand and generic transversal (to differentiate from the homogenising that is often the Eurocentric universal) conceptualisations on the other hand." Yuval-Davis argues that such a movement between situatedness and a transversal gaze is important for building an understanding of racialization that attends to and moves *across* specific times and contexts, and potentially creating contingently common ground. Fundamental to any knowledge project seeking to intervene in identity-based oppression is a sense of movement between the specific and the generic, in order to emplace the personal and the social in ways that are both emotionally and politically sustaining. This chapter, then, attends to the possibilities of movements in feeling rather than to the adoption of particular concepts themselves, although they were sometimes intertwined. Feeling, as sociologist Arlie Hochschild (1983) explains, reveals your location: what you feel you are entitled to; what you feel you owe others. Feminist scholars, in their theorization of affect, have long insisted on feeling as key to positioning the self as feminist; you have to subjectively feel that something is wrong in order to contest it (Hemmings 2011). It is then, perhaps, unsurprising that it was these affective movements that were most conducive to allowing my young feminists to mobilize a sense of sustaining connectedness to others. Such openings toward the world could usefully magnify the significance of lived experience while shrinking the exhausting, defeating focus on the self.

What this chapter, then, aims to show is the promise of the telling of experience in fostering collective orientations, not individual expertise. In everyday life, the individualization noted in accounts of contemporary leftism, neoliberal feminism, popular feminism, and postfeminism was not necessarily most directly countered by the confident wielding of terms such as *structure, inclusion,* and *solidarity.* And while activities like going to protests were important for my participants, particularly in the aftermath of flashpoints such as the Brittany Higgins rape, these were not the ongoing means through which they felt more at ease, sustained, and legitimate in their own bodies. What my young feminists most benefited from was shared conversation that embedded them into imagining belonging in a social world, having specific experiences that were legible but not necessarily identical to others. Such connections were most effectively fostered from the "bottom up," beginning from the minutiae of lived experience. In the everyday, as a space of imperfect repetition, of improvised managing, and of the "local and the particular" (Smith 1987), it was often observation and attention to the small details—feelings of unease at the doctor, one-sided conversations on dates—that enabled my participants to practice a situated "transversal gaze" (Yuval-Davis 2023) through which collective politics begins.

OPENING, CLOSING, OPENING

The kinds of movements I discuss here mirror descriptions of consciousness-raising that have been part of feminist awakenings for some time (Campbell 1983; Hanisch [1970] 2006; Smith 1987). They have occurred through in-person closed groups, feminist "blockbuster" texts (Taylor 2017), and hashtags (Condliffe 2023). In online feminist knowledge cultures, they occurred at different stages of my participants' lives, and they had different durations and movements. I begin with Sumaya, whom I first met when she was nineteen and very much trying to work out who she was. She was working full time in an administrative role straight out of high school but was very much still connected to her high school self. Most powerfully, while she often felt disoriented by the stream of feminist social media she habitually consumed at the time of our first interview, she spoke of how her first encounters with feminist perspectives helped to clarify and provide a grounded vantage point from which to see her own experience. On a personal level, feminism had most powerfully spoken to everyday phenomena she had hazily discerned as odd or uncomfortable, in the all-too-common case of sexual harassment. Sumaya recounted the confusion and dread of her after-school commute:

> When I was in high school, I used to catch the bus from my school to [redacted] and I used to wait at the library for my dad to come pick

me up. And on more than one occasion, I've had random guys talk to me and one time [a guy] just, he would not stop talking to me.

She began talking fast:

I was just waiting for my dad. I didn't want to talk to him. And he was like trying to ask me for my phone number. I ended up telling him—you just lie to people sometimes to get them off your case—and I didn't have a boyfriend—I was only fourteen or fifteen at the time. This is a grown man. And it's like, just go away, just go away . . . I ended up telling him that my phone didn't have a sim card, so I didn't actually have a number. I just used it for games.

Even with some distance, Sumaya's distress was palpable, as she recounted the panicky excuses she attempted to use to foil her harasser on this occasion. For Sumaya, then, hearing other girls' and women's accounts helped to turn the floating unease and panic of dealing with "random guys" into a systemic gendered pattern that was not simply chance, or idiosyncratic, but structural. Further, this pattern could become a clear object against which she could draw her own emotional boundaries: "That's like, that's what all these women are talking about when they say they get harassed by men." She was moved, in particular, by seeing feminist "believability" and authority (Higgins and Banet-Weiser 2023) attributed to teenage women in connection with their own bodily autonomy, opening up another way of understanding the world. For example, she showed me viral posts from Twitter containing critiques of the double standard where teenagers were infantilized as "girls" when attempting to raise their voice politically but referred to as "women" when blamed for their own sexual assault. In discussing sexual harassment and assault in this way, Sumaya's voice was firm and confident; she could locate herself in this broader experience.

Her feminist TikTok also helped to fortify this outward scrutiny of everyday gendered behavior in ways that drew connections with her experience. At her first interview, she showed me TikToks citing the concept of "performative incompetence," exemplified by men "not knowing" how to operate the dishwasher. Sumaya still lived at home and thus hadn't been exposed to co-living dynamics with men beyond this particular context. But it felt clarifying, broadening what she could sense and identify: "It did resonate with me. I'm not sure why. I feel like we've all seen it just like throughout life. Like it's guys in high school, who I talk with sometimes and like, you know . . . they're not stupid, but then the way that they, like, they almost force you to like have to spell it out." Sumaya was outspoken in her politics and noted the resistance under the veil of ignorance: "Like . . . if I, if I make a comment on something, then they will like play dumb and be like, 'Oh, what does that mean?' And then like sort of try and egg me on, there's that side of things."

This vantage point provided a contingent level of self-assurance for her. But at this point in her life, it was still not satisfying enough; it didn't feel enough for Sumaya that feminism had helped to shift her stance on hitherto "normal" behavior by men on the street, and in her everyday life. Sumaya's feminist education at this time was almost exclusively through social media—Instagram, TikTok, Twitter—and she had been immersed in these knowledge cultures for some years now. Consequently, Sumaya felt pushed toward a stance of responsibility—adopting her primary mandate to act in terms of "impact" and "inclusion." Having Muslim heritage through her mother, she took an active interest in what she could learn through social media on Muslim women through history and crises in the Middle East that were often framed through Islamophobia. She felt very strongly about intersectionality, "even though I only learned about this two years ago." She spoke passionately about the importance of feminists acting as a collective "we." But the question of how to understand herself in relation to this "we" was much more difficult.

At this time, Sumaya occupied a position where the "I" felt too big, producing endless loops of self-assessment. She felt a sense of inner conflict between these now ingrained habits of self-monitoring and self-examination and what she felt was ideal intersectional politics. This discomfort burst forth toward the end of her first interview, when Sumaya was thoughtfully critiquing the cruelty of "girlfriend" culture (Winch 2013) in high school, while acknowledging the competitiveness she also felt as a girl. I commented that she seemed to do a lot of reflecting; was that something she was consciously practicing, or had she always done this? Sumaya's words tumbled out: "I think I'm just like obsessed with myself, like really selfish. Yes. To put it bluntly—yes, I—it's a conscious thing—but it's also just, I'm already always thinking about myself. So that might as well, like redirect that energy into like a channel to better myself and like become a better person. So I dunno if that makes sense."

In short, Sumaya was always "obsessively" thinking about herself and her future. She translated this as being "selfish." As a result, she felt she had to atone for this "self-obsession" by ensuring that her feminism was inclusive and "impact[ed] as many people in a positive way as possible," further feeding into the understanding of an individual feminism that had to be continually measured, evaluated, and improved. In the context of the highly individualized online knowledge cultures I have explored, this kind of self-monitoring was common; it was also unsurprising in an environment of incredible pressure on young people to craft linear, successful, future-oriented biographies. But it was troubling to see how this materialized so concretely as Sumaya's discomfort in her own skin.

Another of my young feminists in another phase of life had experienced similar, oscillating travels in her feminist experience. Fiona was a young white woman from rural New South Wales, now employed full time in communications for a public sector organization located in Sydney, where she had moved for academic and professional opportunities. While others, like Sumaya, had been initiated into feminism via social media during their childhoods, for Fiona feminism came at a crisis point in her early twenties. At the beginning of the pandemic in March 2020, Fiona lost her job at a communications agency, being told in her termination interview that she was a "square peg in a round hole." She was also "struggling mentally with a relationship breakdown." This long-term heterosexual relationship had left her with a sense of self-loss, which she described as follows: "I think just not doing things that you enjoy, like for your own self and that's putting it very, very simply, but being like—when was the last time you just did something 'cause you liked it. Not because your partner liked it or your mom liked it or your friend asked you to do it. Like . . . just you—and I couldn't answer it."

At this time, Fiona became aware of the Instagram influencer Florence Given, often derided or minimized in significance by other young feminists, who characterized the aesthetic "Instagram feminism" for which Given was known as ideal "for twelve- to fifteen-year olds." Yet Fiona spoke in admiring terms, carefully positioning Given beyond a fleeting Internet trend:

> She is—gosh, I think she's like twenty-two going on forty years old with her just—words of wisdom—[from] when she went through a breakup and it kind of touches on all the topics of feminism but also a sense of self and . . . without putting it too bluntly, there's this idea

of not needing someone and really finding purpose in your own self. So not necessarily like leaving your partner, it's certainly not like anti-relationship as such, but not settling for something that like, isn't good for you essentially.

She mused,

At the time she was and continues to be like quite a catalyst for my way of thinking. She is—a funky blonde woman who wears fun seventies clothes, but more—more specifically it was the values. And I think it was the first time that I actually started thinking more, like, introspectively about that.

What struck me were the values of which Fiona spoke, suggesting a means of carefully recalibrating, revaluing, and reorienting herself. Given provided a point of reflection—not a mirror straightforwardly showing Fiona who she "was" but a surface against which she could feel and see herself through a different perspective. This perspective allowed an introspective gaze in which the previously invisible, implicit automaticity of being there became an object she could question, an element of "being Fiona" that she was now ready to doubt. Given's own biography, while impressive for Fiona, was less important than her position as an emotional orientation in Fiona's life. As a knowledge object, combined with the other texts that Fiona encountered in her moment of crisis, Given served not as an aspiration to reach for but as the catalyst that helped Fiona to set her gaze inward while also connecting with these questions as a larger social pattern. This helped her feel "a sense of self . . . that I had lost that in that relationship and to say it, it just wasn't right": an affective dissonance (Hemmings 2011) that helped trace out a different "loop" (Hands 2019) of selfhood, one where she felt at odds with her situation.

And yet Fiona had also begun to struggle with how she felt as a feminist. Like Sumaya, she was dissatisfied—but overwhelmed. Given that she had spoken so glowingly of this emotional turning point at this moment of crisis, I asked her if she felt that this sense of self had endured into the present. Fiona responded haltingly, "I think I'd like to say yes, but I don't actually know in reality." As she had become more immersed in online feminist culture, a new set of "oughts" had arisen against which to measure herself. Speaking of the feeling of the emergence of a self and shifting to one that was constantly at odds with the environment she was navigating, she reflected,

> Yeah . . . I often feel conflicted and not just, I guess, in a relationship sense, but even just like aligning with certain things. . . . You're like, oh, if I actually feel that way, like, does that make me a bad feminist?

She explained in more detail:

> I mean, to put it really bluntly it's like, if you feel upset about how a man treats you or makes a comment, let's say something unjust and you get upset about that. And it's like, does that make you a bad feminist? Or if you feel less about yourself because of, I don't know, social media or something like that, like, does that make you a bad feminist? It's just a constant, I guess, internal battle.

Fiona had learned, through her immersion in online feminist culture, that feminists should be invulnerable. Because smart feminists "knew" men could belittle you and that social media presented unrealistic body images, not to mention life images, such knowledge should produce a powerful carapace around the feminist self. The fact that Fiona continued to feel anxiety, uncertainty, and hurt, and even desire for things she felt she ought not to want, was discombobulating. She confided in her first Zoom interview, sitting at home, "I am in a relationship at the moment and I do find it—" then looking behind her and speaking more quietly—

> I'm talking carefully, but I do find it challenging at times because I feel a lot more aware of how I align. Whereas in my past relationship, I think . . . ignorance is bliss, almost. Whereas now I feel a little bit more aware about how I actually feel about certain things. I do find that conflicting and, and probably more challenging—doing—against my behaviors—I don't really know how to articulate it properly. It's like thinking one thing and trying to align with another, while also fitting into . . . I'm not really sure. I don't know how to articulate it.

Fiona's new tentative sense of feminist selfhood was pulled in all directions. The reflective gaze that Fiona adopted now allowed her a certain space to identify and judge her feelings and actions. She wanted to align with the straightness of a feminism that presumed an inoculating confidence against sexism, injury, and oppression. But in effect, she felt discombobulated: these efforts to align twisted her in knots; it wasn't a good fit. Worst of all, knowing the right way to feel but not being able to bring herself into line now suggested a failing on her part.

Fiona and Sumaya struggled. They had become open to the world through a feminist lens, sparking a sideways gaze in which everyday experiences became legible through reference to a structural pattern, requiring a movement between situatedness and broader experience. This opening, at first, felt expansive; it permitted dissatisfaction, hurt, fear, and anxiety but located it within a place beyond the self, to be analyzed as part of a larger social pattern. But dwelling for some time in online feminist cultures made it feel obligatory to move from the permissive to the *agentic*. Adopting the understanding of a self that had all the information, and thus was always in control, they understood themselves as responsible for their feminist actions: feminist guardians rather than beneficiaries. These conflicting feelings thus signaled a lack within themselves; they were ultimately responsible for putting themselves in conflicting situations, for not falling into the correct line.

This movement to a disembedded master view, however, was not frozen in place. An inward gaze could be diverted; a closure could be re-opened. When I met with Sumaya a year later, she had moved from her full-time job in administration into university, where she was studying a creative degree full time while continuing to work casually for her previous employer. I also had the opportunity to meet her in person, as post-pandemic restrictions had been lifted.

Sumaya met me exuberantly. Her smile almost preceded her, and she spontaneously hugged me before we sat down in a pub. Our interview was long, and at the end I asked her to reflect on her declaration of "self-obsession" from the year before and where she was now. Sumaya stated, "Definitely I wouldn't say it the same way now." She attributed it to a sense of isolation, not being able to speak about her feminist ideas with the colleagues she worked with, nor with her "high school friends who, some of whom I was outgrowing a little bit." There was no dialogic outlet for her political consciousness. She explained, "And then so a lot of my focus was on who I wanted to be and who I wanted to keep in my life, how I represent myself and how I am perceived by other people . . . I was sort of obsessed with how other people perceive me and how I perceived myself. So definitely identity, I think, is what I was about. Whereas now . . . I feel a lot more in the world now than I think I did last year."

Rosalind Gill (2023) has written about the increasingly punitive and microscopic gaze that captures young people, but is particularly intensive for young women, in the era of social media. This gaze is continuous, not only enforced by others in physical and online public spaces but also ultimately adopted by young women themselves to assess their deficits and flaws. Sumaya was no exception in this regard. And yet, through beginning university, in a creative arts degree, consistently being placed in contexts of larger social inquiry in which self-identity was not ignored, but not continually scrutinized and foregrounded, Sumaya felt situated. She could step back from the god's-eye view that a corrective, "inclusive" model of social media feminism mandated; the ambit of self-monitoring had shrunk.

Importantly, Sumaya told me she felt "smaller": "In a good way. I think it's good that like, I feel a lot more part of the overall, the puzzle rather. Like I feel like I'm part of the puzzle or I'm part of like the machine in a good way—even though that doesn't sound great—it's more like I'm contributing to something bigger than myself." This world was not necessarily set up to judge her; it simply operated on its own, outside of her: "And now the way that I want the world to view me is just, I don't really care how the world views me actually, I think it is more important how people I love view me and . . . not necessarily how I view myself." The looser sociality and opportunities for creative self-expression that university offered for Sumaya were intoxicating. She spoke of a new best friend with whom she could talk, deeply and analytically, about her experience of being a "mixed kid"; through another unit, she had produced a short documentary on local Indigenous music artists; for another, she was writing a short story, loosely based on but not completely tethered to her own life. In short, Sumaya could now be emplaced in the world, as a small, partial element within it, rather than feeling stretched across it.

For Fiona, these possibilities of reorientation were felt more fleetingly. Touchingly, it was participation in my project itself that allowed her to reoccupy a sense of steady ground. After participating in her first group workshop, she confided during her interview that she had "entered [the workshop] feeling a bit stressed about . . . how I was going to conduct myself," particularly in discussing her experiences as a "privileged white woman," the problematic identity position she had learned she possessed. But as the workshop went on, she felt able to relax. She said she felt it was a "safe space to be able to discuss our lived experiences" in ways that were divergent but also "crossed over" in certain ways: "What I felt was really beneficial," she noted, pausing to collect her thoughts, "was hearing about the lived experience of others [and how] they go about their day-to-day lives; different materials that they, you know, expose themselves to group chats, or certain books that we'd shared in common, how they, you know, cross over and intersect in themselves . . . it gave me a lot of insight that I probably would not otherwise ever have."

Indeed, at the beginning of each workshop, I emphasized that each person's differences, and potential disagreements, were important for informing my project. Fiona felt enlivened by the possibility of sharing a space with strangers where both differences and similarities were cast as useful contributions to a project larger than herself. As she put it, "That's just not something that happens without—I don't know, like, feeling contrived." This sense of potentially contributing to something greater allowed Fiona and others to sidestep the normative intersectional grid allotting worthiness of attention according to identity axes. Against the backdrop of their time-pressured lives, participants had the permission to remain present, and listen, without evaluating or beating others to judgment.

This is not to suggest that I used particularly distinctive methods in my small workshops, comprising a maximum of five participants on Zoom; indeed, my methods for creating a comfortable space mirrored common techniques for fostering inclusive discussion in university classrooms. Rather, Fiona's experience, I suggest, speaks to the paradox that in the seeming historic abundance of means of communication, spaces of face-to-face public encounter that permit speaking and listening at length on personal experience, and that feel purposeful, *are rare*. In her second interview, the following year, Fiona confided that she was saddened that there weren't further group workshops: "I appreciate that it was a few hours of conversation, but those kind of things still really stick with me and resonate with me. So, I really appreciate . . . in those conversations for us, as participants, it was just—no expectation, in a really positive way. So, that was really great. And then I left those conversations being, like, just being able to reflect and giving language to what I felt."

My research project itself was a very modest spatiotemporal intervention into the lives of my young feminists. But the reception of the workshops indicated to me how scarce opportunities were for extended listening and reflection done collectively, simultaneously, and with strangers. Participants overwhelmingly wanted to continue on giving their time to the project. I had designed recruitment for the project to require sign-up for only one stage of the project, the group workshops, hoping that a minority of participants would then want to give their time to the follow-up interviews staged six months, then a year, afterward. Almost all of the original fifty participants, with the exception of two, elected to continue on with interviews, far beyond what I had originally hoped and envisioned. Julie, the young, energetic feminist leader whom I introduced earlier, explained her own decision to continue with the interviews for the project: "I found it really exhilarating and like, like, really uplifting because it was really nice to see just how like similar and how like-minded a lot of the kind of conversations we were having. It was nice to have that kind of solidarity in regard to just like experiencing feminist culture online and how, like, it can be a really positive thing, but it also has had its negative connotations. So that was really, really cool." Julie focused on the likemindedness. I suggest that this was salient in the context of expectations of difference. It was not that the positions occupied by participants in workshops were the same, but that bridges and connections could be found across a group in which differing positions were stressed. The anxiety of the social media intersectional model lay in its counting but also in its containing of difference, arranging identities as fungible units in a unilinear relation of surplus and lack. The permission to diverge produced a sense of surprised delight—"exhilaration," as Julie put it—in potential coalitions of interest.

NOTICING THE MINUTIAE OF THE EVERYDAY

Of course, this kind of facilitated, face-to-face encounter is not the norm on social media. As social media draws together millions in its enclosures, this sociality is not cost-effective, and certainly not easily scalable. It is intensive in resources, energy, and time. But in more ephemeral moments, looking transversally from one's situated experience was also enabled through the practices of noticing undertaken online, when focused on the minutiae of the everyday. I stress that *minutiae* did not encompass abstract political messaging, protest pictures, or feminist popular culture, things that could be appropriated as part of one's brand or position. I mean the details of nonidentical, repeated personal experience that invited attention as in "attending to." These details, focused on the particular, and the specific, especially when offered in the domain of reproductive health or chronic illness, or in connection with dating and romantic relationships, were at first noticed, then parsed attentively by my participants who were seeking answers for a vague, ongoing sense of deficit, trivialization, and actual, ongoing pain.

Take Julie, whom we met in chapter 3. Julie had grown up working-class, "fat," and brown, and had observed a lack in her credibility from high school onward in relation to her reproductive health. She had mentioned to her doctor: "I never have been a regular menstruator. I probably got a handful in my entire life. And my doctor never really bothered to do any tests. When I asked, well, is this an issue? Like, do I need to look into this a bit more? And she's like, yeah, we'll send you for an ultrasound, but it's honestly, you probably just need to lose weight." This message that her size that was to blame for any pain was reinforced "almost every time" by the question "Have you lost any weight? How are you going with weight loss?" even in instances when, Julie said humorously, "like, I'm here because I've got like an infected toe, like what does [my weight] have to do with it?" She observed that her mother also experienced the same treatment:

> My mum has been going to a doctor, I think the same one for like *forty years*. And every time she goes there, she just comes back feeling like shit, because [the doctor] just talks about her weight all the time. My mom has arthritis. . . . She had a burst on her arm recently. And instead of like, actively helping her, [the doctor] just sends her for an ultrasound and said, you know, "Well, you know what I'm going to say to you. Like you just, like I've been saying this to you for years, like you need to lose some weight."

Julie's mother had been shamed by this doctor—presumably for decades—and did not feel she could expect to be treated any better. Many scholars have written on how class inequalities are reproduced through shame, a feeling that "sticks" to those with less recognized cultural capital in spaces of middle-class authority, such as educational and medical institutions (Skeggs 2004). Such feelings are compounded by a classist, ableist, sexist, and racist gaze that always already positions the large, working-class body as unruly and problematic (Harjunen 2016).

But Julie, now, had had enough. On Instagram, Julie had found increasing talk and discussion of "mysterious" symptoms and pain that other women had fought to be recognized as polycystic ovarian syndrome (PCOS). Reading these accounts, Julie was able to compare her own experience with theirs and compose an understanding that women's pain was not only real but also often minimized. She also spoke to other women with similar experiences, such as a friend with endometriosis who had gone through "countless consults, countless doctor's appointments" only to be told "it's just really bad period pain." This repeated encounter with others' unique but similar experiences catalyzed the feeling that what Julie had been told was wrong. This feeling generated an outward move-ment, a search for something different. Julie told me that she had now found a doctor who was "more accepting and receptive to my concerns." It wasn't that her weight was never again mentioned (it was, in connec-tion with other concerns, such as a family history of diabetes), but that she felt she was understood as a whole person. This outward lens in turn helped Julie to identify that it wasn't only a personal problem and that her mother also deserved better. She was not only supporting her mother to seek other medical advice but also actively trying to recommend popular feminist memoirs to her mother for an attitudinal shift ("It's really good, Mum!").

This experience of noncredibility was shared by other feminists of dif-ferent backgrounds and identities. Middle-class white participant Rye had observed from childhood that they experienced different levels of recep-tiveness when visiting the doctor with their father, as opposed to with their mother. But now, with ongoing chronic illnesses, Rye observed wryly, "I'm twenty-eight. I live in a different state to my dad. I can't—take him to ev-ery doctor's appointment. Just, like the day-to-day not being believed—as like being nonbinary is like just a whole extra layer. Like people see me, and think like, 'hysterical woman.' And then I try to tell them my pronouns and they're like, 'Oh, hysterical, quirky woman.'"

Rye mentioned this in a group workshop, prompting the sharing by an-other participant, Kelly, who had endometriosis, about the response to her own pain resulting from the illness with which she had been diagnosed as a teenager, and her surgery by laparoscope (a tube inserted in the abdomen):

I remember I was diagnosed [with endometriosis], like had known for about two years at this point, [I] had a laparoscopy. I went to a doc-tor and said, Hey, [now] it feels different. Like, I don't know what's going on. And they went straight away, okay, well you need a men-tal health assessment because you need to learn how to manage your pain. And I'm like, it's not in my head. Like, do you not read the notes? Like—where's the point where you've come to that conclusion and canceled out everything before that?! And it's not uncommon, like it's terrifying.

Kelly was angry; she had already done a lot reading online about this issue "when I was first going through all of it, and trying to understand it and educate myself so I could stand up against doctors in some cases." She had, for example, found a researcher and women's health activist on Instagram who posted regularly on "what endo is, what PCOS is, what hormone imbalances are, why you should take zinc. Like all of those things that you probably should know, but you have no idea."

Ambitious, smart Kelly had begun working straight out of school due to her neurodivergence and struggle with studies; Rye, by contrast, had undertaken lengthy years of tertiary education. Both turned to social media culture to inform themselves in different ways. Kelly had notably found some authoritative researchers who used social media to back her up in encounters with authority. But Rye's social media knowledge encounters spoke more to the ongoing illumination and resonance that could occur in moving between personal situations and the particulars of others' experience:

> I guess like, like scrolling through Tumblr, you'd come across sort of random posts of like, "Hey, this fucked up thing happened to me today." And it's like, you see like one and you think, oh, that's upsetting and then you see two or three and it's like, "Oh, this is weird." And you start sort of noticing these patterns. And it's like, I would start kind of . . . applying like their feelings of like, oh, this happened and. . . . Like stuff that had happened in my past where like, like, I dunno, a guy has said something gross or I've been in an uncomfortable situation and I've thought, and like, I felt like, oh, this is icky, and this is bad, but I . . . didn't sort of have the words to put to that.

This was a movement that thus did not involve straightforward applicability on the facts, shoehorning one experience into another, like a Russian doll, but a creative thinking and extrapolation of resonances of feeling. This was immensely emotionally sustaining to Rye in relation to their chronic illness, as they had always simply figured "Oh, this is just what life is. And I'm weak." But then, they went on to say,

> to scroll through posts of other people talking about similar things, I think, oh, okay. I feel like this is icky because it is icky. Like, oh my God. And then I remember like a few years ago . . . a lot of people would start posting stuff about like, just the process of getting chronic illnesses diagnosed and just like reading these stories of like people who've gone ten years with a very clear problem and just doctors dismissing it out of hand and just like not being trusted for their own experiences.

And like, yeah, it was just great to kind of—like, it's horrible to read about, but it's great to connect [to] that: I was like, oh my God, this is real.

This detailed, focused recounting of experiences, all different but allowing the occupying of a position of validity in the face of dismissal, was powerful. Although Rye was still searching for a diagnosis, an exhausting endeavor, this wealth of comparative experience allowed them to feel a legitimacy that grounded their expectations.

Another significant arena of the sifting and picking through of everyday experience was in reading thoughtful accounts about relationships, romantic and otherwise, with men. This knowledge production could be seen as one-way if social media interactivity is measured in terms of comments, but it was this very observation and the quiet everyday noticing of patterns that were the most helpful and dynamic forms of knowledge making for my participants. Participants often read and pondered rather than commented, thinking through how this spoke, rather than directly applied, to their own experience and those of people they knew.

Maria, a young Filipina, spoke to me about this in detail. She actively cobbled together snippets of everyday, often humorous, analysis of what men did. She looked to sources such as Discord, Pinterest, and Reddit, although she specified that she mostly hated Reddit outside the "women-centric subreddits, it's just so . . . ew." In these areas of discussion, there was often detailed analysis and extrapolation of insights contained in viral tweets. For example, she learned to identify when emotional extremism was practiced by supposedly stoic men, showing me a thread positing that men's overreactions were actually just a technique to make it extremely hard to set any boundaries (figure 6.1). When men were "dramatic," they noted, this was "a manipulation tactic that men use to make it such a pain in the ass to set a boundary with them that you don't attempt it again."

This could be considered a "hot take," what Jonathan Dean (2023) has observed as a common practice in leftist Twitter, designed to accrue value to the person who can most rapidly issue a pithy, shareable description of a generally known situation. Yet, in the pseudonymous, discussion-oriented culture of these subreddits, Maria found connection in this detail. She compared it to a moment where she was made to feel "really bad" after giving feedback to a male acquaintance on a joke about trans people that did not land with her: "Then I saw that and I was like, wait a minute. . . . It's like you see a post and then you look back at like the experiences you've

○   •••

Men are so dramatic. You can tell a man
"i don't like when you joke about that"
and they'll respond with "ok, fine. I'll just
never speak again."

This is a manipulation tactic that men use to
make it such a pain in the ass to set a boundary
with them that you don't attempt it again

^What they said. Don't give them an inch. They
have absolutely no idea what to do once this
tactic doesn't work.

"Ok fine I'll just never speak again."

"Good deal. You should never speak ever."

30,428 notes   ▷   ○   ⇄   ♥

6.1 "Men are so dramatic." Tumblr post showing a tweet
with Tumblr comments, as viewed on Pinterest, October 9,
2021. Screenshot by author.

had, and you really relate to it. And I guess that's like how I kind of like learn. . . . It helps me—learn from my experiences that, you know, I wasn't being overdramatic really. They were being overdramatic." Maria then drew connections about this imbalance in scrutiny on men's presentation of emotions, in contrast with women's. She showed me another subreddit that critiqued the often repeated assertion that women needed to consider how "men are shamed for showing their feelings under patriarchy," and explained to me how this critical approach resonated with what she had seen in her life. She theorized:

> Men are shamed, but . . . women are also shamed for showing emotion. And I find that, like, women support women, like when it comes to emotion, you know, like if a woman is upset, like it's likely for another woman to console her. I feel like men don't do the same thing for men . . . you know, if you weren't meant to show emotion, then reach out to like your fellow male peers and, you know, be there for them. You don't have to rely on just women, to look after your emotional well-being too.

There was thus a continual movement in Maria's inquiries: she would read and collate small snapshots into everyday behavior, reflect on their application, and then extrapolate and connect them with other insights. In relation to dating, she had sent me a tweet about falling into one-way conversations with men on dates that we discussed in her interview:

Akane Have you ever been on a date with someone who asks you zero questions?

Maria Oh yeah. So I'm online dating for the first time like a couple months ago. Some people are just like, really like expect you to carry the conversation. And at the same time, you know, I would like check, you know, online forums like Reddit and see a lot of men complaining about how women never take the initiative to dating and then I'd be like, oh! But you know, the same thing can be said for men.

[She paused and reflected.]

I can't believe I did that though. Like looking back, I guess I thought, "Oh, maybe there's something wrong with me," but *no*.

Maria often questioned her own "rightness." On a very real, embodied level, she was not confident in her own body. She recoiled from "body positivity," preferring the term "body neutrality." She had come across both concepts through Instagram, but "body neutrality" gave more emotional space to the uneasy relationship she had with her body. Maria was smart and had done well at school, but she had not gained the confidence that marked many (but not all) of my middle-class liberal arts–educated participants. Her proclivity was to slide into self-uncertainty, particularly when she didn't know where she fit. At the time of our first interview, she had spent six years in Australia but did not share the easy attachment to the global term POC by other non-white participants who had grown up locally. The Internet had also caused her to doubt if "Asians" were "real POC." Her tendency was to position her own instinct as potentially wayward, in the face of another contradicting assertion.

But Maria's bowerbird practices of looking, collecting, and building in connection with her everyday experience felt restorative. This repeated outward-inward gaze, located in her own experience but also in connections to others, did not "cure" the ontological uncertainty Maria felt, but did allow her to theorize her experience in a way that provided a sense of legitimacy for herself. It also opened the possibility of situated care for others, such as a close friend in a highly unequal heterosexual relationship: "She just puts in, like, so much work for this relationship and he doesn't do the same for her. And that's really frustrating to see. And, you know, I don't want to ever be in a position like that too. So I guess reading, like this sort of thing helps me to understand, like, why I feel upset at the situation my friend is in." Maria's reading, and the forging of her own curriculum, allowed her to identify her own perspective, and her friend's, as different, while maintaining the careful scrutiny of what her friend was experiencing.

Thus, online feminist knowledge cultures, in moments and in spaces where one could read without being expected to respond, judge, or react, allowed possibilities of quiet resonance. Such moments of noticing, reflection, and revising one's understanding may be understood as lacking in political clout in comparison with social media–facilitated presence at physical protests, in viral tweets, and with popular hashtags—but these possibilities sustained Maria, as well as many of my other young feminists who felt cramped by the noise, the visibility, and the rigidity of other parts of feminist social media.

In concluding, I return to Sumaya to suggest that sometimes—in a world of immense pressure to continually extract more and more from each second —the most powerful mechanisms for theorizing from experience were conversation and time. Early in our second interview, she had shown me a TikTok from her social media feed deconstructing dating culture. The TikTok critiqued how women extracted their "pound of flesh" from first dates, requiring men to fork out considerable amounts to show they cared. At first breath, in explaining it to me, Sumaya framed this as an example of feminism "going too far": "I think it's important for us to call each other out about this. I suppose this one is expectations of men. And how those women's feminism is . . . like privileging women higher than men. That's sort of what it's about. And the patriarchy negatively affects men as well."

The context of this TikTok was vague, so I went on to ask Sumaya about her own experience dating. Sumaya laughed self-deprecatingly and acknowledged she had little interest in dating men herself, not because she was a queer person who was more attracted to women but because men were "gross" on apps in what they felt entitled to from her: "I have not met a single man from a dating app because I think my standards are too high, I have, like, I refuse to settle, like even slightly, and they're so far below my standards anyway, that it's not really a contest." She openly shared how she was completely unused to flirting with men in person. We laughed as she told me how in clubs she would close her eyes while dancing, facing her girlfriends in a circle rather than make eye contact across the room.

Something shifted after about an hour into the interview. We had moved from talking about changes from last year, her move to full-time university, her part-time work, and her struggles in dating. Suddenly, unprompted by me, Sumaya articulated the contradiction she had been attempting to straddle:

> What I had just said about like patriarchy hurting men too . . . just like that disconnect between like, like yes, I support men, but also, oh my God, I hate men. That's the main disconnect that I think I need to sort of work through because right now in this moment I cannot, like, I cannot find a bridge between those two. . . . I am very passionate about the patriarchy ending, not just "for" women, but also for men. And yet,

like my, my actual own personal experiences with men have not been that great. I was like, so why am I rooting for you guys?

Questioning herself, and critical of men's inability to blame the patriarchy for their own problems, she then went on to discuss Andrew Tate with me and her concerns about the extreme misogyny that had exploded online.

I have ended here with Sumaya to sound a small, hopeful note. What I want to indicate is that the breathing space afforded even via the medium of a research interview can sometimes be enough to allow for an opening where one can move and can put theories to work transversally, thinking about the general but also with reference to personal experience. At the beginning of the interview, the identification of a feminism that "privileged women higher than men" was an easily accessible explanation that Sumaya had to hand in reference to this TikTok documenting highly gendered dating expectations. And yet having the time—and a listener—to then reflect on her own personal experience allowed further complexity in working through the dynamics of sexual cultures. What emerged was an acknowledgment of the contradiction she was asked to embody as a feminist, one that involved empathy for men without centering them, and without lowering the bar.

While *connection* has been the central buzzword used by social media platforms to describe their organization of sociality, scholars have questioned how substantive this connection may be, as well as its political ends. My participants were continually searching for feminist connections, with online media seemingly being the most accessible for them. And yet these were elusive. When they found a resonating experience, one that invited them to see themselves as a small, nonfungible part of a larger plurality, they too often then felt they had to move on; they couldn't rest comfortably in the sense that they needed feminism; they had to then become its guardians, its protectors, its agents.

Rather than moving on, this chapter has suggested that my young feminists benefited most from a sense of continual moving *between* a sense of repetitive everyday experience detailed by others that did not necessarily match but could reverberate with their own. Thus I have highlighted the important ongoing, repetitive work of quiet shifts and perspective-taking made possible through the sharing of the minutiae of the everyday. This then allowed them to compose flexible, continuous larger frameworks for seeing the world. To echo Dorothy Smith (1987), this was "creating a way of seeing, from where we actually live, into the powers, processes, and relations that organize and determine the everyday context of that seeing" (8–9).

Smith discusses the everyday as a world of practices of repetition and of locality, in contrast to the "textual," generalizing world of ruling and administration. By privileging this everyday lens, what this chapter has aimed to do is to "shrink" the enormity of achieving collective change, and provide a more feasible framework for engaging with young people and their political negotiations. This is a framework that does not hold them, as they often hold themselves, to impossible structural standards of political efficacy but also does not imbue their practices as "resistant" and "agentic" as an endpoint in analysis. Too often the most impressive accounts of what appears to be collective action through social media, while seemingly inviting hundreds and thousands to participants to come together, achieve only an aggregate of individuals in a "seriality" of practice—that is, a homogeneity of actions that may be repeated and counted (Hands 2019). And yet, when looking behind the curtain, the most sustainable, ongoing forms of endurance often required modest, quiet, and invisible forms of transversal weaving together. I have tried to privilege the small but highly dynamic movements of knowledge making my participants recounted, the importance of felt orientation over the citation of concepts per se, and the contingencies that shape, structure, and make possible these affective movements. This final chapter is not intended to somehow balance out my description of the alienating elements of social media culture, as part of a three-part narrative structure terminating on a happy note. But what I aim to do is bring a different lens to parts of my participants' accounts that could otherwise be buried, to make visible the different lines of possibility that emerge from the dominant intersectional grid I have documented that otherwise so tightly sought to keep people in place.

CONCLUSION

A Call for Everyday Poetry

As "everything" may now be captured online, the sense of surveillance, measuring, and evaluation of all personal activity bleeds into politics, even when the language of such politics is critical, and prima facie names the structural factors of oppression. As such, it is not straightforwardly "popular feminism" (Banet-Weiser 2018), "neoliberal feminism" (Rottenberg 2013), or "postfeminism" (Gill 2007) as distinct feminist sensibilities that problematically construct highly individualistic modes of understanding feminism. In a context where the spaces, temporalities, and structures of encounter with knowledge are so highly *amenable* to the logics of commercial circulation, feminism, in its emphasis on the personal and the interpersonal, is always at risk of being translated into an endless loop of self-surveillance: What ought I to do, as a feminist? How should I have spoken to XYZ, as a feminist? How can I be a better feminist? The abundance and accessibility of online feminist culture is met with a sense of scarcity: not enough time; never enough knowledge; little forgiveness for mistakes that we can no longer afford.

In this book, I have charted a central tension in the movements of online feminist culture: between the essentialization of knowledge and closing down of identity, and the practical possibilities of sustaining collectivity. In this relation, feeling played a central role, forming, informing, and deforming how feminist knowledge materialized in the everyday. It created suturing points between the "everyday" and the "structural," openings and closures that in turn shaped relational possibilities. The online progressive political cultures that constituted part of my young feminists' everyday worlds produced a theory of how to be feminist, and how your identity positioned you to practice such feminism. These cultures are often positioned by scholars and students as more accessible, less hierarchical, and more practical than the knowledges of academia. And yet these knowledge cultures were not often straightforwardly "performative" in Sara Ahmed's (2004b) Austinian use of the word: that is, they did not perform what they purported to do in my young feminists' everyday worlds. These knowledges were implicated in the production of new, universalizing benchmarks of knowledge that regulated personal conduct in the everyday. They raised the standards of what you needed to know to seem "educated." And yet this "theory," described as "intersectional," often failed to hold a meaningful connection to the conditions of the local or the everyday, or allow analysis thereof. In these frameworks, identity categories were fixed endpoints involving an equation of privilege and disadvantage, understood as calculable, fungible units. This then mandated the management of interpersonal comportment according to ritualized presentations of white platforming and taking into account, both online and offline. Producing inclusion as an endgoal, and elevating the interpersonal to the structural in terms of its moral-political significance, such frameworks heightened the stakes of both success and failure for individual young feminists.

As with the coming and going of commercial trends, online knowledge cultures produced ever-moving goalposts of being "in the know." The surfeit of accessible information, in practice, deepened inequalities via classed attributions of value, distancing, and distinction that were needed to parse and make sense of the streams of content. Such cultures fostered the continuing production of exclusions under the guise of inclusion, as Christina Scharff (2023b) has more broadly observed in relation to the class hierarchies of feminist influencer work. They produced languages that required sophistication to speak. Particular terms and identity positions were insisted on in must-know terms, producing new boundaries and hierarchies in terms of who didn't know, and who did, with seeming ignorance revealing a potential moral failure along with the failure to educate the self. Young feminists were confronted with the imperative to continually adopt the right position and with the specter of failing to be good, operating in tandem with my young feminists' different capacities to accrue and demonstrate capital. Highly self-referential, but without an explicit set syllabus that could be meaningfully contested and discussed, this "reactivism," as I have called it, introduced complexity but not necessarily explanatory power into my cohort's everyday lives.

Often, this theoretical underpinning smoothed existing pathways for young white feminists with existing cultural capital to be "good" feminists. At the same time, it turned energy and attention onto the self, creating existential anxieties about one's feminist failures and how one might be called out for their political artifice and lack of true inclusive sensibilities. Young feminists learned by rote how to acknowledge their privilege, understood as a static unit, rather than as a relational exercise of power, and how to defensively note and distance themselves from any "problematic" elements of popular culture, public figures, or global events. Such knowledge cultures thus translated feminist practice primarily as an exercise in position-taking. Positions can, indeed, have political effects, but usually when one speaks for a government, corporation, or other organization that can bring to bear economic, social, and cultural pressure through their declarations. Worryingly, in everyday settings, the position-taking of online cultures reinforced an asymmetry of political responsibility and agency as ultimately residing with the individual. In short, the personal choices in the sphere of talk, consumption, and interpersonal relations had the felt weight of structural decisions to invest, neglect, and let die.

This position-taking put these young feminists in a difficult position. It required the adoption of a microscopic lens—what Rosalind Gill (2023) has called, in other work, the "forensic gaze"—most frequently leveled at the self, and at women in the everyday and in public life, as feminism was conflated with the cultural circulation of objects, news, and stories concerning women. Women's faults and flaws, through the online attention economy, were magnified in their political significance, with absolutely no excuses for those who were wealthy, white, and Western. There was a constant readiness to spot when white women, as licensed subjects of critique, did "white things," made stupid mistakes, or misspoke. Indeed, I often sensed relief, not from my participants of color but from my white participants who sought to demonstrate their good credentials, that it was not them but another white woman who had gotten it wrong.

For my young women participants who felt such a call personally, then, being a good feminist meant spending disproportionate attention and energy to continually distance the self from bad women in the online public sphere and in popular culture. Sometimes, it could feel good to have the right take. But on a personal level, such critique did not fundamentally release the tension of being under the microscope. On an ongoing basis, it further solidified the sense of surveillance in online feminist culture, even as some individually, through their own support networks and cultural and economic capital, were able to carefully navigate the higher stakes of such feminist knowledge cultures.

This exacting understanding of the personal-as-political was also unevenly applied. With the rising popularity of far-right politics becoming part of the background of the everyday, missteps by individual women were seen as missteps that feminism could not afford. But men tended to become central in feminist scrutiny and objects of anger only when responsible for extreme misogyny and violence, the type that is already formally criminalized. With the exception of some corners of TikTok and Reddit, the everyday actions of men in public life were not burdened by the paranoid, binary lens of "good" and "bad" in the same way as those of women. Concerningly for me, as a feminist researcher, it showed how feminist critique, turned inward, could be amenable to the circulation of misogyny, in the intensity with which women's conduct was dissected in stark comparison with the relative lack of indignation against the banal day-to-day self-serving actions of men. The forensic concern with the (re)production of "good women" over the everyday practices of male failure and entitlement exemplifies the narrowing of political vision, in what Olúfẹ́mi O. Táíwò (2022, 11) has critiqued as "supercharging, rather than restraining elite capture" of systems, resources, and social advantage. In making this claim, I am not arguing that my young feminists were in fact misogynists "all along"; I am not arguing that they were "bad feminists." Far from it. I am trying to show how the most "accessible" forms of collective imagination that were open to them through online culture seemed to be inclusive but, against my participants' intentions, also heightened individual responsibility and blame along gendered lines.

As Srila Roy (2022) argues, feminism has long been concerned with governmentality; middle-class feminist women have often sought to govern themselves, and others, in particular ways. This book has focused on online feminist knowledge cultures and is thus particularly focused on how social media, in its frenetic rhythms, its surveillant cultures, and its reduction of complexity into simple, shareable binaries, often intensifies the message that progressive politics is about always being good. Young people are driven in this context to continually account for themselves as good people and, in particular, as good girls. But what I also want to argue is that, in taking a wider view of this contemporary mediated landscape, this emphasis on the good cannot sustain feminism and feminists, neither younger nor older. It deepens inequalities in remaking historical racialized and classed patterns in the demonstration of goodness. And it also feeds into the possibility of actually increasing misogyny against women, even under the guise of feminist improvement, as feminism-as-benchmark becomes yet another measure through women can be said to fail, particularly those that stick out (and they increasingly do, in the media-saturated leadership-driven ethos of the twenty-first century).

I became interested in the everyday take-up of feminism around the time that Sarah Banet-Weiser (2018) began observing that feminism no longer seemed to be something from which one automatically distanced oneself, per Rosalind Gill's (2007) identification of the "postfeminist" sensibility in which feminism, perhaps, was needed once upon a time, but no longer. In the 2010s, beginning with celebrity "coming-out stories" of being feminist, and reaching a crescendo with Hollywood activism around #MeToo, feminism was curiously, startlingly popular. How, I wondered, did this translate into everyday life? At this point in time, and at this point in the book, I ponder whether another cycle has begun, where "feminism," again, has been somewhat displaced by the terms *diversity* and *intersectionality*, once again relegating feminism to a less sophisticated past, as understandings of power, identity, and collectivity are put under the atomizing pressure of social media circuits of travel.

In writing this, I am also reminded of a symposium on transnational media I attended some years ago, when just beginning my scholarly foray into everyday online feminist cultures. I was unnerved, when presenting my findings, at how much the male-dominated room seemed to relish the heated critique of pop star Taylor Swift articulated by my participants— how what I had hoped to be a careful presentation of the conflicts my participants had reported was "lapped up." This, to be clear, is not an argument that women cannot criticize women. Rather, what I am noting is that feminist critique may be easily "amenable" (Hemmings 2011) to nonfeminist purposes in communicative environments simultaneously structured by surveillance and openness, the mainstreaming of feminism, and the accessibility of misogyny. These are also cultural contexts where women are always *already* under the microscope (Fisher 2011). Such scrutiny has intensified in online social media contexts, where anyone may feasibly see such criticism, and where the transnational intensification of misogyny is palpable. Taking this hostile environment seriously is not to abandon critique or criticism but rather to register the heightened challenge in making such critique constructive (Raffnsøe et al. 2022) when too often it reveals, pierces, and denounces without care.

Accordingly, this book has also attempted to attend to what can be *created* and what alternatives are possible in the relationality of everyday life. The second line of movement I have charted tarries with the structures and movements that produce relational feminist possibilities both online and in connected offline spaces. These were minor, everyday moments that helped my young feminists to orient, to breathe, to endure, to be curious. They were not, on the whole, grand citations of resistance against "structural inequality," although being together with others at protests could of course help. These were moments of connection, recognition, and affordance across attention to the particulars of everyday experience. They were most likely to occur where my participants were allowed the space to move beyond polarities of correct and incorrect feeling, and occupy space simultaneously rather than sequentially. Such space allowed participants to ponder and compare where the premise of common ground was of relaying differently lived experiences rather than "identity" or "correct" knowledge to absorb. This kind of quiet expansion and movement could occur in anonymous Reddit forums, in the time taken to listen to podcasts; it could, importantly, take place in a university classroom where trust was built over several weeks. Sometimes it was simply enough to have someone such as an interested researcher listen to you and validate that your experience was worth listening to, even if you didn't have it "the worst" compared with so many other people.

Sometimes, importantly, such expansion could take place in encounters with culture that seemed to be prima facie exemplars of neoliberal or popular feminism. For example, Florence Given, the influencer whom I mentioned in chapter 6, is clearly a feminist brand. For young feminists such as brilliant, acerbic, and time-poor Zala, a working-class participant of Bosnian heritage, Given was described as an inadequate, "basic" iteration of feminism, drawing connections with other Instagram feminisms privileging the aesthetic, the consumable, and the easily shareable. Given's "basic" feminism also came under further scrutiny in 2020, when it was alleged that she had plagiarized ideas from a Black influencer, Chidera Eggerue (see Dean 2023). Yet this did not necessarily mean that the effects of Given's text straightforwardly incorporated her readers into a so-called neoliberal or white feminism. For Fiona, for example, with whom I spent some time in chapter 6, Given's relaying of personal experience felt electrifying, illuminating, an angled surface through which she could newly see elements of her own experience. Fiona's account suggests that the significance of Given as a mediated text was in an encounter of opening space, one that allowed her the wriggle room to look upon her past relationships and produce new ways of being. Literature scholar and English teacher Louise Rosenblatt (1994) calls this the "poem," a coming together of reader and text in a worldmaking that is at once personal and beyond the personal. In contrast to "efferent reading," where a text is reduced to "information," an object to be incorporated or digested or "taken away," in poetic reading, Rosenblatt argues, texts are their own time and space, "an ongoing process" in which text and reader are simultaneous "aspects of a total situation, each conditioned by and conditioning the other" (6). In reading as a "poem," the reader enlivens the text through recall to their own memory, but the visual cues of the text make it seem as though the reader senses something "outside and beyond" the personal (21). In this way, poetic reading is both a personal and a social event where "the boundary between inner and outer world breaks down, and the literary work of art, as so often remarked, leads us into a new world. [The text] becomes part of the experience which we bring to our future encounters in literature and in life" (21). Given is a text, then, whose circulation produces lines of movement according to her readers' frames, orientations, and experiences. Depending on the reader's own history and social position, Given's significance could lean toward constituting yet another drop in the feminist current repetitively circulated in social media, or her significance could extend to providing the space and clarity that some of my feminists so sorely needed day to day.

I have spent some time here to make the point that for scholars, hypothesizing the political effects of feminisms that largely circulate as texts in online culture is immensely complex. The impulse to straightforwardly commute structural principles onto the "personal" too easily produces critique amenable to the first totalizing movement I described, creating standards that cannot be met. "Big" critique of the "structure" straightforwardly translocated onto the domain of the everyday mirrors the punishing self-critique engaged in by anguished participants, such as Alice, who was overwhelmed by the prospect that each of her career, consumption, and life decisions "facilitated capitalism." Leaping from a personal action to the analysis that it is "politically problematic" is often to simultaneously bypass personal circumstance and context, leaving us nowhere to go. But the everyday is a world of the "local and particular," as Dorothy Smith (1987) argues, "ongoingly created and recreated in human sensuous activities" (132). The work of analysis requires not too quickly closing the space between the political and the personal. This kind of rushing underpins the urgent calling out that is often the recourse of online feminist critique. Rather, the political and the personal need to be kept close but in conversation, ontologically resonant but nonidentical, in a continual transversal gaze (Yuval-Davis 2023), situating, looking, and comparing. Understanding the everyday as a political space requires us to consider our actions as limited, situated, and particular, producing conditions of possibility for other actions. For those that work in universities whom I count as an audience for this book, I suggest it is even more important to consider, collectively, what universities can *do* as social media competes and is entangled in the production of new, seemingly commonsense ideas about identity, politics, and responsibility. Against the urgency and the rush of much social media, how can the medium of the university provide the temporality and spatiality for a continuous transversal gaze? What kinds of cultures of feeling can be fostered to provide students with a sense of breathing space? How can texts produce poetic transactions, producing surfaces through which students can review and revise their own narratives?

In the everyday, against a normative frame understanding individual action as a miniature, complete, perfect version of structural action, it is more sustaining—and indeed, more precise, I argue—to understand everyday actions as necessarily incomplete, amenable to other forms of action, as parts of a whole. I emphasize the "sustaining" part because politically my attention to online feminist knowledge cultures has also been to valorize and legitimate the struggles and concerns of my young feminists who took the world on their shoulders. Those that mobilized less cultural and economic capital in my cohort still felt that they had to show they were capable and confident—sometimes even using the language of "privilege" to show that they, too, had read widely and were good feminists. For these feminists, encounters with therapeutic moments of reassurance or encouragement on social media, so easily derided as social media inspo, were crucial elements of getting by.

For others, being feminist imposed a sense that they ought to be at least emotionally impervious to sexism, misogyny, homophobia, transmisogyny, transphobia, and other structural oppressions in their own lives. Those that had any nameable forms of privilege felt, fundamentally, that they did not deserve compassion unless they were extremely good women/feminists/young people. I was particularly struck by this in one instance in which a participant revealed to me that in the days leading up to our second interview, she had been sexually assaulted on the train. She was still reeling from this. We met on Zoom as she couldn't leave her house; she was too afraid to take public transport. And yet, in our interview, she was still concerned with not overstating what had happened to her. There was a sense of continuing deferral of attention to someone who needed it more: "It wasn't as bad as it could have been." She still acutely felt the responsibility to live her politics in an exemplary fashion. She felt guilty that she was reneging on her environmental politics by now relying on her car, not public transport, to get around. She articulated a future-oriented responsibility to take care with discussing what had happened to her, in ways that were both politically impactful and sensitive to her readers who were deadened by callout culture. I was moved by her commitment, and her principles, but also deeply saddened.

I hope, then, that this book, in its attention to the minor, to the everyday, and to the emotional politics of personal experience, helps move beyond reductive framings of the "strong woman," and the "outspoken feminist." Rather than trying to show "what" kinds of feminism and feminists were the most effective and powerful in speaking to the social structures that are set against them, my aim has been more modest: to show, in these times of intensifying lack, competition, and violence, how and if feminisms in their different mediations benefit their subjects—those usually disempowered by their gender—in the everyday. This book has conjectured what it might look like to move away from the need to continually prove one's worthiness of attention, in the conceptualization of the political as the continual taking up of individual corrections, improvements, and burdens. In doing so I have sought to provide another space for quiet endurance and for care.

REFERENCES

INTERVIEWS

What follows is a list of participants who are mentioned in this book. All names have been changed to de-identify participants. Ages are given for the first year they participated in the project.

Ade (age twenty-four), interviewed by the author in October 2021–July 2022.

Alice (age twenty-six), interviewed by the author in November 2021–August 2022.

Bella (age twenty-three), interviewed by the author in October 2021–August 2022.

Bernie (age twenty-six), interviewed by the author in November 2021–July 2022.

Cathy (age twenty-four), interviewed by the author in September 2021–June 2022.

Crystal (age twenty-two), interviewed by the author in September 2021–August 2022.

E (age twenty-six), interviewed by the author in November 2021–September 2022.

Elise (age twenty-eight), interviewed by the author in October 2021–June 2022.

Fiona (age twenty-seven), interviewed by the author in October 2021–August 2022.

Gabi (age twenty-three), interviewed by the author in October 2021–July 2022.

Greta (age nineteen), interviewed by the author in October 2021.

Harriet (age nineteen), participated in a group workshop in June 2021.

Hayley (age twenty-seven), interviewed by the author in September 2021–June 2022.

Holly (age twenty-five), interviewed by the author in October 2021–July 2022.

Jenny (age twenty-one), interviewed by the author in November 2021–August 2022.

Jillian (age twenty-seven), interviewed by the author in October 2021–July 2022.

Julie (age twenty-two), interviewed by the author in November 2021–August 2022.

Katie (age twenty-eight), interviewed by the author in October 2021–July 2022.

Kelly (age twenty-five), interviewed by the author in November 2021–August 2022.

Kristen (age twenty-seven), interviewed by the author in September 2021–August 2022.

Lakshmi (age twenty-eight), interviewed by the author in November 2021–August 2022.

Leila (age twenty-five), interviewed by the author in October 2021–August 2022.

Liz (age twenty-eight), interviewed by the author in November 2021–August 2022.

Marcela (age twenty-six), interviewed by the author in October 2021–August 2022.

Margot (age twenty-one), interviewed by the author in November 2021–July 2022.

Maria (age twenty-four), interviewed by the author in October 2021.

Marina (age twenty-seven), interviewed by the author in October 2021–June 2022.

Nina (age twenty-one), interviewed by the author in September 2021–July 2022.

Ollie (age twenty-two), interviewed by the author in September 2021.

Pippa (age twenty-five), interviewed by the author in October 2021–July 2022.

Priscilla (age twenty-six), interviewed by the author in November 2021–August 2022.

Rosie (age twenty-three), interviewed by the author in October 2021–July 2022.

Rye (age twenty-eight), interviewed by the author in November 2021–August 2022.

Sara (age twenty-two), interviewed by the author in September 2021–June 2022.

Shae (age twenty-one), interviewed by the author in September 2021–July 2022.

Shona (age twenty-one), interviewed by the author in October 2021–July 2022.

Sonya (age twenty-eight), interviewed by the author in September 2021–August 2022.

Sumaya (age nineteen), interviewed by the author in October 2021–July 2022.

Thea (age twenty-eight), interviewed by the author in September 2021–July 2022.

Zala (age twenty-one), interviewed by the author in November 2021.

Adkins, Lisa, and Celia Lury. 1999. "The Labour of Identity: Performing Identities, Performing Economies." *Economy and Society* 28 (4): 598–614. https://doi.org/10.1080/03085149900000020.

Ahmed, Sara. 2004a. *The Cultural Politics of Emotion*. Edinburgh: Edinburgh University Press.

Ahmed, Sara. 2004b. "Declarations of Whiteness: The Non-Performativity of Anti-Racism." *Borderlands E-Journal* 3 (2).

Ahmed, Sara. 2006. *Queer Phenomenology: Orientations, Objects, Others*. Durham, NC: Duke University Press.

Ahmed, Sara. 2012. *On Being Included: Racism and Diversity in Institutional Life*. Durham, NC: Duke University Press.

Ahmed, Sara. 2019. *What's the Use? On the Uses of Use*. Durham, NC: Duke University Press.

Andrejevic, Mark. 2013. *Infoglut: How Too Much Information Is Changing the Way We Think and Know*. New York: Routledge.

Andrejevic, Mark. 2020. *Automated Media*. New York: Routledge.

Andrews, Kehinde, Kimberlé Crenshaw, and Annabel Wilson. 2023. *Blackness at the Intersection*. London: Bloomsbury Academic.

Ang, Ien. 2003. "I'm a Feminist but . . . 'Other' Women and Postnational Feminism." In *Feminist Postcolonial Theory*, edited by Reina Lewis and Sara Mills. New York: Routledge.

Awkward-Rich, Cameron, and Hil Malatino. 2022. "Meanwhile, T4t." *TSQ: Transgender Studies Quarterly* 9 (1): 1–8. https://doi.org/10.1215/23289252-9475467.

Bailey, Moya, and Trudy. 2018. "On Misogynoir: Citation, Erasure, and Plagiarism." *Feminist Media Studies* 18 (4): 762–68. https://doi.org/10.1080/14680777.2018.1447395.

Banet-Weiser, Sarah. 2012. *Authentic: The Politics of Ambivalence in a Brand Culture*. New York: NYU Press. https://www.jstor.org/stable/j.ctt9qfmw0.

Banet-Weiser, Sarah. 2018. *Empowered: Popular Feminism and Popular Misogyny*. Durham, NC: Duke University Press. https://doi.org/10.2307/j.ctv11316rx.

Baraitser, Lisa, and Laura Salisbury. 2021. "'Containment, Delay, Mitigation': Waiting and Care in the Time of a Pandemic." *Wellcome Open Research* 5: 1–16. https://doi. org/10.12688/wellcomeopenres.15970.2.

Bartky, Sandra Lee. 1997. "Foucault, Femininity, and the Modernization of Patriarchal Power." In *Feminist Social Thought: A Reader*, edited by Diana T. Meyers. New York: Routledge.

Bauman, Zygmunt. 2000. *Liquid Modernity*. Cambridge: Polity.

Bennett, W. Lance, and Alexandra Segerberg. 2012. "The Logic of Connective

Action: Digital Media and the Personalization of Contentious Politics." *Information, Communication and Society* 15 (5): 739–68. https://doi.org/10.1080/1369118X.2012.670661.

Berlant, Lauren. 2011. *Cruel Optimism*. Durham, NC: Duke University Press.

Berliner, Lauren S., and Nora J. Kenworthy. 2017. "Producing a Worthy Illness: Personal Crowdfunding Amidst Financial Crisis." *Social Science and Medicine* 187:233–42. https://doi.org/10.1016/j.socscimed.2017.02.008.

Beta, Annisa R. 2022. "Fight the Patriarchy: Digital Feminist Public Pedagogy and Post-Feminist Media Culture in Indonesia." In *Gender in an Era of Post-Truth Populism*, edited by Penny Jane Burke, Akane Kanai, Rosalind Gill, and Julia Coffey. London: Bloomsbury. https://www.torrossa.com/en/resources/an/5205786.

Bobel, Chris. 2007. "'I'm Not an Activist, Though I've Done a Lot of It': Doing Activism, Being Activist and the 'Perfect Standard' in a Contemporary Movement." *Social Movement Studies* 6 (2): 147–59. https://doi.org/10.1080/14742830701497277.

Bratich, Jack. 2010. "Affective Convergence in Reality Television: A Case Study in Divergence Culture." In *Flow TV: Television in the Age of Media Convergence*, edited by Michael Kackman, Marnie Binfield, Matthews Thomas Payne, Allison Perlman, and Bryan Sebok. New York: Routledge.

Brock, André. 2011. "Beyond the Pale: The Blackbird Web Browser's Critical Reception." *New Media and Society* 13 (7): 1085–103. https://doi.org/10.1177/1461444810397031.

Brunsdon, Charlotte. 2005. "Feminism, Postfeminism, Martha, Martha, and Nigella." *Cinema Journal* 44 (2): 110–16.

Bucher, Taina. 2018. *If... Then: Algorithmic Power and Politics*. Oxford: Oxford University Press.

Bull, Anna, and Kim Allen. 2018. "Introduction: Sociological Interrogations of the Turn to Character." *Sociological Research Online* 23 (2): 392–98. https://doi.org/10.1177/1360780418769672.

Campbell, Karlyn Kohrs. 1983. "Femininity and Feminism: To Be or Not to Be a Woman." *Communication Quarterly* 31 (2). https://doi.org/10.1080/01463378309369493.

Campeau, Kari, and Yee Thao. 2022. "'It Makes Everything Just Another Story': A Mixed Methods Study of Medical Storytelling on GoFundMe." *Technical Communication Quarterly* 32 (1): 33–49. https://doi.org/10.1080/10572252.2022.2047792.

Carastathis, Anna. 2016. *Intersectionality: Origins, Contestations, Horizons*. Lincoln: University of Nebraska Press.

Carbado, Devon W. 2013. "Colorblind Intersectionality." *Signs: Journal of Women in Culture and Society* 38 (4): 811–45. https://doi.org/10.1086/669666.

Cattien, Jana. 2019. "When 'Feminism' Becomes a Genre: *Alias Grace* and 'Feminist' Television." *Feminist Theory* 20 (3): 321–39. https://doi.org/10.1177/1464700119842564.

Cetina, Karin Knorr. 2007. "Culture in Global Knowledge Societies: Knowledge Cultures and Epistemic Cultures." *Interdisciplinary Science Reviews* 32 (4): 361–75. https://doi.org/10.1179/030801807X163571.

Cho, Sumi, Kimberlé Williams Crenshaw, and Leslie McCall. 2013. "Toward a Field of Intersectionality Studies: Theory, Applications, and Praxis." *Signs: Journal of Women in Culture and Society* 38 (4): 785–810. https://doi.org/10.1086/669608.

Code, Lorraine. 2006. *Ecological Thinking: The Politics of Epistemic Location.* New York: Oxford University Press.

Collins, Patricia Hill. 2015. "Intersectionality's Definitional Dilemmas." *Annual Review of Sociology* 41 (2015): 1–20. https://doi.org/10.1146/annurev-soc-073014-112142.

Condliffe, Zoe. 2023. "Solidarity, Rage and Justice: Transformation and Consciousness-Raising for Contemporary Feminist Activism." PhD diss., Monash University.

Crary, Jonathan. 2001. *Suspensions of Perception: Attention, Spectacle, and Modern Culture.* Cambridge, MA: MIT Press.

Crawford, Kate. 2009. "Following You: Disciplines of Listening in Social Media." *Continuum* 23 (4): 525–35. https://doi.org/10.1080/10304310903003270.

Crenshaw, Kimberlé. 1989. "Mapping the Margins: Intersectionality, Identity Politics, and Violence Against Women of Color." *Stanford Law Review,* no. 6, 1241–300.

Curthoys, Ann, and Jessie Mitchell. 2020. *Taking Liberty: Indigenous Rights and Settler Self-Government in Colonial Australia, 1830–1890.* Cambridge: Cambridge University Press.

Dabiri, Emma. 2021. *What White People Can Do Next: From Allyship to Coalition.* New York: Harper Perennial.

Daniels, Jessie. 2016. "The Trouble with White Feminism: Whiteness, Digital Feminism, and the Intersectional Internet." In *The Intersectional Internet,* edited by Safiya Umoja Noble and Brendesha M. Tynes. New York: Peter Lang.

Daniels, Jessie. 2021. *Nice White Ladies: The Truth About White Supremacy, Our Role in It, and How We Can Help Dismantle It.* New York: Seal Press.

Davies, Margaret. 2008. "Feminism and the Flat Law Theory." *Feminist Legal Studies* 16 (3): 281–304. https://doi.org/10.1007/s10691-008-9096-z.

Davis, Kathy. 2008. "Intersectionality as Buzzword: A Sociology of Science Perspective on What Makes a Feminist Theory Successful." *Feminist Theory* 9 (1): 67–85. https://doi.org/10.1177/1464700108086364.

Dean, Jonathan. 2023. "From Solidarity to Self-Promotion? Neoliberalism and Left Politics in the Age of the Social Media Influencer." *Capital and Class* 48 (4): 519–41. https://doi.org/10.1177/03098168231199907.

Dimitrovska, Natasha. 2024. "'Woman Is Not Wolf to Woman': Solidarity, Struggles and Contradictions in Digital Feminist Activism in the Balkans." PhD diss., Monash University.

Dobson, Amy Shields, and Anita Harris. 2015. "Post-Girlpower: Globalized Mediated Femininities." *Continuum* 29 (2): 143–44. https://doi.org/10.1080/1 0304312.2015.1022943.

Edell, Dana, Lyn Mikel Brown, and Celeste Montano. 2018. "Bridges, Ladders, Sparks, and Glue: Celebrating and Problematizing 'Girl-Driven' Intergenerational Feminist Activism." In *An Intergenerational Feminist Media Studies*, edited by Jessalyn Keller, Jo Littler, and Alison Winch. Abingdon: Routledge.

Edmond, Maura. 2022. "Careful Consumption and Aspirational Ethics in the Media and Cultural Industries: Cancelling, Quitting, Screening, Optimising." *Media, Culture and Society* 45 (1): 92–107. https://doi.org /10.1177/01634437221099615.

Elias, Ana, Rosalind Gill, and Christina Scharff. 2017. "Aesthetic Labour: Beauty Politics in Neoliberalism." In *Aesthetic Labour: Rethinking Beauty Politics in Neoliberalism*, edited by Ana Sofia Elias, Rosalind Gill, and Christina Scharff. London: Palgrave Macmillan. https://doi.org/10.1057/978-1-137-47765 -1_1.

Enloe, Cynthia. 2011. "The Mundane Matters." *International Political Sociology* 5 (4): 447–50. https://doi.org/10.1111/j.1749-5687.2011.00145_2.x.

Errázuriz, Valentina. 2021. "A Digital Room of Their Own: Chilean Students Struggling Against Patriarchy in Digital Sites." *Feminist Media Studies* 21 (2): 281–97. https://doi.org/10.1080/14680777.2019.1668451.

Essed, Philomena. 1991. *Understanding Everyday Racism: An Interdisciplinary Theory*. Newbury Park, CA: Sage.

Euritt, Alyn M. 2022. "Podcasting's Transmedia Liveness." In *The Routledge Companion to Radio and Podcast Studies*, edited by Mia Lindgren and Jason Loviglio. London: Routledge.

Federici, Silvia. 2020. *Revolution at Point Zero: Housework, Reproduction, and Feminist Struggle*. Oakland, CA: PM Press.

Fisher, Anna Watkins. 2011 "We Love This Trainwreck! Sacrificing Britney to Save America." In *In the Limelight and Under the Microscope: Forms and Functions of Female Celebrity*, edited by Diane Negra and Su Holmes. London: Continuum.

Fuchs, Christian. 2015. *Culture and Economy in the Age of Social Media*. New York: Routledge.

Gajjala, Radhika. 2001. "Studying Feminist E-Spaces: Introducing Transnational/ Post-Colonial Concerns." In *Technospaces: Inside the New Media*, edited by Sally Munt. London: Continuum.

Gill, Rosalind. 2007. *Gender and the Media*. Cambridge: Polity.

Gill, Rosalind. 2023. *Perfect: Feeling Judged on Social Media*. Cambridge: Polity.

Gill, Rosalind, and Christina Scharff. 2011. *New Femininities: Postfeminism, Neoliberalism and Subjectivity*. Basingstoke: Palgrave Macmillan.

Gilroy, Paul, and George Yancy. 2015. "What 'Black Lives' Means in Britain." *New York Times*, Opinionator (blog), October 1. https://archive.ny times.com/opinionator.blogs.nytimes.com/2015/10/01/paul-gilroy-what -black-means-in-britain/.

Gleeson, Jessamy. 2016. "'(Not) Working 9–5': The Consequences of Contemporary Australian-Based Online Feminist Campaigns as Digital Labour." *Media International Australia* 161 (1): 77–85. https://doi.org/10.1177 /1329878X16664999.

Goonewardena, Kanishka, Stefan Kipfer, Richard Milgrom, and Christian Schmid. 2008. *Space, Difference, Everyday Life: Reading Henri Lefebvre*. New York: Routledge.

Gülçiçek, Demet. 2024. *Travelling Theory and Women's Movements in Turkey: Imagining Europe*. Abingdon: Routledge.

Hage, Ghassan. 2000. *White Nation: Fantasies of White Supremacy in a Multicultural Society*. New York: Routledge.

Halberstam, Jack. 2018. *Trans*: A Quick and Quirky Account of Gender Variability*. Berkeley: University of California Press.

Hall, Stuart. 1988. *The Hard Road to Renewal: Thatcherism and the Crisis of the Left*. London: Verso.

Hands, Joss. 2019. *Gadget Consciousness: Collective Thought, Will, and Action in the Age of Social Media*. London: Pluto Press.

Hanisch, Carol. (1970) 2006. "The Personal Is Political: The Women's Liberation Movement Classic with a New Explanatory Introduction." https:// www.carolhanisch.org/CHwritings/PIP.html.

Haraway, Donna. 1988. "Situated Knowledges: The Science Question in Feminism and the Privilege of Partial Perspective." *Feminist Studies* 14 (3): 575–99. https://doi.org/10.2307/3178066.

Hardt, Michael, and Antonio Negri. 2000. *Empire*. Cambridge, MA: Harvard University Press.

Hardt, Michael, and Antonio Negri. 2004. *Multitude: War and Democracy in the Age of Empire*. New York: Penguin.

Harjunen, Hannele. 2016. *Neoliberal Bodies and the Gendered Fat Body*. London: Routledge.

Haslop, Craig, Jessica Ringrose, Idil Cambazoglu, and Betsy Milne. 2024. "Mainstreaming the Manosphere's Misogyny Through Affective Homosocial Currencies: Exploring How Teen Boys Navigate the Andrew Tate Effect." *Social Media + Society* 10 (1): 20563051241228811. https://doi.org /10.1177/20563051241228811.

Hemmings, Clare. 2011. *Why Stories Matter: The Political Grammar of Feminist Theory*. Durham, NC: Duke University Press.

Hillis, Ken, Michael Petit, and Kylie Jarrett. 2012. *Google and the Culture of Search*. London: Routledge.

Hiruy, Kiros, and Rebecca Anne Hutton. 2020. "Towards a Re-Imagination of the New African Diaspora in Australia." *African Diaspora* 12 (1–2): 153–79. https://doi.org/10.1163/18725465-bja10010.

Hochschild, Arlie Russell. 1983. *The Managed Heart: Commercialization of Human Feeling*. Berkeley: University of California Press.

Hodkinson, Paul, and Sian Lincoln. 2008. "Online Journals as Virtual Bedrooms? Young People, Identity and Personal Space." *Young* 16 (1): 27–46. https://doi.org/10.1177/110330880701600103.

Jackson, Sarah J., Moya Bailey, and Brooke Foucault Welles. 2020. *#HashtagActivism: Networks of Race and Gender Justice*. Cambridge, MA: MIT Press.

Jarrett, Kylie. 2015. *Feminism, Labour, and Digital Media: The Digital Housewife*. New York: Routledge.

Jarrett, Kylie. 2022. *Digital Labor*. Cambridge: Polity.

Jenkins, Henry. 2006. *Fans, Bloggers, and Gamers: Exploring Participatory Culture*. New York: NYU Press.

Jeong, Euisol, and Jieun Lee. 2018. "We Take the Red Pill, We Confront the Dick-Trix: Online Feminist Activism and the Augmentation of Gendered Realities in South Korea." *Feminist Media Studies* 18 (4): 705–17. https://doi.org/10.1080/14680777.2018.1447354.

Kafer, Alison. 2013. *Feminist, Queer, Crip*. Bloomington: Indiana University Press.

Kanai, Akane. 2020. "Between the Perfect and the Problematic: Everyday Femininities, Popular Feminism, and the Negotiation of Intersectionality." *Cultural Studies* 34 (1): 25–48. https://doi.org/10.1080/09502386.2018.1559869

Kanai, Akane, and Rosalind Gill. 2020. "Woke? Affect, Neoliberalism, Marginalised Identities and Consumer Culture." *New Formations* 102: 10-27. https://doi.org/10.3898/NewF:102.01.2020.

Kanai, Akane, and Caitlin McGrane. 2021. "Feminist Filter Bubbles: Ambivalence, Vigilance and Labour." *Information Communication and Society* 24 (15): 2307–22. https://doi.org/10.1080/1369118X.2020.1760916.

King, Tiffany Lethabo. 2015. "Post-Indentitarian and Post-Intersectional Anxiety in the Neoliberal Corporate University." *Feminist Formations* 27 (3): 114–38.

Lacey, Kate. 2011. "Listening in the Digital Age." In *Radio's New Wave*, edited by Jason Loviglio and Michelle Hilmes. New York: Routledge.

Lâm, Maivân Clech. 1994. "Feeling Foreign in Feminism." *Signs: Journal of Women in Culture and Society* 19 (4): 865–93. https://doi.org/10.1086/494943.

Lee, Jane, Miles Herbert, Allison Chan, Laura Murphy-Oates, Joe Koning, and Miles Martignoni. 2023. "Why Were Neo-Nazis at an Anti-Trans Rally in Melbourne?—Podcast." *The Guardian*, March 22, sec. Australia news.

https://www.theguardian.com/australia-news/audio/2023/mar/22/why
-were-neo-nazis-at-an-anti-trans-rally-in-melbourne.

Lewis, Gail. 2013. "Unsafe Travel: Experiencing Intersectionality and Feminist
Displacements." *Signs: Journal of Women in Culture and Society* 38 (4): 869–92.
https://doi.org/10.1086/669609.

Listnr. 2021. *It's a Lot with Abbie Chatfield.* https://listnr.com/podcasts/its
-a-lot-with-abbie-chatfield.

Lo, Jacqueline, and Mayu Kanamori. 2013. "Returning Memory to Earth: Towards Asian-Aboriginal Reconciliation." *Crossings: Journal of Migration and
Culture* 4 (1): 67–78. https://doi.org/10.1386/cjmc.4.1.67_1.

Luft, Rachel E., and Jane Ward. 2009. "Toward an Intersectionality Just out
of Reach: Confronting Challenges to Intersectional Practice." In *Perceiv-
ing Gender Locally, Globally, and Intersectionally*, edited by Vasilikie Demos
and Marcia Texler Segal. Emerald Group. https://doi.org/10.1108/S1529
-2126(2009)0000013005.

Lugones, Maria. 2003. *Pilgrimages/Peregrinajes: Theorizing Coalition Against Multiple Oppressions.* Lanham, MD: Rowman and Littlefield.

Marvin, Carolyn. 1990. *When Old Technologies Were New: Thinking About Electric
Communication in the Late Nineteenth Century.* Oxford: Oxford University
Press.

McDowell, Linda. 1997. *Capital Culture: Gender at Work in the City.* Oxford:
Blackwell.

McRobbie, Angela. 2007. "Top Girls? Young Women and the Post-Feminist Sexual Contract." *Cultural Studies* 21 (4–5): 718–37. https://doi.org/10.1080
/09502380701279044.

McRobbie, Angela. 2009. *The Aftermath of Feminism: Gender, Culture, and Social
Change.* Los Angeles: Sage.

McRobbie, Angela. 2015. "Notes on the Perfect: Competitive Femininity in Neoliberal Times." *Australian Feminist Studies* 30 (83): 3–20. https://doi.org/10.1080
/08164649.2015.1011485.

McRobbie, Angela. 2020. *Feminism and the Politics of Resilience: Essays on Gender,
Media, and the End of Welfare.* Newark, NJ: Polity Press.

Mendes, Kaitlynn. 2022. "Digital Feminist Labour: The Immaterial, Aspirational and Affective Labour of Feminist Activists and Fempreneurs." *Wom-
en's History Review* 31 (4): 693–712. https://doi.org/10.1080/09612025.2021
.1944353.

Mendes, Kaitlynn, Jessalynn Keller, and Jessica Ringrose. 2019. "Digitized Narratives of Sexual Violence: Making Sexual Violence Felt and Known Through
Digital Disclosures." *New Media and Society* 21 (6): 1290–310. https://doi
.org/10.1177/1461444818820069.

Mohanty, Chandra Talpade. 2003. "'Under Western Eyes' Revisited: Feminist

Solidarity Through Anticapitalist Struggles." *Signs: Journal of Women in Culture and Society* 28 (2): 499–535. https://doi.org/10.1086/342914.

Mohanty, Chandra Talpade. 2013. "Transnational Feminist Crossings: On Neoliberalism and Radical Critique." *Signs: Journal of Women in Culture and Society* 38 (4): 967–91. https://doi.org/10.1086/669576.

Moreton-Robinson, Aileen. 2000a. *Talkin' Up to the White Woman: Indigenous Women and Feminism*. St. Lucia: University of Queensland Press.

Moreton-Robinson, Aileen. 2000b. "Troubling Business: Difference and Whiteness Within Feminism." *Australian Feminist Studies*. https://doi.org/10.1080/713611977.

Moreton-Robinson, Aileen. 2006. "Whiteness Matters: Implications of *Talkin' Up to the White Woman*." *Australian Feminist Studies* 21 (50): 245–56. https://doi.org/10.1080/08164640600731788.

Morse, Margaret. 1998. *Virtualities: Television, Media Art, and Cyberculture*. Bloomington: Indiana University Press.

Moss, Rachel. 2021. "What 'Peg the Patriarchy' Actually Means, from the Person Who Coined It." *HuffPost UK*, September 15. https://www.huffingtonpost.co.uk/entry/what-does-peg-the-patriarchy-mean_uk_6141b5dce4b064 0100ac44ad.

Mull, Amanda. 2020. "The Girlboss Has Left the Building." *The Atlantic*, June 25. https://www.theatlantic.com/health/archive/2020/06/girlbosses -what-comes-next/613519/.

Nakamura, Lisa. 2015. "The Unwanted Labour of Social Media: Women of Colour Call Out Culture as Venture Community Management." *New Formations* 86 (86): 106–12. https://doi.org/10.3898/NEWF.86.06.2015.

Nash, Jennifer C. 2019. *Black Feminism Reimagined: After Intersectionality*. Next Wave: New Directions in Women's Studies. Durham, NC: Duke University Press.

Noble, Safiya Umoja, and Brendesha M. Tynes. 2016. *The Intersectional Internet: Race, Sex, Class, and Culture Online*. New York: Peter Lang.

Orgad, Shani, and Rosalind Gill. 2021. *Confidence Culture*. Durham, NC: Duke University Press.

Ortega, Mariana. 2006. "Being Lovingly, Knowingly Ignorant: White Feminism and Women of Color." *Hypatia* 21 (3): 56–74. https://doi.org/10.1111/j .1527-2001.2006.tb01113.x.

Ouellette, Laurie, and Julie Wilson. 2011. "Women's Work: Affective Labour and Convergence Culture." *Cultural Studies* 25 (4–5): 548–65. https://doi.org /10.1080/09502386.2011.600546.

Pain, Paromita. 2021. "'It Took Me Quite a Long Time to Develop a Voice': Examining Feminist Digital Activism in the Indian #MeToo Movement." *New Media and Society* 23 (11): 3139–55. https://doi.org/10.1177/1461444820944846.

Pariser, Eli. 2011. *The Filter Bubble: What the Internet Is Hiding from You*. London: Penguin.

Paul, Christopher, and Miriam Matthews. 2016. *The Russian 'Firehose of Falsehood' Propaganda Model: Why It Might Work and Options to Counter It*. RAND Corporation. https://www.jstor.org/stable/resrep02439.

Pedwell, Carolyn. 2014. *Affective Relations: The Transnational Politics of Empathy*. London: Palgrave Macmillan.

Pereira, Maria do Mar. 2017. *Power, Knowledge, and Feminist Scholarship: An Ethnography of Academia*. London: Routledge.

Phillips, A. A. 2006. *On The Cultural Cringe*. Carlton: Melbourne University Press.

Proctor, Hannah. 2024. *Burnout: The Emotional Experience of Political Defeat*. London: Verso.

Puar, Jasbir K. 2007. *Terrorist Assemblages: Homonationalism in Queer Times*. Durham, NC: Duke University Press.

Raffnsøe, Sverre, Dorthe Staunæs, and Mads Bank. 2022. "Affirmative Critique." *Ephemera: Theory and Politics in Organization* 22 (3).

Rambukkana, Nathan. 2015. *Hashtag Publics: The Power and Politics of Discursive Networks*. New York: Peter Lang.

Rault, Jasmine. 2017. "White Noise, White Affects: Filtering the Sameness of Queer Suffering." *Feminist Media Studies* 17 (4): 585–99. https://doi.org/10.1080/14680777.2017.1326557.

Repo, Jemima. 2020. "Feminist Commodity Activism: The New Political Economy of Feminist Protest." *International Political Sociology* 14 (2): 215–32. https://doi.org/10.1093/ips/olz033.

Rivers, Nicola. 2017. *Postfeminism(s) and the Arrival of the Fourth Wave: Turning Tides*. Cham: Springer. https://doi.org/10.1007/978-3-319-59812-3_6.

Roberts, Steven, and Karla Elliott. 2020. "Challenging Dominant Representations of Marginalized Boys and Men in Critical Studies on Men and Masculinities." *Boyhood Studies* 13 (2): 87–104. https://doi.org/10.3167/bhs.2020.130207.

Rogers, Baker A. 2023. "TERFs Aren't Feminists: Lesbians Stand Against Trans Exclusion." *Journal of Lesbian Studies* 28 (1): 24–43. https://doi.org/10.1080/10894160.2023.2252286.

Ronson, Jon. 2015. *So You've Been Publicly Shamed*. New York: Riverhead.

Rosenblatt, Louise M. 1994. *The Reader, the Text, the Poem: The Transactional Theory of the Literary Work*. Carbondale: Southern Illinois University Press.

Rottenberg, Catherine. 2013. "The Rise of Neoliberal Feminism." *Cultural Studies* 28 (3): 418–37. https://doi.org/10.1080/09502386.2013.857361.

Roy, Srila. 2015. "The Indian Women's Movement: Within and Beyond NGOization." *Journal of South Asian Development* 10 (1): 96–117. https://doi.org/10.1177/0973174114567368.

Roy, Srila. 2022. *Changing the Subject: Feminist and Queer politics in Neoliberal India*. Durham, NC: Duke University Press.

Savolainen, Laura, Justus Uitermark, and John D. Boy. 2022. "Filtering Feminisms: Emergent Feminist Visibilities on Instagram." *New Media and Society* 24 (3): 557–79. https://doi.org/10.1177/1461444820960074.

Scharff, Christina. 2023a. "Are We All Influencers Now? Feminist Activists Discuss the Distinction Between Being an Activist and an Influencer." *Feminist Theory* 25 (3): 454–70. https://doi.org/10.1177/14647001231201062.

Scharff, Christina. 2023b. "Creating Content for Instagram: Digital Feminist Activism and the Politics of Class." *Astrolabio*, no. 31, 152–78.

Schindel, Katrin. 2024. "The Politics of 'Including Everyone': Digital Feminism, Popular Intersectionality, and White Femininities in the Neoliberal Age." PhD diss., Kings College London.

Sedgwick, Eve Kosofsky. 1997. "Paranoid Reading and Reparative Reading; or, You're So Paranoid, You Probably Think This Introduction Is About You." In *Novel Gazing: Queer Readings in Fiction*. Durham, NC: Duke University Press.

Singh, Rianka. 2018. "Platform Feminism: Protest and the Politics of Spatial Organization." *Ada: A Journal of Gender, New Media, and Technology* 14. https://doi.org/10.5399/uo/ada.2018.14.6.

Singh, Rianka, and Sarah Sharma. 2019. "Platform Uncommons." *Feminist Media Studies* 19 (2): 302–3. https://doi.org/10.1080/14680777.2019.1573547.

Skeggs, Beverley. 2004. *Class, Self, Culture*. London: Routledge. https://doi.org/10.4324/9781315016177.

Smith, Dorothy E. 1987. *The Everyday World as Problematic: A Feminist Sociology*. Boston: Northeastern University Press.

Smythe, Viv. 2018. "I'm Credited with Having Coined the Word 'Terf': Here's How It Happened." *The Guardian*, November 28. https://www.theguardian.com/commentisfree/2018/nov/29/im-credited-with-having-coined-the-acronym-terf-heres-how-it-happened.

Sobande, Francesca. 2019. "Woke-Washing: 'Intersectional' Femvertising and Branding 'Woke' Bravery." *European Journal of Marketing* 54 (11): 2723–45. https://doi.org/10.1108/EJM-02-2019-0134.

Sobande, Francesca, Akane Kanai, and Natasha Zeng. 2022. "The Hypervisibility and Discourses of 'Wokeness' in Digital Culture." *Media, Culture and Society* 44 (8): 1576–87. https://doi.org/10.1177/01634437221117490.

Spinelli, Martin, and Lance Dann. 2019. *Podcasting: The Audio Media Revolution*. New York: Bloomsbury.

Steele, Catherine Knight. 2021. *Digital Black Feminism*. New York: NYU Press.

Steele, Catherine Knight, Jessica H. Lu, and Kevin C. Winstead. 2023. *Doing Black Digital Humanities with Radical Intentionality: A Practical Guide*. New York: Routledge. https://api.taylorfrancis.com/content/books/mono/download

?identifierName=doi&identifierValue=10.4324/9781003299134&type
=googlepdf.

Stephenson, Peta. 2007. *The Outsiders Within: Telling Australia's Indigenous-Asian Story*. Sydney: UNSW Press.

Stiegler, Sam. 2024. '"Are You Still in Touch with Your Participants?': The Implications of Asking Questions About Other People's Research." *Cultural Studies—Critical Methodologies* 25 (2): 124–32. https://doi.org/10.1177/15327086241281923.

Stryker, Susan, and V Varun Chaudhry. 2022. "Ask a Feminist: Susan Stryker Discusses Trans Studies, Trans Feminism, and a More Trans Future with V Varun Chaudhry." *Signs: Journal of Women in Culture and Society* 47 (4): 789–910. https://doi.org/10.1086/717737.

Sullivan, Shannon. 2014. *Good White People: The Problem with Middle-Class White Anti-Racism*. Albany: SUNY Press.

Syed, Khalida Tanvir. 2012. *Through White Noise: Autonarrative Exploration of Racism, Discrimination, and the Doorways to Academic Citizenship in Canada*. Rotterdam: Sense.

Táíwò, Olúfẹ́mi O. 2022. *Elite Capture: How the Powerful Took Over Identity Politics (and Everything Else)*. Chicago: Haymarket.

Taylor, Anthea. 2017. *Celebrity and the Feminist Blockbuster*. New York: Palgrave Macmillan Springer.

Tiidenberg, Katrin, Natalie Ann Hendry, and Crystal Abidin. 2021. *Tumblr*. Cambridge: Polity.

Tompkins, Jessica E., and Ashley ML Guajardo (née Brown). 2024. "Gatekeeping the Gatekeepers: An Exploratory Study of Transformative Games Fandom and TikTok Algorithms." *Games and Culture* 0 (0). https://doi.org/10.1177/15554120241244416.

Veracini, Lorenzo. 2011. "Introducing: Settler Colonial Studies." *Settler Colonial Studies* 1 (1): 1–12. https://doi.org/10.1080/2201473X.2011.10648799.

Warner, Michael. 2002. "Publics and Counterpublics." *Quarterly Journal of Speech* 88 (4): 413–25. https://doi.org/10.1080/00335630209384388.

Watercutter, Angela. 2022. "TikTok's New, Terrible Trend." *Wired*, May 13. https://www.wired.com/story/tiktok-depp-heard/.

White, Michele. 2006. *The Body and the Screen: Theories of Internet Spectatorship*. Cambridge, MA: MIT Press.

Williams, Raymond. 1990. *Television: Technology and Cultural Form*. London: Routledge.

Winch, Alison. 2013. *Girlfriends and Postfeminist Sisterhood*. Basingstoke: Palgrave Macmillan.

Winter, Jessica. 2022. "The Johnny Depp–Amber Heard Verdict Is Chilling." *New Yorker*, June 2. https://www.newyorker.com/culture/cultural-comment/the-depp-heard-verdict-is-chilling.

Yin, Siyuan, and Yu Sun. 2021. "Intersectional Digital Feminism: Assessing the Participation Politics and Impact of the MeToo Movement in China." *Feminist Media Studies* 21 (7): 1176–92. https://doi.org/10.1080/14680777.2020.1837908.

Yuval-Davis, Nira. 2023. "Antisemitism Is a Form of Racism—or Is It?" *Sociology* 58 (4): 779–95. https://doi.org/10.1177/00380385231208691.

Zeng, Natasha. 2024. "Asianness in Motion: Online Cultures and Everyday Spatio-Temporality." PhD diss., Monash University.

Zuboff, Shoshana. 2019. *The Age of Surveillance Capitalism: The Fight for a Human Future at the New Frontier of Power*. London: Profile.

INDEX

knowledge cultures: access to information conflated with knowledge, 17; and attention economy, 81; class hierarchies, 170; consciousness-raising, 148; everyday, theorizing, 13–18; labor of, 15, 21; management of belonging in, 15; "online knowledge cultures," 5; rearticulation of experience through, 146–47, 151–52; as sensibility directed toward "updates," 15; social media feminism as set of, 8

Lacey, Kate, 138
Lâm, Maivân Clech, 19, 118
leadership, 6, 23–24, 28; activism conflated with, 84–85; argumentative style, 99–100; "be the change" injunctions, 23, 83, 118; as building capacity in local community, 85; and burnout, 96–100; competitive relation with the self normalized, 83; in deferred sense, 96; disavowal of lack, 89–90; expected of those with existing material privileges, 83–84; experience as intellectual property, 101; good versus "neoliberal white," 63; and individual struggles for survival, 98–100; international degrees promoted, 84; language of in university marketing material, 83–84; as mandatory now and in the future, 82; obligations of white middle-class feminists, 63, 82; pathways of potential, 83–90; and platforming, 63–64; "proving people wrong," 88–89; as resource for others' journeys, 82, 91–95, 101; self-advocacy, 98–99; upward trajectory, challenges to, 96–100; "women in STEM" discourses, 90; youth programs for others, 86–87. See also girlboss feminism; "good" feminism; journeys of leadership
"leaning in," critique of, 110
legislation of intersectionality, 59
lesbian identity, 115–16
Lewis, Gail, 10, 58
likemindedness, 157
liking, algorithms of, 34
Lil Nas X, 41
Lincoln, Sian, 33
"liquid modernity," 2

"listening in" and "listening out," 138
LiveJournal, 33
loving perception, 91
low-stakes social spaces, 26, 126, 145
Lugones, Maria, 16–17, 55, 57, 68; bird's-eye view, concept of, 61, 64

Malatino, Hil, 116
Mamamia (podcast), 139
marginalized others, 67; activists as, 85–86; amplifying and platforming, 63; categorization of, 81; disadvantage, ranking, 65, 68–72, 76–77, 144; question of how to uplift, 10; safe spaces for, 54; status of as knowledge objects, 57–58, 93. See also non-white feminists
Matatas, Luna, 110
Matjila, Bobo, 139
McCall, Leslie, 22
McRobbie, Angela, 8–9, 85
men: emotional extremism practiced by, 161–63, 162; left off the intersectional grid, 81; "performative incompetence" of, 149–50; and rape culture, 45–46, 75–76
mental health, 34
Met Gala controversy (2021), 18, 65, 108–10, 111
#MeToo movement, 7, 49, 173
Michigan Womyn's Music Festival, 115
Middle East, feminists from, 35–36
Middle Eastern, as orientalist term, 95
misogyny, 21, 104–5; in boys' schools, 128–29; increased under guise of feminism, 172–73; mainstreaming of online, 39–41, 126, 129–30, 173. See also right-wing politics
Mohanty, Chandra Talpade, 10, 93
Moreton-Robinson, Aileen, 7, 59
movement: across specific times and contexts, 147; affective, 147, 152; noticing minutiae of the everyday, 157–64; between opening and closing, 148–57, 169–70; repeated outward-inward gaze, 163–64; taking time to understand experience, 165–67; transversal gaze, practice of, 26–27, 147, 148, 176

Nash, Jennifer, 10, 58–59, 91
neoliberal feminism, 105–8, 145, 147, 169

www.ingramcontent.com/pod-product-compliance
Lightning Source LLC
Chambersburg PA
CBHW030831270326
41928CB00007B/990